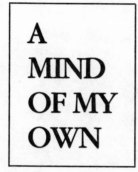

A
MIND
OF MY
OWN

A MIND OF MY OWN

The Woman Who Was Known as Eve Tells the Story of Her Triumph over Multiple Personality Disorder

Chris Costner Sizemore

William Morrow and Company, Inc.
New York

Grateful acknowledgment is made for permission to excerpt from "Traces of Eve's Faces"; reprinted with permission from *Psychology Today* magazine, copyright © 1982 (P. T. Partners, L.P.).

Library of Congress Cataloging-in-Publication Data

Sizemore, Chris Costner.
    A mind of my own / the woman known as "Eve" tells the story of her triumph over multiple personality disorder / Chris Costner Sizemore.
        p.   cm.
    ISBN 0-688-08199-1
    1. Sizemore, Chris Costner—Mental health.   2. Multiple
personality—Patients—United States—Biography.   I. Title.
    RC569.5.M8S594   1989
616.85'236'0092—dc20
[B]   89-32629
                                                                  CIP

A Greene Communications Book

Printed in the United States of America

First Edition

1   2   3   4   5   6   7   8   9   10

BOOK DESIGN BY JAYE ZIMET

To Don, Taffy, Bobby, Tommy, Jimmy, and Christi,
my family, who filled my life with love
and made my struggle worthwhile

Preface

Following three previous books about my decades of mental illness, this one, at last, is about my wellness. And about the peace this wellness has brought to my family. This memoir, then, is a story of love rising above mental illness; and the word *love* was rarely used in earlier accounts of my life.

Among those, *The Three Faces of Eve* and *The Final Face of Eve* focused on my ordeals in the fifties with the disorder known as multiple personality. And in those books—published decades before MPD was officially recognized by the American Psychiatric Association—my illness seemed more important than who I was. But I *was* many women. Then, in 1977, my account of the entire forty-four-year ordeal was published as *I'm Eve.* That autobiography helped me resolve multiplicity. Since then, I have been only one person. *Myself.*

However, as psychiatric patients know better than most, mental health is never a simple accomplishment, and rarely a solitary feat. This book confirms these principles. The last fourteen years in the public eye have certainly brought many triumphs, successes, and opportunities my way. But they have also been years when, privately, I endured many anguishes. These pages recount such memories with the hope that by my revelations of the private pain I have endured in order to become well and remain healthy, others may be helped.

Being one person is not easy. Adjustment has become my life.

7

And my family's as well. Even though my birth certificate indicates that I was born in 1927, I emerged as a woman in 1974 whom none of them knew. To their credit, my family not only helped me grow strong and independent but also resolved conflicts in their individual relationships with me. They loved me before any of us knew who I would become.

This book is also the story of MPD itself—a controversial disorder that was misunderstood throughout my struggles with it. In the eighties, however, MPD has found legitimacy among mental-health professionals. As both a former sufferer of that disorder and, subsequently, an advocate for patients' rights, I was privileged to play a part in accomplishing that legitimacy. So this memoir recounts how health has enabled me to contribute to society's understanding of my former sickness.

To readers who may not know the details of my life, as told in the previous books, I offer a brief summary.

For more than forty years, I simultaneously coexisted as three or more personalities in one body. My psychiatric problem was the neurosis MPD. It's a defense mechanism by which the personality creates other satellites to face realities that appear unbearable. I initially experienced such multiplicity in 1929 at the age of two. That was the first time I can remember vacating my body and then watching as someone else acted in it.

As a young child, I was not aware that other people did not have such experiences. Even though I was considered unacceptable at school in my hometown of Edgefield, South Carolina, it wasn't until I was a young wife and mother that I became fully aware that I was indeed different from others. It was then that I began to have severe headaches, feelings of inertia, blackouts, and long periods of amnesia.

In 1952, two psychiatrists in Augusta, Georgia—Drs. Corbett H. Thigpen and Hervey M. Cleckley—diagnosed my problem as MPD. I was under their constant care for two and a half years, and it was from my case history that they wrote their book, *The Three Faces of Eve,* on which the motion picture of the same name was based. During this period, the two psychiatrists identified three personalities, or alters, functioning overtly in my life. For publishing purposes, the doctors gave these alters the pseudonyms of Eve Black, Eve White, and Jane.

I subsequently sought help in vain from six psychiatrists until the early seventies. That's when Dr. Tony A. Tsitos, a psychiatrist in Annandale, Virginia, and Dr. Tibor Ham, a physician in Vienna, Virginia, cooperated in helping me get well. Under their care, the long-standing amnesia gradually diminished its hold on my mind.

The results of that therapy, detailed in *I'm Eve*, indicated that I had exhibited twenty-two personalities, or alters, since the first alter emerged in 1929. And among these twenty-two alters, ten were poets, seven were artists, and one had taught tailoring. Today, I paint and write, but I cannot sew. Yet these alters were not moods or the result of role-playing. They were entities that were totally separate from the personality I was born to be, and am today. They were so different that their tones of voice changed. What's more, their facial expressions, appetites, tastes in clothes, handwritings, skills, and IQs were all different, too.

Because of these differences, my daughter, Taffy, named each of the alters that emerged after the disappearance of Eve Black, Eve White, and Jane. Taffy chose names that related to my alters' habits or idiosyncrasies, such as the Purple Lady, who was obsessed with that color, or the Strawberry Girl, who was obsessed with that fruit, or the Retrace Lady, who refused to retrace her tracks.

The emergence of these alters generally followed a pattern: There were always three at a time. In each trio, there was one that functioned as the *wife/mother image;* another would always be a fun-loving, lively type, a *party girl;* and the third would usually appear to be "normal" but *intellectual.*

This book, however, begins on the day in 1974 when I, as the birth personality, finally resurfaced in my own life. Technically, I was forty-seven years old at the time. But I remembered so very little that I was deeply confused. I had to catch up on a lifetime of many lives, and that process has taken years.

This book, then, details that process and the life I have enjoyed, once my mental health was restored.

—Chris Costner Sizemore
Bradenton, Florida

Acknowledgments

With love and gratitude I acknowledge the following members of my family for their support during the writing of this book: Don Sizemore, Bobby Sizemore, Taffy Fecteau, James "Tommy" Fecteau, Jimmy Fecteau, Christi Fecteau, Elise Walton, Louise Edwards, and Elen Pittillo.

I thank Charles "Chuck" Brandon, Phillip M. Coons, M.D., Adam Crabtree, Harriett Henderson, Richard P. Kluft, M.D., Stanley Krippner, Ph.D., John Russell, Ph.D., Moshe Torem, M.D., Tony A. Tsitos, M.D., and Mary Jo Voorhees for their kind assistance. I also express appreciation to Dr. Lois Crider, chiropractor, for special care and friendship.

My special thanks to two very good friends: Lisa Drew, my editor for a second time, for her unswerving belief in me and for her insightful suggestions throughout this work; and Mary Yost, my literary agent, whose support helped me to accept, calmly, the responsibility of this effort and whose guidance helped greatly during the writing of this book.

I am grateful to Preston Garrison, executive director of the National Mental Health Association; to Pam Davis, Richard "Dick" Hitt, Tom Sovine, and Dee Talty, all of whom are directors of state mental health associations; and to MHAs across the country for their invaluable support. I am also grateful to the manuscript curator and the librarians of the William R. Perkins Library, Duke University, for their help in researching the Chris Costner Sizemore Papers. To Randall Elisha Greene, for his conscientious editorial services, my deepest appreciation.

To thousands of people throughout the world—therapists, pa-

11

tients, and families—who have encouraged my efforts: thank you. And a warm remembrance to David Caul, M.D., deceased.

All names in this book are authentic and legal, except for those of my alters (which are authentic but not legal names) and the following pseudonyms, noted on their first appearance in the text: Sybil Dorsett *(Chapter One)*; Evelyn Lancaster *(Chapter Two)*; Earl Lancaster, Bonnie White, Jane Lancaster, and Ralph White *(Chapter Three)*; Rita *(Chapter Seven)*; Hillside Strangler and Mrs. Anderson *(Chapter Nine)*; Judy, Kate, and Tara Sue *(Chapter Ten)*; and Olivia, Angie, and Vijna *(Chapter Eleven)*.

Contents

PART I

Saying Good-bye to Eve

$$\boxed{1}$$

I t was a hot July day when I finally emerged from what could be described as forty-four years of hiding in the mind. I felt as though I had been awakened from a deep sleep and then thrust out, thrown into the middle of the world. I was being held like a child in my daughter's arms, and the first thing I saw was her face. Big tears were running down her cheeks, and she was saying, "Mamma, you're all right. Mamma, you're going to be all right, Everything's all right."

She seemed so pretty, this woman, and it felt good to be in her presence. I knew she was my daughter and that her name was Taffy. I had gotten glimpses of her the day before. But I still felt as though I had not seen her in a long, long time, and that feeling frightened me.

My illness—I would come to understand—had estranged me from my *selves* and had estranged my family from me; but it had not caused me to view either my family or my friends as strangers. Instead, it had made *me* the stranger. I lacked a full knowledge of who I was. And having been locked away from the human interactions that build relationships but not having been locked away from the knowledge of who my family and friends were, I knew them but they didn't know me. All they knew was that, over the decades, I had been many women, many selves—a victim of multiple personality disorder. But when I emerged, all I knew was that suddenly I had become a victim of aloneness.

I began to tremble, but my daughter continued to hold me,

gently comforting me, patting me with her dainty hands as though *she* were *my* mother. I felt dizzy. I attempted to close my eyes and could feel them fluttering. My thoughts slipped out as words: "I don't know what to do. I need somebody to do something."

That's when I became aware of the man behind us. He laid his hand firmly on my shoulder, and said, "Don't do that anymore. Don't *ever* do that again."

I wasn't sure what he meant. But when I looked directly at him, I knew who he was—my therapist, Tony A. Tsitos, M.D.— and I understood that we were in his immaculate and tastefully decorated office. But even though I knew where we were, it was as if I had never been in this room before. How, I wondered, could I know these people and yet know so little else? My mind seemed like a large blank canvas on which only a few lines and colors had been randomly placed.

I felt my fingertips against the wood of the chair. I felt my palms move against the dress I was wearing and discovered that it was a soft, nice material. Somehow I knew it was silk. And though my daughter and my therapist didn't seem to be aware of what I was doing at the moment, I felt my hair and slowly ran my hands along my body. The touch of me felt good. And that's when I became aware that I had a body, as if I were discovering something obvious, but wondrous, which I should have known all along.

After a pause, my therapist said, "You're not the Purple Lady, and you're not the Retrace Lady, so it's up to you. Do you want to tell us who you are?"

I looked at him as if he were a damn fool. He returned my quizzical gaze with a questioning one. Then I said, "Why, I'm Chris Sizemore."

"That's fine." His voice was steady, revealing no excitement. "And how old are you?"

"Thirty-three."

At that, he looked at Taffy—who was then twenty-six years old—and he nodded. I looked at my daughter, too, and saw surprise flash across her face.

Then I smelled coffee, somehow knew it was coffee, and the fragrance was so rich that I commented on it. He asked if I would like a cup.

"I sure would. It's been a *long* time since I've had anything to eat."

"And I'd like coffee, very black," Taffy interjected, letting out a deep sigh. Her voice cracked with emotion.

Dr. Tsitos asked his receptionist to bring two coffees for us and hot tea for him. While the beverages were being served, I looked down at my feet and was startled. My shoes were burgundy-colored, with pointed toes and straps that went across my ankles. I thought they must be the ugliest pair of pumps imaginable. *Did I buy these?*

"Do you want sugar or cream in your coffee?" he asked, interrupting my concentration. Strangely, I didn't seem to know how either would taste, so I said neither. Then, after being handed the steaming cup of black coffee, I took my first sip. The taste was stimulating, and so was the experience of drinking. I could feel the liquid trickling all the way down inside my body and warming me all over. That felt wonderful.

Moments later, my therapist began working with me again— this time continuing for about two hours. He asked if I had a headache, and I said that I didn't. He asked if I was experiencing any other pain, and I wasn't. He asked if I remembered conversations from the earlier portion of our therapy session, and I thought for a moment, then said that I did. He also asked where I lived, what month and day and year it was, who my husband was, and who my children were. To these and other simple questions, I gave the right answers: *10320 Layton Hall Apartments in Fairfax, Virginia; July 9, 1974; Don Sizemore; Taffy and Bobby.*

But what became clear to them—though not yet to me—was that, though I possessed a vaguely reasonable memory of other people, my family and friends, I could recall little about my own life. Only their lives. This did not seem particularly strange to me at the time, but I could see by their expressions that my words, my actions—maybe even who I was?—appeared to be extremely important and puzzling to them. Never since that day have I seen such expressions of surprise on anyone's face as I saw on theirs. So I assured them, "I'm okay. The only problem I have is that I'm so frightened."

My therapist responded methodically but with care. "And what are you frightened of?"

"I don't really know I just don't feel like I know what to do with myself." As I paused, I could feel Taffy's hold on me remaining secure, unfailing.

"And are you having any unusual feelings?" he asked.

"Yes. I feel empty." I thought about that, then added, "And I don't hear anyone talking anymore."

A reassuring smile crossed his face as he asked, "Will you explain that?"

The answer seemed very clear to me. "There should be voices in my head, but I don't hear any."

"That's all right," he said. "Actually, that's fine."

When he paused again to sip his tea, Taffy whispered, "Mother, are you certain that you don't want a tranquilizer?" I assured her that I did not, though my trembling persisted.

I knew what was wrong: I was scared of life. It was not alien to me to be a human being, nor was having a family totally alien. These were not surprises when I emerged. The puzzlement, I realized, was how to deal with the *reality* of me being alone in their midst.

When I explained this, my therapist said, "You don't have to do that alone, Chris. From this day forward, you don't have to be anybody else. It's up to you. You can progress as one person. You can get well and you can stay well. But it will be up to you— provided you are strong enough to fight that battle. Are you up to it?"

It was such a powerful question and I felt so weak that all I could say was "I don't know."

"Mamma, I'll help." These simple, sweet words came from my daughter, and in saying them, the tone of her voice suddenly changed from a mother's to a child's.

After more questions and answers, my therapist gave me a tranquilizer and other prescriptions for medication, then asked me to try to relax. As the medicine began to take effect, I listened as he and Taffy talked.

"And what do you think we have seen?" he asked.

"It's the creation of a new personality," she said.

"That's only what it appears to be," he said, pausing to look at me carefully. Then he said softly to Taffy, "We are witnessing the arrival of the nucleus of the personality. It is she who creates the *others.*"

An interesting theory, I reflected while the two of them continued their discussion. But I could not stop thinking about the others: *Where are they?* I knew that *they* must be frightened, too, because Retrace Lady thought yesterday that she had killed Purple Lady. The distraught Retrace Lady was telling this to my therapist in the conversation about which he had asked me: She had been driving home from vacation and had run over Purple Lady; then, when she and Taffy and Bobby got home, Taffy had brought out Purple Lady's self-portrait; when Retrace Lady saw it, she screamed, begging Taffy to call the police to search for the woman she had hit.

These were the events that both Retrace Lady and Taffy had described to my therapist before I had emerged. But what they did not tell him was that yesterday, when Retrace Lady screamed, the shock was so great that *I* came out. It was terrifying. I remained out all day and fell asleep at night. But I dared not make myself known. Realizing that it had been many years since I existed, I simply listened, watched, and absorbed everything I could. I eavesdropped on my life.

At one point yesterday, Retrace Lady discovered me. I could feel her horror, but she did not react beyond that initial recoiling. Throughout the night, we stood at bay in my mind. She seemed as astonished to sense my presence as I was at being discovered. That's probably why, when she awakened this morning to find that both Purple Lady and Strawberry Girl were still absent but that I remained and she was not alone, Retrace Lady screamed again.

That particular sound somehow seemed familiar. It was a remarkable scream. Wordless, primitive, sustained, it scarcely seemed more human than the midnight wail of an old steam locomotive.[1] And yesterday's scream seemed to horrify Don. He ran from the bathroom, gathered Retrace Lady in his arms, then put his hand over her mouth so that the neighbors would not hear through the thin walls of our Fairfax apartment building.

It felt strange—chilling, in fact—to be in my husband's arms. Somehow, I knew his name. I knew his face. And I recognized his lean, well-shaped hands as they pressed against my mouth. But in his eyes I could see that I was a stranger to him, and he was distraught, as if overflowing with anger and frustration and contempt. That was another reason I remained hidden yesterday and am so frightened today. How can I go home alone to face *him*?

Near five o'clock, my therapist asked if I felt secure enough to drive home. Taffy reminded me that she did not drive, and when I thought about it, I realized that, yes, somehow I did know how to drive. So I assured them that I would be fine. But on the way home I became excited. My doctor had confirmed that, at long last, I was the personality that therapy had been seeking.

Was I really well? I felt fresh and new, but also drained and hollow. It was an eerie mixture of moods, which seemed to dangle me in a delicate balance. Thankfully, the car seemed to drive itself along the highway.

"Taffy, I think we should take a trip to see my father and mother," I said.

"That might not be such a good idea," my daughter responded. "Let's talk about it when we get home."

Weeks later, Taffy would explain that my comment had been her clue. In 1974, my mother, Zueline Hastings Costner, had been dead for nearly a decade—since April 1965, five years after my thirty-third birthday. So when I had said in the therapist's office that I was thirty-three, Taffy realized that I had apparently lost whole aspects of my memory over a long span. This meant that if today was a milestone in my healing process, I still had a long way to go.

When we reached the Layton Hall Apartments and our drab, dark unit on the second floor, my daughter told me very gently that there were some things I did not remember. Again, as she had done in the doctor's office, Taffy put her arms around me, and she explained that my mother had been dead for a long time.

"Mamma's dead?" Instinctively, I knew that my daughter would not lie to me, but I could not believe *this*. I became nervous, as Retrace Lady had. I told myself that the reason I didn't remember was because Retrace Lady was back. That I wasn't well. That it was *she* who didn't remember Mother's death.

After telephoning the therapist, Taffy gave me some medication. Gradually, my nervousness diminished. My senses dulled. My body relaxed. But my heart did not stop grieving. It was a confused mourning. My tears were for Mother, for the *others* who would not come back to me, but also for myself.

Or maybe my therapist had been correct this afternoon? It really did seem to be *me*—not one of the others—who was here, alone in the body. Earlier today, it had been easy to come through while Retrace Lady was bent with the pain of a headache. But now I felt as though I were in a room with no doors. There was no place to run, and I could not remember a time when I had no escape.

That night Taffy didn't tell the family what had happened during the long, significant therapy session. She appeared to be protecting me, even though I suspect that even she was uncertain as to who I was.

Once she had gotten me relaxed on the long couch in the living room, she paused long enough to telephone her husband, Tommy, and to ask him to come to our house. Then she began preparing supper. I watched while my petite, dark-haired daughter worked efficiently in the kitchen. She knew where everything was. She began cooking without a recipe, as if she knew exactly what my husband and son liked to eat. And she worked with a familiarity, as if the kitchen were her own. That's when I remembered that Taffy *had* been doing this for years, whenever the *others* had been ill. Since her marriage to Tommy—in what, the late sixties?—she had often been housewife and mother to two families. Hers and mine. So in terms of duties, tonight was just like any other. She had four men to feed: my husband and son, plus her husband and son.

But there was one crucial difference. Tonight there was a new mother in the house. She seemed to believe it, and I was beginning to believe it. I was just in no condition to understand what it all meant.

It soon became apparent that neither Don nor Bobby noticed the change. When my fifteen-year-old son came racing into the house, he headed straight for the refrigerator. Seeing him was so wonderful that I rushed to embrace him.

Years later, Bobby would explain his reactions that night: "For some reason, nobody told me, 'Mom is back. Mom is Mom.' So I didn't really look for any differences. What I did see was a lot of emotion, a lot of crying and tiredness. You looked lethargic. Like somebody who had just come home after a long journey. But we had lived through many nights when you came from therapy and cried. Maybe that's why, at the time, it seemed like just another night."

And in many ways it was. Bobby ate his supper and went to his room, as I somehow understood he had been doing for years. Then Don came home, and neither he nor I was demonstrative. Obviously tired from a long day at work, he moved silently in the house. That's when I realized most clearly the life to which I had returned. My husband of what was then twenty-one years had come home to be alone. I could see by his demeanor that he expected to spend another night keeping a respectable distance from his wife the mental patient. He didn't ask Taffy how the therapy had gone. He ate the food she fixed, then he went to his chair and watched television until he fell asleep.

He seemed so sad. He acted like a boarder, a bachelor living in someone else's house. He was not unkind. He did nothing abusive. He just didn't seem to notice that his wife was a new woman. He didn't seem to notice me at all.

But I was soon to understand why Don might not have paid much attention to a new personality, even if he had been told there was a new one in our home that night. Since our marriage, in 1953, he had endured at least nine other personalities manifesting themselves in me. Therefore, having a new wife appear in what was then my forty-seven-old body was nothing new to Don Sizemore. He had lived with the phenomenon of multiple personality disorder for nearly a quarter of a century. And he had been told numerous times over the years that I was cured, only to have a new personality interject herself into the family's lives. So I suppose the last thing Don wanted to hear was that a new Chris had come on the scene. That's probably why Taffy didn't tell him; and as frightened as I was, I had no intention of doing so, either.

That night, after Don and Bobby had gone to bed and Taffy had taken her family home, I began exploring the things in our apartment that apparently belonged to me. There were mementos, correspondence, and a host of diaries. One letter, dated two months earlier, was from Corbett H. Thigpen, M.D. He wrote in a chatty style that implied a longstanding familiarity with me and my family; and with no apparent hesitation, Dr. Thigpen offered advice even though his letter acknowledged that nearly two de-

cades had elapsed since the mid-fifties when he was the psychiatrist in charge of my case. Specifically, he encouraged me to visit
Duke University where, he predicted, physicians in the department of psychiatry might welcome an update on my case. One
Duke psychiatrist, he noted, had been particularly intrigued in
recent years by *The Three Faces of Eve*.[2]

A chill ran down my spine. Though I didn't seem to remember much about my life, I somehow knew with certainty
that *I* had been *Eve* and that the book mentioned in this letter
had been written about me. I also knew Dr. Thigpen. But other
than the Purple Lady, Retrace Lady, and Strawberry Girl, I could
not recall any others. Which one of them, I wondered, had
been Eve?

As I continued reading my former psychiatrist's letter, I was
even more surprised by his subsequent comments. He praised
my abilities as a writer and predicted that readers in America
would welcome my story because, in his opinion, it had resolved
happily and successfully.[3]

What was this man talking about? Maybe Retrace Lady had
been planning to write a book, but she was no longer here. And
for decades I had been an absentee landlord in my life, so what
did I have to write about? It all seemed absurd—particularly the
line "a story with a happy ending." To my amusement, I reflected,
*Dr. Thigpen should have been here yesterday when Retrace Lady
screamed!*

Later that evening, since I was plagued with insomnia, I began
reading a diary that began, "The year 1974." It was no surprise to
see that the others had different handwritings or different perspectives; multiplicity made sense to me. What did surprise me
was that there seemed to be no hint in the diary about the
singleness. Where did it come from? An entry written by the Purple Lady made it clear that, as recently as a month earlier, there
was no single personality:

> Today I saw Dr. Tony Tsitos. Usually I can't talk about
> myself to other people, but with him it was easy. Natural. I told
> him about the three personalities now in existence.
> The Purple Lady—Me
> The Strawberry Girl

The Retrace Lady

These are Taffy's nicknames for us. She calls me the Purple Lady because I like the color and, of course, the blankets. The Strawberry Girl rushes out for strawberries or strawberry pie, etc. I know her. The Retrace Lady, I don't know. She simply doesn't want to retrace her tracks. Walking, driving, etc. On our trip to South Carolina, she drove miles on back roads to keep from coming back [to] I-95.

I also told Dr. Tsitos my thinking about the problem. That my marriage is my big problem. It's so hard to live without a man's love. I need someone to care, and someone to need me.[4]

In fact, reading entries by each of the others, it became apparent that they didn't anticipate having to deal with me. They wrote of entanglements and struggles among the three of them, with each convinced that getting well meant simply that one of *them* would be the sole survivor. They wrote of increasing changes, night after night, from one personality to another. The Purple Lady, who thought she was fifty-eight years old, indicated that "they flip . . . as one would rapidly change television stations." The Retrace Lady, who thought she was forty-six years old, agreed. She indicated that the transitions were "becoming more painful and more often," usually accompanied by headaches, which often resulted in incoherency.

And they wrote about Don.

To Retrace Lady, Don was an enigma. Following a personality change that required special medication from the family doctor, she wrote, "I attempted to discuss it with Don, but he didn't want to know." The next day her entry noted, "It worries me that Taffy has to assume Don's responsibilities for my care. I can't be alone at this time, and he's going to leave me anyway. He could have helped this weekend and let Taffy rest and enjoy her family. I must do something."[5]

By June 10, however, Retrace Lady seemed more conciliatory: "Today is Don's birthday. I want to make it as pleasant for him as possible. My illness can't be easy for him. Often, I wonder if he chooses to ignore because he can't accept or because he doesn't know how [to cope]." And nine days later, she wrote of her concern for what Strawberry Girl (who thought at the time that she was twenty-six years old) had told the therapist during that session: "S.G. succeeded in getting out. She talked with Dr. Tsitos. Telling him that she wasn't sick, therefore better prepared to live than the other two. Asked him what was wrong with liking strawberries. Informed him that she was not going to go to bed with Don. Her voice was brassy, loud and vulgar, and I was so embarrassed. Dr. Tsitos was very kind when I came out. I couldn't stop the tears that flowed. . . ."[6]

The turning point appears to have begun around June 16, because Retrace Lady subsequently provided details about how, in mid-June, the therapist changed the medications that the others had been taking: "Dr. Tsitos . . . withdrew Equagesic and began Bellergal Spacetabs to be taken twice daily. He cut Tofranil from eight daily to three daily and started Navane three times a day. The first two days I was too sleepy to function. Now I'm so nervous I could jump out of my skin. . . ." Three days later, Retrace Lady wrote, "I have come to realize, as I suspected all along, that Purple Lady and Strawberry Girl are indeed a part of my personality. It's difficult for me to accept that the crude, rebellious, strawberry-eating creature is a part of me. The Purple Lady doesn't bother me. I don't want to be like her, but I don't find her repulsive."[7]

Thereafter, events tumbled one upon the other so that, not unlike a play that ends with all the cast dead onstage, within two weeks the others would be gone. Absent from my somehow unified awareness. But none merely faded away. "I hate and despise Dr. Tsitos," Strawberry Girl wrote in her childish script. "He refuses to help me. He will come to realize that he is helping the wrong girl, because I'm not going to die."[8]

Underneath that entry was a boldly written, mysterious style of handwriting for a terse response that reads as though it could almost have been my own: "Dr. Tsitos is helping the wrong girl all right, but the right one isn't you, little girl."[9]

Nonetheless, Strawberry Girl got the last word. Two days later, she wrote, "You and Dr. *Tit-so* can go to hell!" And she added what would become her last entry in the diary: "Strawberry season is over anyway."[10]

In a sense, it would be Strawberry Girl's epitaph, because she would soon disappear—but not before enjoying a few final, idiosyncratic pleasures. Within the week, she would wash Retrace Lady's medicine down the drain and then drink consecutive cans of strawberry Shasta until the more sedate Retrace Lady finally became annoyed. "She says she will kill herself in order to destroy me," Retrace Lady would write when that evening had ended. "I find myself so weak I can hardly dress myself. I can't help but wonder if I may indeed be dying."[11]

Somewhat removed from the competitiveness and threats being hurled between Strawberry Girl and Retrace Lady was the Purple Lady. She believed herself to be far older than the others, but she could not distance herself from the approaching crisis in their lives. Throughout June, Purple Lady wrote of her desperation and sadness. Possibly sensing the nearness of her demise, she worked rapidly as an artist, sometimes painting several pictures in a day. By mid-month she was temporarily blinded, and the incident was even more disturbing to her because Strawberry Girl had predicted it.

Somehow, the trauma of this temporary blindness became the final persuader. On June 25, Purple Lady wrote her farewells and an informal will in the diary:

> I'm sorry I ever went to Dr. Tsitos. He promised to help me, but he is helping Retrace Lady instead. Of course I should have known better than to trust any man! I am packing my things away so they won't be in anyone else's way. She can throw them out if she likes.
>
> I feel as though I have been deceived. But what difference does it make anyway? If I die, I won't have to fight this losing battle any longer. I hope Retrace Lady will love and appreciate my children, and I hope she will go ahead and do the book. I would hate to let Elen down.
>
> I would sure like to see my father one more time. He loves me, and I, him. We understand each other best.
>
> I finished my portrait tonight. Possibly my last work of art. P.L. I would like Taffy to have my book, *The Here and the Hereafter.* P.L. For Bobby I leave the painting. He also wanted Strawberry Girl's, but it isn't mine to give. To all my family, I leave to you all the love I have to give. God bless. Purple Lady.[12]

During the next two weeks, she would increasingly fade into the background, and by July 8, Retrace Lady would view the Purple Lady's disappearance as a hit-and-run accident. But accident or not, Purple Lady never returned.

However, long before the perceived accident near Centerville, Virginia, Purple Lady's fading had an effect on Retrace Lady. "Today is bad, one of the hardest days I have had," she wrote after reading Purple Lady's informal will in the diary. In this passage, Retrace Lady explained some reasons for her emotional state:

> I am tired, and I am very confused. I feel sad because Purple Lady is leaving or is gone. She so wanted to live.
>
> Don was so nice last night [helping me when the insomnia and headaches were so bad], but he is back to normal tonight. For several nights I have dreamed that [he] is breaking my glasses, and I am panic-stricken.
>
> Taffy . . . came up today and did my laundry for me. No woman ever had a better daughter than I. I'm sure she has no idea how grateful I am nor how much she means to me. . . . Headaches continue.[13]

It was as though both Purple Lady and Strawberry Girl had premonitions of, or at least some unexplainable intimations about, the imminence of what therapists now term *unification,* or the blending of multiple personalities into one.

But at the time, Retrace Lady did not. Or if she did, she refused to consider the possibility that all three of them would disappear and be replaced by another. After the passing of another week, she would write, "I can't help but wonder if I may be dying! I can't seem to accept that. I feel I will live. . . . Told Dr. T. about my dream of Don breaking my glasses. He thinks it represents a barrier that Don manifests to keep me from doing something I want to do."[14]

By the start of July, therefore, the end for the others and the beginning for me were only days away. But that period resulted in a chaotic and emotional state of dying and rebirth that exacted a great toll on the body. During the next four days, no entries were made in the diary, partly from the stress but more specifically because the family was vacationing in West Virginia. And there was a third reason. During the trip, Retrace Lady—who earlier in the summer had come to dominate the writing of the diary—seemed to discover my presence. It was as if she sensed *another* standing in the mind's wings but could not determine who it might be. Yet account for it or not, my presence silenced her.

But like Strawberry Girl, the Retrace Lady did not pass without one last night of enjoyment. Over the years, she and a friend, Harriet Henderson, had frequented a supper club in northern Virginia. Their evenings had been escapes from the tedium of working days in ladies' specialty shops, reprieves from the difficulties of middle age and parenthood and married life. That supper club became the Retrace Lady's haven, in which she lost herself in an atmosphere of music, good conversation, and anonymity. And all three loved music: Strawberry Girl loved soul music, Purple Lady classical music, and Retrace Lady enjoyed pop music.

So during the vacation, when Don took Retrace Lady and Bobby to a supper club in Clarksburg, West Virginia, something clicked within her. Suddenly, she felt festive. She had a martini, very dry and intoxicating, followed by a couple of Brandy Alexanders. Slowly, the recent months of worry about headaches, personality changes, and survival over the others seemed of increasingly less importance. A small combo began playing a song she liked, and she asked Don to dance. He agreed. While they danced, Bobby sat at the table and seemed to admire their grace and agility on the dance floor. And emotion overwhelmed the Retrace Lady.

This was exactly what she had wanted for years. Many times she had begged Don to go with her and Harriet to the northern Virginia club, but he had consistently refused. Now, unwittingly, he was giving her what she had always wanted. *The irony of it.* As the Retrace Lady pondered that thought, she became lightheaded and eased her weight onto Don's grasp. He seemed to think she was being affectionate and, uncharacteristically, he responded in kind. He tightened his hold on her and they danced under his strength, his rhythm, his control. Later, during the meal, she realized that their conversation was friendly, bordering on warmth. Bobby joked with them. The evening seemed as if nothing could tarnish it.

Then she became ill. Maybe from the drinks or the dancing or mixing alcohol with the medication she had been taking, but she spent nearly two hours in the supper club's rest room, where she vomited and suffered from dry heaves.

After she had recovered, they left, but Don snapped at her as they went to the car, "My God but you've made a fool of yourself tonight, girl."

"I didn't misbehave," she protested. "What did I do wrong? I *know* I was in complete control all the time."

He said nothing in response as they crossed the dark parking lot. But when they reached the car, he said, "You were so wasteful. I paid too much for the meal and the drinks to have you throw them up. Don't you know how weak you are, how sick you've been? You had no business drinking and dancing."

"I didn't know I was going to make myself sick," she said, crying. "And I wouldn't have dreamed of causing you to waste your money. I was just enjoying myself so. *Just once. . . .*"

En route to the motel, Don resumed his complaint that she had made a fool of herself. But this time she got angry.

"You make it sound as though I intended to get sick. Intended to waste your money," she said.

"No, I didn't," he responded. "I just said that nine dollars was a lot to waste."

The next morning Retrace Lady wrote her final entry in the diary and penned a note to Taffy. The first recounted the supper-club incident and ended, "Taffy, darling, I thank you for making life easier for me." The second was written on narrow paper and contained the Retrace Lady's farewells:

Taffy darling:
   Please get this in my diary if I am unable to do so.
   I know that I am dying. I have known for a week now, so there is no need deceiving myself.
   Dr. Tsitos has really tried to help me, and I truly tried to become the main personality. But when anyone would ask me who I was, I always answered, "Retrace Lady." And that is who I am. Only a small, intricate part of the total personality. So I too must go.
   I don't want to die, but your theory of life and death make

it much easier for me. I can go away feeling that I will be born again, therefore I will be with you again. With you, Bobby, Tommy, Jimmy, and, yes, even Don. All my children.

I am very tired and sick. I can hardly see to write. . . . Tell Dr. T., also, that I tried. I love you.

Mother,
Retrace Lady[15]

The following day, a Sunday—yesterday—would be when Retrace Lady was driving through Centerville toward Fairfax. The vacation was over. Purple Lady, seen by Retrace Lady as the hit-and-run victim of her driving, would disappear. Her life was over. Then, this morning, Retrace Lady would walk into the therapist's office. It would be her last journey. Her life was over. Hours later, *I* would walk out.

But what have I walked out to? The others have left, allowing me finally to begin living in a normal way. One person, one life. But they took some crucial things with them. Other than their cryptic notes in these diaries, they seem to have taken into the black disappearance of my mind all traces of memory about who they were and what they did. They took the memories of decades when I was hidden. Without knowledge of their pasts, how can I understand—or ever hope to fit into—the life to which I have returned?

I have no answer for that. All I possess are the furnishings in a dreary apartment and all the clothes and mementos, the correspondence and memorabilia, that once belonged to the others. My God, what has this healing gotten me into?

Again I have no answer. All I have is a pen and this diary. Dr. Thigpen says I write well. Let's see. I'll write the entry for July 9:

In Dr. Tsitos's office today she came out and told him of an incident that occurred near Centerville, Virginia. She thought she (Retrace Lady) saw a person cross the road in front of her. She stopped the car suddenly, and in so doing, she threw Taffy against the dash. . . . Retrace Lady got out and looked for the woman dressed in purple, but there was no one there. She was sure she had struck the woman. She even thought she felt her hit the bumper. (I think this may have been when Taffy hit the dash.) When they got home, Taffy brought out a self-portrait of Purple Lady, and the reaction was most unexpected. . . . The shock was so great that 'I' came out. . . .[16]

Reflecting on those painful days of July 1974, but allowed the distance of more than fourteen years, I know that I could not be affirming today that I am mentally well if I had not gone all the way through the healing process. Prior to that time, most of my *alters* (the term therapists now use for personalities perceived by an MPD patient) had made the same commitment: to resolve the disorder. None of them made that commitment out of a desire to die. All of them loved life; they all wanted to live, to be the single survivor once the disorder had ended. Yet none liked the way they had to live, locked within the disorder and competing with the others for one body, one mind, one memory, one lifetime.

In retrospect, I'm not sure that it was the commitment of my birth personality for the disorder to end. Today, I am that same birth personality. But when I was two years old, I retreated *into* the disorder. Therefore, unification[17] at the age of forty-seven meant the consistent end of not only the disorder but also of my retreat from responsibility for my own life. My alters wanted the disorder to end, but I don't think that I did—certainly not until long after July 1974. Prior to that time, the alters were in control of my life. So it was their choices and their retreating that thrust me back onto center stage, whether I wanted that emergence or not. The only other option at that time was for the body, devoid of a personality, to die as a result of what might be described as a psychological vacuum.

Even my obnoxious alter, the Strawberry Girl, wanted the healing, because she wanted to live, wanted to be the survivor. I now believe that's why she regressed, increasingly assuming a mentality younger than her initial perspective of being twenty-one years old. It was as though she understood that unification for them was somehow linked to getting back, to rediscovering what had initially triggered the disorder, then proceeding forward again from that moment in order to reconstruct a whole, integrated life.

Though the Strawberry Girl's regression led to her demise, it made the recall of all my alters' memories easier for me, once the unification had taken place. And unlike the classic MPD case of Sybil Dorsett, I accomplished my own integration. Despite the confusion of my days and nights, I was organizing my own per-sonalities and life throughout 1974. But in Sybil's case, it was her therapist who did these things for the patient; Cornelia Wilbur, M.D., purposely regressed each of Sybil's alters until all were the same age. Then she brought each alter forward to Sybil's actual age. Sybil's was a healing process made orderly by a clinician highly skilled in hypnosis; it was a process from outside the pa-tient.

In contrast, mine was primarily self-willed. Dr. Tsitos, a highly competent psychoanalyst, did not structure my regressions. In fact, he did no regressions in therapy with me. If a regressive state began with one of my alters, my therapist pursued it. But he consistently reminded me that I, the patient, could do this orga-nization myself. And he said that if I did, then the integration—when it was achieved—would hold.

However, the personalities' unification that occurred in July 1974 was merely the climax of a much longer process toward integration. It had taken nearly twenty years of therapy to get me to that point, and it would take three more years of therapy to secure this wellness. And this interim, follow-up therapy began with the recall of all my former alters' experiences—a phenome-non that only my mind could accomplish, at its own pace and in its own manner.

At this fragile stage following the unification, my identity was defined by what I could recall. I seemed to exist only as deeply as the memories I could claim of my former alters. On July 16, my diary entry referred matter-of-factly to one significant memory loss: "I (my recall) obviously blocked part of the past."[18]

But memories did start coming back to me, and most of them were pictorial flashes or images. The earliest were in the form of dreams. During the first two weeks after the unification, these dreams intermingled imagination with what I would subse-quently recognize as re-creations of actual scenes from my alters' lives. Some dreams came during sleep, but others occurred while I was awake, watching late movies on television.

Were these dreams actually memories from the unconscious realm where I had hidden for decades? Or were the dreams my mind's way of reconciling its awareness of both the conscious and the unconscious selves I had been? The answers were not clear, but the dreams were:

In one dream I was lying on a bed in a colorless room. A woman brought a baby and laid it in my arms and told me to breast-feed it. I looked at the child, and it had no face except a small round opening for a mouth. When the child's mouth touched me I began to scream. It felt like the touch of death. I awakened.

In another dream I was searching for houses. I found one I liked. It was tall and airy. A lot of rooms and space. So I told the realtor I would take it. Then the walls opened up and fell all around me. Yet it didn't seem to bother me. I kept searching for a house. I would find a house, and the same thing would occur. After four or five times having the walls collapse, I woke up.

The next dream did not upset me, either. I found myself in "another" place. The people there had white, round heads and larger, black bodies. On the sides of each body was a round button. The people looked like painted objects, but these "things" could talk, though I saw no evidence of mouths, ears, eyes etc.
One of the female "things" opened up a cabinet in the wall and handed me a baby to feed. The baby was like the one in the earlier dream. I told her I could not feed it.
She laid the baby down on a table and went to a wall that had sockets like electric units. She plugged her little round button into one of the sockets. When I asked her why she did that, she said the child couldn't feed itself and that someone else had to do the eating for it. That everyone helped everyone else there.[19]

These dreams seemed to express my inner turmoil during those initial weeks of oneness. I was obsessed with being normal.

For the first time in decades, I was like everyone else—at least in the sense that I was one person. But I was paralyzed by fears. I had no idea how to be a mother to my children. It didn't matter that Taffy was grown and had a family of her own, or that Bobby was a teenager establishing his independence. I needed to mother. I needed a house to make into a home. And new to life, I feared death, destruction, and failure.

The truth of my story was frightening—mainly because it was impossible to know what that story was. A fourth dream expressed this fear. It involved my former psychiatrists, my husband and my current psychiatrist:

> I was in a basement. Very dark, damp and cold. I was seated at a table against the back wall. On the front wall there was a stair to the right of me and a door on the left. Down the stairs came a man dressed like an old movie gangster—overcoat, hat over his eyes etc.
>
> The man came up to the table, put two five hundred dollar bills on it and said to me, "This is *not* to tell!"
>
> "But I *have* to tell," I said.
>
> The man opened the door to leave, and as the light struck his face, I saw that it was Dr. Corbett H. Thigpen.
>
> In all, three men did and said the same things. A second man was Dr. Hervey M. Cleckley, and the third was Don.
>
> I picked up the money to look at it. At that moment Dr. Tsitos was standing in front of me, and he said, "Ah, ha. I caught you."
>
> I started to cry and told him I wasn't going to take the money, but I had to tell and I was only going to tell the truth.
>
> "If all you're going to tell is the truth," Dr. Tsitos said, "then it's all right."
>
> That's when I awakened.[20]

The day I told Dr. Tsitos about these dreams was also the day that I took him the first draft of a manuscript about my childhood. It had been written by my cousin, Elen Sain Pittillo. Ultimately, this text would form the basis for *I'm Eve*, the autobiography I coauthored with her.

He seemed most interested in the fourth dream. "I understand Don's role," he said. "For some time, you have been saying that Don thinks you get sick to spite him—"

"Talk about ego!" I snapped, interrupting.

"—but I don't quite understand about Thigpen and Cleckley."

I did not respond. I had no concrete reasons for my fears of my former psychiatrists. I simply felt the fears. When I continued to remain quiet, Dr. Tsitos did not pursue that. Instead, he shifted the subject to himself.

"The part about me may be good," he said. "It may mean that you and I have a good rapport."

Suddenly, I realized that my therapist shared something in common with me. Living was new to me, but he was also having to adjust to a new patient. Me. "And we're certainly going to need that," I said, laughing.

He stood and walked from behind his desk. He sat in the chair across from me. "I accept you as you are, Chris, and your problem for what it is." There was a new warmth in his voice. "As long as you trust me enough to tell me, I will not question the validity of what you say about yourself or your illness."

"Then why did you say, 'Ah, ha. I caught you,' in my dream?"

"Maybe you now sense that I know what you do, that I know how you create your 'other selves,'" he said. "I'm only searching for the truth. And it's clear from your dreams that your mind is ready to deal with the truth and that you're ready to tell it."

He encouraged me to continue working with my cousin on the book. He described it as good therapy But he cautioned that the unification of personalities was not yet a full integration. He said the worst might be ahead.

I did believe I was ready to talk and, more specifically, ready to start living. I made a two-hundred-dollar deposit with a California-based sportswear company to operate a clothing franchise with my sisters (even though the company would subsequently dissolve and our money would be returned).

And I planned trips with the family. Though none of them, except for Taffy, seemed to realize that I was a new person, I had to discern how I fitted into their lives. During one of these outings, a drive to Hershey, Pennsylvania, I studied each of them as if

I were planning to paint their portraits. Late that Sunday night, I wrote my observations:

> The day was a bit confusing, but interesting. Both my children are strongly opinionated and usually disagree, though it seems like healthy opposition. I tried to enter into their conversations, only enough to see what makes them tick. I'm happy about what I discovered of their independence and individuality.
>
> Don and Jimmy understand and respect each other, grandparent to grandson. And more importantly, they enjoy being together.
>
> My son-in-law Tommy is the strong, silent type, but he understands Taffy and enjoys being with her. I got the distinct impression that the two of them prefer doing things alone, rather than as a part of a family unit. Perhaps Don and I may also enjoy being alone? I don't really know. Time will tell.
>
> My greatest delight comes from discovering that Taffy and I can speak openly and honestly without anger. This is a hidden blessing.
>
> But the day ended badly because Tommy's car broke down. In the midst of the turmoil I told them it had been a good day anyway, and they laughed at me.
>
> Still, it *was* a good day. I was able to study all members of my family, separately and as a part of the whole. I think my adjustment into the group is working out fine. So the day was good because we were together.[21]

By our next family trip, however, Dr. Tsitos's cautions proved correct. At Edisto Beach with my twin sisters, Elise "Becky" Walton and Louise "Tiny" Edwards, there began a period of recall that lasted for more than six weeks and grew progressively more intense. The first recall started with a severe headache, though that pain lasted only a short while. During that suffering, however, I saw myself as a little girl. Afterward, Tiny said that I acted and even sounded like a little girl. Was this possible?

In the recall, a neighbor had insulted me, and one of my aunts sided with him. She kept calling me "a bad girl," and I kept repeating that I wasn't. "I'm just a little girl, I'm not bad," I could see myself saying, though I could not actually hear the sounds. Yet somehow I knew everything that was being said, and I could see who they were talking about. I could see the bad little girl. It just wasn't me.

Or was it?

2

According to modern psychiatry, the *association* of ideas or images or impulses causes memories to emerge into normal consciousness.[1] For example, we see a tree. Immediately, our minds associate that image with trees we have previously seen, and simultaneously, we recall memories that we had associated with trees on earlier occasions. But when memories cannot readily be associated with ideas or images or impulses, then our minds consciously experience *dissociation.*[2] For most of us, dissociation is fleeting in everyday life. But for MPD patients, dissociation *is* life.

And because I had endured this dissociative illness for more than four decades, the period of recall during August and September 1974 proved to be extremely difficult. It necessitated almost daily sessions with my therapist and, when possible, constant companionship while I was at home. My life—or more accurately, my *lives*—passed before my eyes. I thought I was going to die. It was terrifying, redefining the word *confusion.* And when it became clear that I wasn't dying, I thought I was going insane.

Yet how could I tell my family what was happening in my mind? It was all so bizarre that, for a time, I isolated myself from all of them except Taffy. For nearly six weeks, I never went to the table to eat. Each day I bathed quickly, changed clothes, then rushed back to the long couch in our living room. That room, being the largest space in the apartment, was the only area where

I did not feel enclosed or trapped. I did not want to leave. It seemed safe, a haven as secure as the Strother Place's attic had been when I was a child.

I needed that haven because I was afraid to sleep. I feared getting lost again in my unconsciousness. So I watched television, tried to read, did anything to avoid the depths of unconsciousness. And when exhaustion finally demanded it, I often slept sitting up. Basically, I was experiencing such enormous intimacy within my mind that I could not bear closeness with anyone else. This was so intense that I rarely went to bed with Don.

Despite this outward chaos, my inner experiences with recall were systematic and ordered. Beginning with the age of two, my life passed in review. Day after day, week after week, era upon era, it was virtually a ceaseless envisioning of who I had been, of those whom my former alters had known, and of the things the alters had done. As well, it was chronological, with few regressions or repetitions of scenes: Once I recalled a spot of time, I would not see it again.

But beyond the process itself, there was another aspect that made this recall riveting. The people in these scenes were not visions. They appeared to be real. And the significant scenes that I saw have not faded in my memory. I can recall them today, nearly as vividly as they first appeared to me:

Daddy is wearing white long johns, and they have buttons and a flap in the back. Trimming a holly Christmas tree, he is tying oranges, apples, and popcorn on it. There is a fire in the hearth, and the oaken water bucket is filled with nuts. A beautiful doll is under the tree. But I am in the featherbed, and I lay my head back down. I don't want him to know that I'm awake. . . .

The dragon in the ditch is lying flat on its back. It's a man! He has red hair, a red mustache, and there's mud on his face. His coat is like a tapestry, homemade and woven, but he's dead. . . .

The man in the saw pit is in three parts. Mother is holding me as we watch other people gather around the body. She is wearing an apron and her hair is jet black. . . .

Mother is bleeding beside a hearth where the bricks are

uneven. A jar is broken. It's a half-gallon fruit jar, and so
much blood is flowing from Mother's arm. Blood is
everywhere. I hide my head under the pillow. I move to get
Daddy, but I am also under the pillow. The me who is running
has red hair. At the door, she has to step down onto a round
rock. From there, a path leads to the barn and Daddy. . . .

It's the day my sisters are born. The Red-headed Girl goes
through a turnstile gate, across the pasture, through a creek,
up a hill, and into the house. Mother is in a bed in the corner,
and the twins are in the Red-headed Girl's bed. My bed. . . .

The most remarkable aspect was how quickly this material
came to me and how rapidly the scenes moved. I didn't have to
think about it. The recall simply came—not as thoughts but as
pictures unlike any I had ever seen. It was as though a river of
many currents flowed steadily in my mind; and within these currents, reflections filled with people were also in motion. Seemingly unaware that they were being watched, these people were
living out moments of time in their lives. My life?

What I saw was like a montage effect in a film, except that
these moments moved from left to right, then out of view. All
were in vivid color, like watching channels being switched on a
television set, and all were without sound. But beyond the vivid
colors of the foreground scenes, the backgrounds were always
red or black. It was as though the people were standing or walking on blackness but enveloped in redness. And these backgrounds were smokelike, with the reds and blacks flashing like
strobe lights.

However, these scenes were unlike switching TV channels in
one crucial way: I had no control over them. I was simply the
audience for unedited excerpts of a movie of all my many lives.
Yet I seemed to be hidden within each of the women in these
scenes. And mine was a peculiar film. There were no voices or
environmental noises linked directly to the scenes; the only
sounds I heard were the normal ones within the apartment itself
or from outside along the streets of Fairfax.

At Mt. Carmel Methodist Church the family is gathered for
dinner on the ground. The Singing Girl is wearing an

organdy dress with a huge white bow in the back, and she is eleven or twelve years old. . . .

Daddy has his head hung between a mechanical rake and the side of a building. A man came to help. He moved the rake so Daddy could get his head out. . . .

Grandfather Hastings is dead. Daddy is putting quarters on his eyes. Mother is crying.

Daddy comes to sit with the Big-eyed Girl, Becky, and Tiny on the woodpile. It is under a silver maple, but for some reason the girls call it a cottonwood tree. . . .

A goat is standing on top of Daddy's convertible. Big riding rocks are beside the car. The Poet knows that women used to stand on these rocks to mount horses. . . .

A chain gang is moving along the street. Daddy is wearing a gun, and he is a guard there. Through a window with bars the Liar is watching the prisoners. . . .

The Freckle Girl is standing in a long blue dress. She is waiting for her date, and they are going to the prom. She waits a long time, but he does not show up. . . .

In a sense, I was coexisting in two eras: the one in which I actually lived during those months of 1974, intermingled with the successive eras I was revisiting. I was aware of what was going on in our apartment at the same time that I was seeing mind pictures. And these pictures continued whether I closed my eyes or left them open. Asleep or awake. In fact, keeping my eyes open made me feel more comfortable, because that seemed to maintain a hold on reality.

Chris Costner is seated in a tall chair at a switchboard. Later, she will be called Eve Black in a book. Even though she is working as a telephone operator, she wears a silk dress. But she has it on backward. The buttons are supposed to go down the back, yet she has them going down the front. . . .

Chris Costner is in a beauty pageant at Augusta. She is wearing a long white dress. She is laughing the way she does when she is drinking. . . .

Dr. Thigpen is hypnotizing the other Chris. In his book he will call her Eve White. On one wall of his office is a print of Pan in the forest with animals. On the other wall is a pencil drawing of a minaret. . . .

It is the day that Don and Jane are getting married. Mother is in a bed in the sitting room. When Don and Jane leave, Grandmother and Taffy see them off. Somewhere else, Don is bringing a big corsage to the car, but Jane doesn't know what it's for. . . .

Except for recognizing myself at the age of two, I knew that none of the women in these scenes were actually me; all of them were alters. Yet it was apparent that they *had* lived my life and that, until this recall, I had no idea what had caused them to live my life or how they had lived it or who they had been.

All I seemed to have in common with them was an understanding of multiplicity. But even in that distinction, this recall was different. It was the opposite of multiplicity. Viewing these eras, I could see that during the disorder one alter from a recess of space inside my mind had been able to watch another when she was "out" in the body. However, recall was the reverse. This time it was as though I were outside of my mind and looking in, watching these memories being replayed on my mind's center stage.

Taffy is a new baby, and her mother is the Freckle Girl, who is wearing a red nightgown. It has a long skirt and a halter top. A heater is angled in the corner of the room, and the mother is holding the baby in a pink blanket. Taffy is tiny. She has no hair. It is the room where she was born, and she is so beautiful. . . .

Strangely, I felt few emotions at the time about myself in relation to what I was seeing. Yes, this was my life, but somehow I had not lived it. Yes, I recognized the people and the events, but I had not been there. All I felt was extreme fatigue. Emotions would come later.

Although Dr. Tsitos kept careful tabs on how this recall was progressing, my daughter became my real therapist through this stage in the healing process. Every morning Taffy was at our door by five-thirty. My son-in-law, Tommy, would carry young Jimmy inside and place the sleeping child on the couch. Then Taffy and Jimmy would stay with me all day, not leaving until my husband and son had been fed supper.

Hers was a daily, fourteen-hour vigil of love. She pampered me. She cleaned the apartment, got the groceries, and did other household duties, but she suggested nothing that would disturb me. She alone understood the importance of this recall to my ultimate wellness. She sat beside me and listened, often asking, "What are you seeing now? Which personality is it?" When scenes were perplexing, she tried to help me unravel who it might be and what might be happening. When a scene was funny, she laughed with me. And when I was overcome with exhaustion or confusion, she held me.

Somehow, Taffy remained unemotional throughout all of this, as if she had been given a therapist's training to care for me during this phenomenon. And it was then that our mother-daughter bond began. In a sense, as she reviewed my former lives with me, Taffy and I assumed the equivalent of a shared life together. Being in my presence while my mind gathered memories from the life I had missed with her, Taffy and I regained what MPD had stolen from us.

On August 23, this recall took on a new and frightful dimension. My remembering reached 1957, when a surgeon in Georgia, William E. Barfield, M.D., operated on my body—then controlled by alters known as Jane and the Blind Lady. A third alter during this period would subsequently assume the pseudonym Evelyn Lancaster, as she coauthored *The Final Face of Eve* with Jim Poling.[3] But what made this recall different from the rest was that I became *part* of it; and even stranger, I became part of a remembered event that had originally occurred while my alters were presumed unconscious. It was an *abreaction,* or the release of emotional energy attached to repressed memories. My diary explained:

I was wide *awake,* but I experienced Dr. Barfield
performing surgery on me. I could see people standing around

me. They wore green gowns, masks and hats. I could hear them talking surgical lingo. Heard Dr. Barfield say, "She has two endometriomas. One's the size of an orange; the other, a bit larger."

Worse still, I could *feel* them cutting my stomach. I was in absolute agony, and Bobby was frightened to death. This continued for about two hours, and I was surprised that I was not covered with blood.

I must surely be losing my mind. I can't tolerate another of these experiences.[4]

But I did endure others. A second abreaction occurred three days later, causing me to face the fact that my past included an abortion and a hysterectomy in 1964. Two alters at that time— the Bell Lady and the Turtle Lady—had been competing for Don's affections, because the alters wanted a third child. But Don was uninterested and distant. Better than they, he understood how difficult the family's circumstances were. He alone had been taking care of the finances, and there was barely enough money to support a mentally ill wife and *two* children. A third child was out of the question. But a third alter who also existed at the time, the Card Girl, knew that a pregnancy was not out of the realm of possibility.

Capricious and uninterested in Don, the Card Girl viewed an unwanted pregnancy as her means of escape. With distorted logic, she believed that if she could manipulate circumstances so that the Turtle Lady became pregnant, then Don would seek a divorce and the Card Girl would be free. So she tricked Don and the Turtle Lady, and a pregnancy developed. Don became furious but insisted that she have the child. The Turtle Lady attempted suicide. The Card Girl, frustrated that her scheme had failed, insisted on the abortion.[5]

Ten years after that 1964 surgery, I found myself in 1974 not only learning about this tragedy for the first time but also *reliving* it. As with the earlier abreaction, I saw the actual surgery room. I saw the medical staff at work on my body as they performed both an abortion and a hysterectomy. I heard their comments, some of which they would not have dared say to a conscious patient. And I felt the pains: "The cutting feeling was

searing, burning. I heard a woman screaming and suddenly realized it was me."6

Another three days passed, and a third abreaction occurred in
the presence of Don, Bobby, my sister Tiny, and her son Chuck.
Its significance at the time seemed to be that the recall's chronology was breaking down. But more emphatically, this reliving
was not just a mental and emotional process. What I remembered
actually recurred.

Afterward, my sister said that the abreaction had interjected
itself into an otherwise normal evening. She recalled that the two
of us had been conversing, when suddenly I got quiet. She said
that I regressed rapidly until I seemed to be acting and talking
like a little girl. She said that within seconds I began tearing off
my clothes, then I fell on the floor and was screaming, "Mamma,
I'm burning. Mamma, I'm burning!"

My sister was initially frozen by shock but then responded by
rushing to the kitchen for my medication. When she returned
with the pills and a glass of water, she said I was still screaming
but now rolling on the floor. The torn clothing left much of my
upper body exposed.

This clamor aroused Don and the boys from adjacent rooms.
Responding to the crisis, they held me while she attempted to
force medication down my throat. In the struggle, she spilled
water on my arm.

"Oh, that feels good," she heard me say, and I seemed momentarily relieved yet still in pain.

Tiny ran for my robe. Bobby rushed to get a wet towel. During the lull, Don pointed out to Chuck that a puckered childhood
scar on my upper right arm had turned a fiery red. But when
Bobby returned with the wet towel and placed it on my arm, I
stopped screaming and relaxed. Later, when the towel was removed, she remembers that the puckered scar seemed cool and
white but that the terry cloth was steaming hot to the touch.

Her memory is that it took nearly an hour for the abreaction
to cease and the medication to take effect, calming me, allowing
me to slip from the regression.7

These abreactions got Don's attention in a way that, according to what I was recalling, nothing had been able to do in years.

He seemed deeply embarrassed that someone other than he or Taffy or Bobby had witnessed my crisis; yet my husband also seemed concerned about me. I later learned that Don even consulted with Dr. Tsitos—something he had not done since my therapy in the fifties.

And Don had reason to be concerned. Emotionally, I had fallen apart. I was panic-stricken. For about two days, I paced the apartment like an animal that had been captured, trapped, and caged. I could not be still. My sister, who extended her visit to care for me, said I talked incessantly—sometimes in the present but mostly from the past—as if I were reliving my life in a jumbled fashion that seemed more like an emotional breakdown than a healing process. It was as though all my alters were talking at once, screaming memories that only they possessed. Tiny said I was so consumed with energy that she had to follow me around until I dropped from exhaustion, and only then could she feed me. By August 30, my therapist was called, and he prescribed a new medication. It immediately reduced the anxiety, but it did not stop my talking.

Something had been triggered within me. Regaining memories had given me new perspectives. For the first time, I realized that my life had been controlled by at least *twenty-two* personalities during the prior forty-four years. The sheer chaos of that was troubling enough. But I also realized who Don had been while at least nine different alters had come and gone during what was then our twenty-one-year marriage.

To his credit, Don had not abandoned me or any of my former alters. On the contrary, he had worked every day during each of those years to make certain that there was money for doctor bills, food, clothing, transportation, and a place to live. He had been an attentive father to our son and daughter. He had been dependable, coming home every night and going to work every morning. He had never failed to live up to his vows to provide for me or our home. But my anguish was that for nearly two decades Don had also been *ashamed* of my illness.

I had finally seen that shame when he realized that my sister and nephew were witnessing the abreaction, and that my son and nephew had seen me half-naked on the floor. I also knew that this shame had been brewing within Don for decades because, during the recall of earlier incidents when my alters had experienced crises in public, I had seen that same expression on his face, that same disdainful lingering in his eyes until those scenes passed out of view in my mind.

I wrote in my diary on September 2, "I know this is very hard on him and that it embarrasses him, but I can't help myself anymore than I do. . . ."[8] That was the day Don and I discussed my health, him, and our marriage.

"You don't need help anymore," he said, bent over the kitchen sink, his back to me. "Dr. Tsitos says you don't have multiple personality anymore. He says you're all right. You're well."

I studied the back of Don's head as if it were a map to an uncharted land. "I only seem well because I'm on medication," I said. "Can't you see the pills keep me acting like a normal human being?"

He continued to face the wall, but his remarks were aimed at me. And these words seemed to have been prepared after considerable thought. "I *see* that everything has worked out. There won't be any more changes in you, and the doctor has found medicine to keep you calm. You're well. You've got some savings, and you'll be getting more money soon from the Japanese translation of that book with Poling. Plus, you and Elen will be working on another book. That will bring money, too." Then he turned toward me. I have never seen a face so filled with pain, yet so resolute.

"You're saying we should get a divorce, aren't you?"

"I'm saying that I've got a life to live, too, Chris. From now on, you'll just have to do the best you can."

Divorce was not a new subject in our home. The weeks of recall had confirmed that. But divorce was an untimely subject, given what I was enduring. Yet I had to admit that this man was virtually a stranger to me. And I to him. Handsome and dependable and long-suffering as he still was at the age of fifty-one, I had not chosen him. I had not married him. My alter named Jane had made those choices. Moreover, he did not know *me* now. At least he did not acknowledge that I was different from the women my alters had been. Maybe our marriage *was* as long gone as the alter he had first loved in the fifties—but how could I tell this man that he had loved an *illusion*? How could I make him understand that, finally, I was the real person inside the woman who was his wife?

"That's it," I said, and Don looked at me with suspicion, as if he thought I were switching personalities again. "All these years you thought that when I got well, I would be *Jane* again."

"She had a beautiful personality," he said in a faint voice, "but I didn't expect her to come back. I never remember any of them returning."

"Then who *did* you think I would be, once I got well?"

"I just thought you'd be a wife and a mother who wouldn't need help anymore. I thought the doctor bills would end. I thought that, instead of emergencies, we would finally have an *emergence.*" The words didn't sound like Don, but they were clearly expressing his sentiments. He was serious.

"And if we do get a divorce, will you help me?" I responded. "Bobby's still in high school. He has needs I can't meet. And I still don't remember very well, so when Tiny leaves I'll need someone to help me—"

"Help you do what?"

The conversation halted on a dime. It had actually gotten nowhere. That was clear. Either he could not understand what I was going through or he didn't want to. I couldn't determine which it was, but I knew that the difference mattered. And there was no love in his voice or his words, or in his eyes. "You did want Jane back. Didn't you?" I asked again.

"I wanted somebody who would help *me* for a change."

"And you don't think that day will ever come with me?"

For the first time, an emotion other than coldness flashed across his face, and he said, "Girl, you don't *know* what I've been doing all these years, working for, expecting, waiting on that day."

"You're right, Don," I said. It was useless to argue that as an MPD patient, my awareness had somehow *not* been out of touch with him or Taffy or Bobby. Only myself. "So maybe this is it? Maybe we should end it."

We sat silently for several long minutes. The kitchen smelled of food getting cold and stale. The apartment seemed unnaturally still. And I realized that if I were certain I could exist on my own, then I *would* let him go. I also realized that there must have been many times over the years when he had thought the same thing: Had he been certain at any point that I was well and able to exist without him, then he would have gone.

Finally, I had to ask the inevitable question: "If we divorce, will you support me and Bobby?"

"I'll always look after my boy. But you've got money in the bank and more on the way. So if we split up, then, no, I won't pay your bills. I've done more than enough of that."

I had to give him that. During the last two decades, Don had paid over $100,000 in medical bills for my therapy. He had been forced to sell our homes three different times. Yes, long ago he had paid more than most husbands. But it was also becoming clear that I had paid a high price, too. It all seemed like such a vicious circle. That evening, when I wrote about this conversation in my diary, the last line in the entry beseeched: *God, what is life anyway?*

By the following Friday, I was so despondent that I took an overdose of sleeping pills, mixed with some of the other medications I had been taking. When our son, who was fourteen at the time, came home from school, he found me crawling along the apartment floor, my mind slipping in and out of consciousness. Bobby called a cab and rushed me to our family physician, Tibor Ham, M.D. The doctor saved my life, and I spent the remainder of that night on the living room couch. Hour upon hour, only one thought echoed in my mind: *saved for what?*

From this chaos, the next couple of weeks became a roller-coaster ride. During therapy sessions in early September, my therapist placed great importance on the abreactions. "At this time, Chris, your personality is such that you are recalling scenes which could normally be accomplished only under hypnosis. This in itself is a phenomenon," he said.

"But they're not phenomena," I protested. "They're *real.*"

"As real as they may appear, I suggest they are more likely to be illusions."

"You wouldn't say that if they happened to you."

"Probably not," he responded. "But just because we disagree on what to call these 'happenings,' I am not uncaring about what they may be doing to you. I do care. And what I think they're doing is ensuring that you will stay well."

"Then when will I *feel* well? When will all of these abnormalities cease?"

"I can't answer that," he said. "Your mind is its own healer now."

"And who is going to heal my family?" I asked, then proceeded to tell him about my conversation with Don about divorce and about my concerns that a divorce might harm Bobby.

"You should not base such discussions upon your feelings for what might be best for Bobby," he said. "It's just as unhealthy for a teenager to live in an unhappy atmosphere as it is for him to live in the aftermath of a divorce. Divorce is acceptable, as long as your son's life continues to run smoothly *after* the divorce. If Bobby can continue to do things with, and see, his father; if Bobby can be confident that he can still go to a good high school and then a good college; if Bobby can feel assured that you'll be well, even though you're living apart from his father—if your son can have a sense of security about all these concerns, then divorce will not harm him."

"But how can *I* give that to my son? If peace of mind doesn't come in a pill bottle, I don't have it to give. I'm sinking, Doctor. I feel as though all three of us—Don, Bobby, and I—are slowly drowning in the flood of confusion that has been my life. And Bobby's so vulnerable."

"We won't let you drown, Chris," Dr. Tsitos said. "If pills have been a problem, we'll try something else to help you relax. After all, when you're uptight, you can't swim or tread water, now can you?"

"But what if I don't want to swim?"

"Oh, but you do," Dr. Tsitos responded. "Life is too new to you. That's all." That day he replaced my medications with the use of relaxation tapes, and he encouraged me to begin work on the book with Elen. But he cautioned that, like the recall and abreactions, reviewing facts for my cousin to write about all my former alters could trigger many difficult, emotional moments. And he warned that this stress could be accompanied by more aftereffects of MPD. Ten days later, I would discover how right he was.

Elen and I began work in mid-September. From the start, this process of going back over my life created enormous stress. Often I would find myself, in mid-session, feeling disoriented. A few times Elen observed behavior that seemed to indicate my alters were resurfacing. And entries in my diary evidenced that my handwriting was again taking varied forms: some like the penmanship that the Purple Lady and the Retrace Lady had used; others, however, were unrecognizable to me. After our first week of work on the manuscript, I wrote in the diary:

> I'm not over the shock of finally facing the fact that I created the other personalities. But even realizing this, I wonder if I am strong enough to stop?
>
> I view myself as a dressmaker, and establishing a lone (one) personality forever is like making a new garment. Should I find the task too great, I'll go back and wear the old one.
>
> I'm like a sick bee in a garden of beautiful flowers. The nectar is here, but how do I know it won't make me worse? I don't. So I can only take a sample and hope for the best.[9]

Existing in this fragile state, I returned home in early October to discover that Don had talked to a lawyer in my absence. My first hint was a call from the bank indicating that they had returned several of my checks. I was incredulous. I told the bank employee they had to be mistaken because the checking account had nearly four thousand dollars in it.

"No, ma'am," the woman said. "The account has been closed."

I grabbed my bankbook and scanned its entries. They included two deposits transferred from my savings account— thirty-three hundred dollars and eight hundred dollars—but withdrawals of less than five hundred dollars for checks I had written during the trip. And among those entries, I also saw traces of different penmanship. "Is there no end to this?" I moaned.

That night when I confronted Don, he admitted that he had transferred all the money from our joint checking account into one listed solely in his name. And he said he had seen an attorney When I asked why, Don said that I had more than enough money in my savings account, so he had closed the joint checking account for self-protection.

"I can't predict what you'll do," he added. "I could come home one night to find this apartment empty, the bank account drained, and you run off somewhere with Bobby. So I just took measures to protect myself."

"And how does making my checks bounce protect you?" I asked. "Do you have any idea how humiliating this is?"

His face was unemotional as he responded, "It just evens the score, Chris. You've still got *your* savings. I didn't touch that. But I did take *our* money so that, for the first time in years, I'd have some back-pocket money, too."

"This is what people do in preparation for a divorce," I said. "Just admit that's what you're up to."

"You're wrong," he said. "All I'm doing is funding *two* sets of dreams. This way, you've got money to write your book, and I've got money to fix up the homeplace."

I understood Don's motivations. *The land. Southerners and the lure of land.* Years before, following the death of his mother, Don had inherited the Sizemore farm and family home in Chatham County, North Carolina. But we had never been able to restore the aging farmhouse or to farm the land. Doctor bills and household costs had taken every available dollar. Yet he had always dreamed of fixing up the place and moving there. According to what I had recalled, some of my alters shared that dream, too. Anything would be better than what our family had known: a lifetime of living in trailer parks and apartments, with only brief interludes in houses that Don ultimately had to sell. So it was a dream that I had inherited along with all the other memories of my past. But his usurping the household money suddenly changed this shared *dream* into a one-sided *scheme.* He was obviously planning his escape from our marriage.

I felt numb. Stunned. "So when are you leaving?" I asked, realizing that our discussions in the past were just that. History.

"Oh, I'm not going anywhere. I'll see this thing through until Bobby finishes high school. But I make no promises after that."

"My God," I whispered, "that's two years from now. We can't go on like this for that long."

"We've done it for twenty-one," he mumbled. "What's two more?"

The prospects seemed unbearable. "*You* may have done it for twenty-one, but I didn't," I responded. "That's what you will not understand. I haven't been around for ten minutes of our marriage. I just got here in July."

"Please, Chris, don't start that—"

"But that's where we must start. Until you see that I'm not all those women who came before, we are never going to unravel this. You've called nine different wives 'Chris,' and none of them were me. That's what you've got to accept. But what I've got to accept is even harder: I've got to take responsibility for the fact that *I* created all those others, and by not coming back and not regaining control of my life sooner, I unwittingly allowed *all* our lives to sink into this mess. So I know the pain of truth, Don. And no matter how hard the last two decades have been on you—and I'm sure they have been awful—we both have to accept the truth. I must bear the guilt of what my illness has done. But don't think you can escape guilt, either. Believe me, fella, if you walk out now, you will have to bear the guilt of divorcing a woman you never even married, much less got to know."

For several seconds, Don sat breathlessly. Had my words finally been convincing to him? Then he rubbed his face and said, "Why can't we just live together as friends? That's what I used to do with the others, whenever they didn't accept me. It worked then. Why can't it work a couple of years longer?"

"It worked with the others because, somehow, they knew they were transients in some other woman's life," I said, not entirely certain that I was correct. "They tolerated the circumstances because each one knew she had only a short period in which to live." My heart was burning, with pains not unlike the searing ones I had experienced during the surgery abreactions. "But I'm not like the others. Like it or not, I'm the real thing, Don. And I've come home inside my own body to make something of my life. Until you accept that fact, we're headed for disaster."

"I'm so terribly depressed," I wrote a week later. "I want to do something drastic to show Don how strongly I feel about our situation, but I can't." I was immobilized because my lawyer had advised me to be cooperative and to do whatever Don suggested. As a result, all I could do was be patient; but patience bred depression and stress. "I had a blinding headache this morning," the entry continued, "and I searched my mind for the 'usual' help. But it wasn't there. There is only emptiness and a great ache in my heart." The next day I wrote, "The horrible void continues."[10]

In a sense, I was like those wandering souls who, according to legends, anguish because they are trapped between lives. My alters could no longer intervene, and I had no idea how to live in this singular situation. My therapist would not permit me to get a job until he was certain there would be no more aftereffects of MPD. And I did not dare touch my savings, because I had no idea what the future held. The result was that I had no available money. Don received the only paycheck and kept it; and now he had sole control of our household money. So I was trapped, possessing a new life but no means with which to live it. By mid-October, I reached the depth of my dilemma:

> There is no one I can talk with, nor write to, who will recognize the truth. The pain I feel is so great, the emotional ache so deep, that I stand in the shadow of my soul and weep; my heart is bursting with unshed tears. But that is the strength of truth. Once you catch a glimpse of it, nothing else will suffice.
>
> When I returned home the problem was waiting. My whole world crashed around me, and yet I still stand. I feel that I want to die, but I live on. Worse, I want "the girls" to lean on, but I can no longer find them. The old coping method fails me, and I must face the world alone.
>
> I thought this was what I wanted—being one person—but the real me is disappearing and what remains is foreign to me. Almost a false being.
>
> I did not recognize that in blocking the coping mechanism I was going to lose my identity. This much I have learned: it is not wise to play God. It was *my [alters]* that kept *me* in *balance*. Now I have such a mental block I can no longer use them. I fear I may have, indeed, loosed a monster.
>
> In time, perhaps, I will grow into a real person again, but for the present time I walk on water. I pray my love ones will

be able to understand me, and to love me, no matter what I become.

Yet I wonder: has Don done this to me, or I to myself?[11]

My only hope for income seemed to be the book that Elen and I were writing, but complications had surfaced in that project. I believed that my former therapists, Drs. Thigpen and Cleckley, had held since the fifties documents that concerned rights to my story as an MPD patient in conjunction with *The Three Faces of Eve*. When I could not locate copies of these agreements—signed by my alters while they were under Drs. Thigpen and Cleckley's psychiatric care—I sought help from my lawyer.[12]

The initial result was a letter from Dr. Thigpen in mid-October. His letter implied that neither he nor Dr. Cleckley would prevent me from publishing my autobiography.[13] And I read his statement—rightly—to mean that neither of them would use the old documents to interfere with this new book's contents, as they had previously done during the writing of *The Final Face of Eve*. So I put this worry aside, believing—again rightly—that in subsequent months my attorney would handle the negotiations and clear the way for publication of the book on which Elen and I were working. Anyway, I had more pressing concerns at home.

Don and I began living silent lives. Neither of us disturbed the other. Each went in separate directions. He worked during the week and stayed to himself at nights in our apartment. I spent my weekdays gathering material for Elen's drafts of the book and weekends with her or other family members, where I could gather their memories concerning the major events of my life. My own memories still seemed so slender, so distant, and so devoid of feelings. Don used his weekends for trips to the North Carolina farm where work was in progress to clear the land. Don lived on his paycheck, and I reluctantly lived off my savings. Bobby kept busy with high school activities and, showing great maturity, did not take sides with either of his parents.

Occasionally, Don and I did battle in the subtle ways. Since Don handled the household money, he did all the shopping. However, when I would empty the grocery sacks, they contained such a motley assortment of items that no housewife could have produced an acceptable meal from any combination he had selected: sardines, artichokes, calves' liver, brussels sprouts, prunes, cornflakes, boxes of Jell-O, powdered milk, and enough cheese to supply a pizza parlor. But I insisted on trying.

To make matters worse, it became apparent during my meal preparations that the period of recall had not given me the knowledge of how to cook. It seemed incomprehensible that my mind could have reviewed an entire lifetime and still not found within its recesses something as basic as the skills necessary to operate a kitchen. But that was the case. When I mentioned this to Bobby, he laughed and said, "That's understandable, Mom. When the other personalities were here, we ate a lot of TV dinners."

That devastated me. I struggled through the evening's cooking tasks and continued chatting with Bobby, but I anguished over what this bright, cheerful young man had endured. He seemed undaunted about the current troubles in our home. Instead, he talked about wanting to go to the University of Kentucky or Duke University when he finished high school. And he wanted to study journalism. But I had quietly grieved, knowing that I could not afford tuition at Duke or an out-of-state school if Don and I were divorced.

"When the time comes, I hope we can manage that, son," I said. "But things don't look good. Dad and I may be separating. And if that happens, I may not have the money to send you."

"I can get a job, Mom," the fourteen-year-old said, cheerfully. "And everything will work out. You'll see."

On my next visit to the therapist, he said that if Don didn't put more effort into our marriage, then I would have no choice but to get a divorce. "The way you're having to live is only making you more nervous," Dr. Tsitos added. "And I don't see how you can overcome the aftereffects of MPD unless your life becomes organized, purposeful, and secure to the point that you can know what to expect, day to day."

"That's why I've got to get a job," I said, almost begging.

"I don't think that's wise, not just yet. You already have too many pressures, and the stress of starting a new job could be very detrimental to the healing process. The timing is all wrong."

"But I've got to do something, *anything,* to change our family's situation. If I don't, I feel like I'm going to have a nervous breakdown."

Dr. Tsitos smiled, straightened his tie, and unfolded his hands. Behind his uncluttered, well-polished desk, he looked more like a bank auditor than a psychiatrist. "Your mind has triumphed over a forty-four-year ordeal of mental illness," he said. "It's highly unlikely that it will succumb now to a breakdown. But your heart is a different matter. That's what I'm concerned about. You seem halted in your tracks by fear, but I don't know what you're afraid of."

"I'm afraid that someday I'll look up and find that I'm completely and totally alone."

"And why do you fear this?"

"I feel so unworthy," I said, my voice shattered by emotion. "The other day Don said that I had *used* him. I told him that was strange because, looking back and recalling how he related to my alters, it seemed that *he* had used me, that he had secretly thrived on my illness and had gotten excitement from having so many different wives—even the ones who rejected him. Doctor, I now know that the man enjoyed a virtual harem in his bedroom, and the worst part is that *I* created all those women even though I was none of them. Perhaps I can also see that *we used each other* over the years to satisfy whatever needs existed. But the point is, Don never had a monogamous marriage; because of the disorder, he could sleep around without ever leaving his bedroom. And I made that bizarre circumstance possible. In retrospect, it all seems such a waste."

"But you've got the chance now to correct all that, if you so desire. You and Don can establish a normal marriage, provided he is also willing to put his share of effort into it. Is that not how you see it?"

"Not if I have to do it alone, I don't. It isn't worth the effort," I said, as slow, hot tears fell from my cheeks onto my dress. "Why is it, Doctor, that I must struggle so hard simply to exist? Why can't I just die? My life is so empty of good deeds and my future so devoid of hope. What am I all about? Dear God, *somebody* has got to give me a purpose."

But no one could do that for me, Dr. Tsitos reiterated, just as no one could answer these questions for me. I had to answer the questions, and I had to determine my purpose in life. And from that day, I began trying.

At first I turned to painting. Seven of my former alters had been artists, and during their short lifetimes they created a sizable body of work that evidences many different styles, techniques, and visions. Surely I could do that, too, even though I was acutely aware of the fact that I had not attempted a day of painting since the unification in July. But after my session with Dr. Tsitos, I felt resolute, so I set up their easel, selected several tubes from their shelf of acrylics, and prepared brushes for work on a crisp, white canvas. Within the hour, however, it was apparent that there seemed to be no beauty left in my soul. As the day languished on, I began drinking whiskey and rationalizing that this would help restore my creativity. Instead, by late afternoon I was drunk, depressed, and self-pitying. "I feel drained of all that is worthwhile," I wrote that night in the diary. "What must I do to rise above this? Am I going the wrong way? *Alcohol.* If I know that this is not the right way, then why do I do it? Is it because it dulls the pain of being alive?"[14]

This pain of living became acute during the last weekend in October. I was surrounded by Don, Bobby, and Taffy and her family during a casual family gathering at our apartment. It was not a special, or even a memorable, evening. We were playing the card game rook. The others seemed to be having fun, so I laughed and conversed with them even though my behavior was a mask. As the game progressed, I looked carefully around the card table. Their expressions implied that no one suspected I was anything other than happy. We continued to play the hands of cards rapidly, and the game became competitive. Perhaps to ease tensions, Taffy interjected suggestions about how we could spend Thanksgiving and Christmas together. Ideas for menus and decorations and special activities were as plentiful as the nachos Taffy had made. It seemed like such a pleasant evening. But throughout, I could not stop wishing that I could just die.

Memories of other, comparable evenings began flooding my mind, and I suddenly realized that this evening was different. For the first time in years, my family was not preoccupied with me as a sick mother. In fact, this evening they were relaxing and planning as if my illness were merely a distant memory. But the difference did not stop there. I also realized that my way of remembering had changed. It must have begun weeks before, but I did not notice until this evening that I was remembering the way *normal* people described the process. I was merely thinking in words, rather than recalling in images.

It was a peculiar revelation. It excited me. I finally understood that normal persons do not remember exclusively in flickering images, the way MPD patients do. Normal people remember in a complex, intricate manner that involves words and feelings as well as the recall of odors, sounds, and images. And, indeed, my mind seemed to be functioning normally.

"Come on, Nan," five-year-old Jimmy said, nudging me. "It's your turn." Startled, I looked around to see grins on all the faces around the card table. Then I saw that during my musings my hands must have slowly relaxed, exposing my cards to the others. A burst of laughter filled the room. Embarrassed, I joined in with a nervous giggle, and we started that hand over. The remainder of the evening was so carefree that we hardly seemed like the same family.

Later, when everyone had gone, and Don and Bobby were asleep, I wrote in the diary:

> All my secret agonies are worthwhile, so long as my family and loved ones are spared my suffering. This way is better than the old. Somehow, they were able over the years to handle my disorder, and now, by the living God, I must learn to handle in private these pains of growing. And I will. Without overindulging in alcohol. Without being afraid of tomorrow. I can handle it because I have lived through the horrors of the past.
>
> I must concentrate on the present and live each day to the fullest. Tomorrow will take care of itself. Chris, ole girl, you're on your way up.[15]

The next day I began calling friends, most of whom had not seen me since the final stages of MPD had gotten so bad nearly six months earlier. It was a frightening step. Somehow, I knew who these people were, yet I also knew that I was not the woman they had befriended. Would they notice the changes in me? Would they like me as well as they had my former alters? Or would they reject me on sight? Telephoning first, I decided, would give me clues.

To my surprise, the phone calls went well. One of the first was to Harriet Henderson, the woman who had also worked at various ladies' specialty shops when I did. She seemed delighted to hear from me, and that gave me courage. She had been a true friend to the Retrace Lady, the Purple Lady, and even the Strawberry Girl. Beginning in the late sixties, Harriet had introduced them to a painting class and had shared those casual evenings with them at a suburban supper club. More important, Harriet was one of the few people whom my alters had told about the struggles with MPD, so I felt a deep need for her friendship.

During the conversation, she did not ask about my mental health. She never had. Instead, she asked about my art. I told her that I had done very little over the summer but that Elen and I were now working on a book. Harriet became very excited about that and said she would arrange an art show for me when the book was published.

When I hung up the receiver, I felt a deep sense of relief. Nothing in Harriet's voice had indicated that the new *me* created a problem for her. It was as though she had been expecting this all along. So I made more telephone calls. For the most part, each person's reaction was similar to hers. By the end of the day, I was surprised to find that I had begun to like myself, too. I had not previously realized that during the decades of my disorder, I had actually enjoyed being more than one person. At the time, I thought that I hated multiplicity, and I *had* hated the disorder's inconveniences and discomforts. Then I realized that I had never hated the reality of the disorder itself. Not, that is, until now.

The difference had come as a result of days like this one. Finally, I had spent twenty-four hours in which I enjoyed being one person. And this enjoyment evoked new perspectives. The following evening I wrote in the diary reflections on how my sister Tiny had comforted me back in August when the first period of recall had been so agonizing:

When the headache was over I found that Tiny was on her knees and holding me in her arms. She said she heard me saying, "Please, God," and that she had prayed for God to give me whatever it was that I was asking for, or to let me be whatever I wanted to be.

This makes me realize that the people I love, and who love me, want me to be happy. They *will* accept whatever makes me happiest or gives me peace.

Can I, then, be a lesser person than the others who came before me? I cannot. I dare not disappoint my family and friends because they so loved me, even when I did not love myself.[16]

One major obstacle, however, continued to weigh upon me. Don and I were living even more like puppets on the strings of a possible divorce. I had been advised to give Don no grounds for divorce—meaning, among other actions, that I should return "to sleep" in our marital bed. Apparently, Don had been given the same advice, because he did not protest my return one uneventful night. But there was little sleep to be had. Lying together, yet straining to avoid the slightest touch, only increased my anxiety. In the morning, Don awakened mumbling complaints that he would have to work another day without sufficient sleep. And I became more and more exhausted, angry and torn.

Part of my frustration was rooted in the fact that, even though I was forty-seven and a mother, *I* had never been in love and had never made love. Romantic feelings, and the periods of my life when they were felt, had belonged to my alters. This revelation had been one of the most painful truths to surface during the nearly four months since my emergence into adulthood. As I had gleaned a fragmentary recollection of my former alters' sexual experiences, it became apparent that their moments of passion had not been mine. I had not been in control of this body when they felt a man's strong arms holding it against him. I had not felt the sensations from warm kisses or a look of affection from across the breakfast table or the sensualness of just being in love. While they made love, I was somehow lost in the recesses of my mind.

Reflecting on my alters' memories of conversations over the years with Mother and other women, I had written in late October, "I thought the time came in a woman's life when she no longer needed, or wanted, a man. Maybe that's true for some women, but not me. Without this, I am not a whole person. Yet things are happening so slowly. My life, though really just begun, is running out."[17]

Rationally, I knew from my recall that at least some of my alters had known passion and sexual pleasure, even though many of them—particularly the "party girl" types—had actually been frigid. Their excessive flirtations had betrayed that secret to any man who cared to notice. In addition, through the scenes that passed before my eyes I had been shown my alters' passions in action. I had watched as they toyed with strangers, then slipped to the safety of a collective unconsciousness, beyond the strange man's reach. And I had watched as some lost their innocence; as others longed to do so but could not. In a sense, I had been a voyeur upon my body's lifetime of secrets. So, no, I could not reasonably justify my feelings of having been denied this crucial aspect of living. But sex is not a reasonable drive. "I just want more of the same, and soon," I confessed to my diary, "or it will be too late for me, forever."[18]

Inevitably, these secondhand memories of passion became an obsession. I was like a teenager, but in an aging body. What I knew about sex, but had not intimately felt, began to color all my thoughts, to edge all my emotions and to direct all my motivations. But unlike an innocent girls', my passions were intermingled with resentment and anger. I might not be able to claim sensual memories of love acts with Don over the years, but I possessed enough knowledge about them to understand the range of joys and frustrations, of intimacies and estrangements, which had brought our marriage to its shattered state. And this knowledge added a dark determination to my obsession.

How else can I explain what I did? One ordinary, unromantic night in early November, I unleashed all these emotions on my husband. And I did so without the slightest warning.

The evening had begun with no promise of a shift in our routine. Midway through my preparations for supper, Bobby phoned to say he was spending the night with friends. When Don came in from work, he was silent as usual. I went through the motions of preparing dinner. We ate, made small talk, and watched television, almost oblivious of one another.

By eight o'clock, Don was napping in his chair; I got up and walked to the bathroom for a long, hot soak in the tub. I did not feel the slightest desire for sex. All I thought I yearned for was the relaxation of a steamy tub, the refreshing sounds of splashing water, and after that the exhilaration of drying off with a thick towel.

After a long soaking, I slipped into my gown and got into bed, where Don already was lying, his back to me. I looked at him and suddenly recognized in him distant memories the *others* had left me. I felt I wanted to reach out and touch Don. I knew none of the other personalities had been assertive sex partners, so when I put my hand on Don's back, I know he was surprised, to say the least.

My own advances continued, and Don began to respond. I became an experimenter, trying everything from a vast storehouse of recall. The sex between us became more and more uninhibited, and the veneer that barred me from my true emotions for nearly four months began to crumble. Feelings of unworthiness, ugliness, and subjection slipped from me like the perspiration that flowed from all parts of my body. Anger and frustration and loneliness fueled my desires and lovemaking until their burning seemed to purge my soul.

When it was over, I felt complete, whole, cleansed, and vindicated. I felt confident that at last I had finally communicated to Don that this woman in his life was no mere shell of a creature and certainly not just another mental patient whose spirit had been broken. Instead, I was somebody. I was the singular, unique person he could finally acknowledge tonight.

And this Chris Sizemore, I realized, had finally become a healed and life-loving woman, a wife capable of anything that any other woman could offer him, a personality to be reckoned with. These facts had now been made clear to him. And to me. That thought gave me such peace. I curled under the covers and easily fell asleep. My mind danced with contentment and resolve. Hereafter, whatever Don chose to do about our marriage would be all right, because a void inside me had been filled. I would not be starved of life's joys. Never again.

3

"*I* have never *quite* been able to get the *feel* of you, Chris," my cousin Elen said during our mid-November work sessions on the book. "I can define other people, describe them, analyze their behaviors and their backgrounds. But not with you. Somehow, you don't add up."

"I've never been just one person, at least not the same person," I said. "And until now, I've never been a whole person, a *real* person. Maybe that's why you find me such a blur."

"But parts *should* add up to the whole. Otherwise, how on earth can we write this thing?" Elen said, the months of sorting through boxes of my diaries and correspondence and memorabilia having exacted an extraordinary toll on her.

Maybe we're talking new math here, I thought, remembering the homework Bobby breezed through each night. *Maybe two plus two equals four even though four is not simply defined as two plus two?* But feelings of inferiority overcame me, and I could not say this to Elen. After all, it was my bright and accomplished cousin who was nearing the completion of her doctorate at Duke University, while I was just a therapy patient with a tenth-grade education. Yet my reticence did not prevent my mind from churning. Surely the answers were nestled somewhere within.

If so, then understanding myself was going to be like playing *Jeopardy!* on television: Given the answers, phrase the correct questions. Maybe the unification had given me the essentials from my alters' previous existences, but I did not feel *defined,* or *complete,* as simply the sum of their memories and desires, their talents and skills. Impossible as it seemed, I already knew that I was more than that. Seven of my alters had been painters, and their works had evidenced talent and style; yet the few times since July that I had gone to the easel, the results seemed sophomoric. Similarly, a few of my alters had been seamstresses, but I seemed all thumbs when attempting a basic task like repairing a button. But if I *was* not the sum, did this mean I was just one more part? This thought disturbed me even more, and I asked Elen about it.

"You were always there," she said. "You had to be. You created them. They were merely parts of you, satellites that surrounded the hidden *you* as a means of protection." It was a theory that my cousin would question, probe, and evaluate throughout the writing of *I'm Eve.* "It's the only process that makes sense. When you needed them, they surfaced and you withdrew. That accounts for periods when two or three *others* were you. But when each crisis was over, you always came back."

"That may account for me saying, 'I'm thirty-three,' when Doctor Tsitos asked my age back in July," I mused, "but why don't I feel as though I've lived *through* all that I remember?"

Neither of us could answer that. All I possessed was a host of memories and a few feelings about what those events meant. Nor was working on this book making me feel I was coauthoring an autobiography. Instead, I felt as if I were researching a *biography* of twenty-two women whose experiences, diaries, correspondences, and relationships were somehow a significant part of my mind but only a distant part of my heart. These perspectives made me deeply reliant upon Elen, but my concerns were even more complex. Intellectually, I knew that we were writing my life story, no matter which alters had lived which parts of it. How else could my mind have recalled their experiences had those events not contained meaning for me? Yet I was dealing with dilemmas deeper than my intellect. For example, the Freckle Girl had given birth to my daughter, but somehow I knew Taffy was mine. The Bell Lady had been Bobby's mother, but my heart claimed Bobby, too. My body loved its own. It intuited bonds to my children whether at the time I understood these feelings or not.

Yet I didn't know how any of this was possible. I only knew that, pertaining to my children, the answer was: *It just is.* The same was true, in different senses, for my parents, my aunts, my sisters, and my cousins. Then why could I not feel a similar bond of love toward Don? Was it because my husband and I did not share that same primal, genetic linkage that held me to the children?

As a result of our solitary night of sex, my husband no longer ignored me, but I got no indication that the intimacy had caused him to love me again, or even to like me. Asserting myself sexually had not produced emotional intimacy. It was as though being forced to acknowledge my existence had only created confusion in Don. He came and went, day after day, like a man in mild shock. When discussions about divorce arose, his comments were no longer terse and determined. He now acted like a man who had no idea what to do.

Taffy removed several decks from the Card Girl's collection and placed them on our dining-room table. "Why don't we just forget it and play cards," she said. But seeing my resolute expression, she smiled, stopped pressing the issue of a card game, and said that I looked lovely. Like a guest of honor.

"Thank you," I responded. But I didn't feel pretty in one of the Retrace Lady's casual winter dresses. How, I wondered, could I look nice when I was wearing my own hand-me-down?

Taffy then went into the kitchen that the Purple Lady had decorated. "If we aren't going to forget it, we *must* have popcorn," Taffy said.

Don was wearing his favorite flannel shirt, a gift from the Turtle Lady one Christmas. I could not remember where he had gotten his khaki slacks, but I had contributed: I had pressed them. He looked relaxed but weary as he poured soft drinks for our grandson, Jimmy, then fixed coffee for Taffy and himself.

Minutes later, Bobby telephoned to say that basketball practice would run late, and Taffy suggested that we put together a giant picture puzzle. Their scheme was transparent. Don and Taffy were doing everything they could to dissuade me. But I remained determined. "You know what I've got to do," I said. "So forget the cards and the puzzle."

Don and Taffy exchanged several nervous glances, then the joking and laughter were dispelled like a sunny afternoon chased by gray-black clouds in advance of a slow summer rain. "Are you sure you want to watch it?" Taffy asked, concern solidly expressed in her voice.

"We've run from it for seventeen years. I won't hide anymore. I can't."

So the four of us encircled the television. We looked like small, anxious children awaiting either punishment or a reprieve in the principal's office. And we were baffled children, uncertain about which it would be.

As a promo announced during a commercial break, "Coming up, Joanne Woodward in her Academy Award–winning performance, *The Three Faces of Eve,*" Taffy explained to her five-year-old son, "Jimmy, this movie is about Nanny."

November 16, 1974, had been a long time coming, and at great sacrifices. None of our family had ever seen this 1957 movie based on our lives. My alters had been barred from its world premiere in Augusta, Georgia, because Drs. Thigpen and Cleckley believed that seeing it could be highly detrimental to the stability of the patient who, they had wrongly claimed, was cured. So while limousines and celebrities gathered at the gala in Augusta, the subject of that movie was hospitalized to undergo one of the surgeries I would subsequently relive in abreaction. Fame in anonymity began. And from that day, the movie launched our family on a run. We uprooted ourselves from community to community, futilely trying to escape discovery while *The Three Faces of Eve* was shown, then rerun, year after year. It became our *great unknown,* and like a bounty hunter's victims, we fled it for years without ever knowing what it was about.

Yet its wide acceptance by moviegoers solidly established Eve's fame, and my psychiatrists' fortunes. A year after finally seeing this film, I would learn from published reports that *The Three Faces of Eve* had sold about a million copies since the book's publication in 1957, and that the movie had grossed $2 million.[1] In contrast, I had received free therapy from Drs. Thigpen and Cleckley, but nothing from the book's earnings and only seven thousand dollars for motion-picture rights from Twentieth Century-Fox. Otherwise, Don, Taffy, and I were known only by the pseudonyms of Earl Lancaster, Bonnie White, and Jane Lancaster, respectively, and we had to live with notoriety long after both the book and the movie had become classics.

Anonymity, I thought. *It's a fine name for that darkened recess of the mind where alters abide. Where they watch and hear but are not seen and heard, except when they choose to come "out." The world according to MPD.* Yet waiting for the movie to begin, I felt no resentment or excitement or fear. Instead, in tune with the mood of Robert Emmett Dolan's eerie music dubbed to the film's opening credit frames, only emptiness and a longing swept within me.

Then Alistair Cooke appeared on our television screen. Speaking about "Dr. Jekyll and Mr. Hyde" and intoning in his British accent, the famous author sounded professorial, as if he were reciting the introduction to an educational program about archaeology. And the film's black-and-white format added to this musty, unsettling mood. Suddenly, I felt a twinge of our perpetual fear: *What, in God's name, has this movie shown the world about me?* But I also felt a sharp loss because I remembered somet ˙ that the recall had not made clear. At one point in this movie's production, Jane had been scheduled to be flown to Los Angeles and placed behind a translucent screen. She was to have been interviewed by Cooke as part of this introduction. Upon learning this, she had been ecstatic. She planned her wardrobe and dreamed Hollywood dreams. But when Nunnally Johnson called from Hollywood, Dr. Thigpen decided that it was not advisable for Jane to go. So the film was completed without anyone telling her that the cameo appearance had been scrapped. Now, suddenly armed with this memory, I felt numb as Joanne Woodward appeared on the television screen.

Minutes later, when the actress portrayed Eve White being stricken by a headache, five-year-old Jimmy broke the tension in our living room by saying, "Look, Mom. Nan had headaches then, too." All of us laughed, though nothing was really funny. Maybe we laughed because it all seemed so real, yet so very different from our memories?

As more scenes progressed, I reflected that Joanne Woodward

appeared utterly fragile, yet also full of life. So plain and pitiful as
Eve White, yet vibrant and daring when Eve Black's antics began.
And much later, so plastic and transparent as Jane. At one point, I
gasped, realizing that while the actress was portraying the
"switch" of personalities, the phenomenon seemed authentic,
as if one of my psychic sisters were actually emerging from within her.

Then Don surprised us all by joking in reaction to the scene
where David Wayne, playing the-soon-to-be-divorced Ralph
White, is astounded. It *is* a comical moment. On the set re-creat-
ing Eve White's hospital room, Lee J. Cobb, playing Thigpen, calls
Eve Black forth to introduce herself to Ralph. Without assistance
from the camera, Joanne Woodward's entire demeanor changes
from Eve White's moroseness to Eve Black's defiance, and Ralph
White looks as if he has seen a nun transformed into a Martian.
Reacting, David Wayne stutters and protests. Yet even in his be-
fuddlement, Wayne appears far more sophisticated than the real
Ralph White could ever have been.

"Ole *Ralph's* got his hands full," Don quipped, "and the fool
don't even know it." There was no edge to Don's voice. No anger
in his humor ˉ fact, I was convinced that I heard compassion.
And it didn't seem directed either toward self-pity or toward the
man who had been Taffy's birth father. The compassion seemed
to be intended for my ears.

Despite breaks for TV commercials, the remainder of the
ninety-five-minute film passed quickly. When it ended, our collective tension had been replaced by an overwhelming sense of relief. We moved to the dining table and started playing gin
rummy. To my surprise, Don and Taffy immediately began exchanging their personal theories about my illness. It was the first
time the two of them had ever done that in my presence. But I
might as well have been absent, because neither of them included me in their discussion. Don said he thought the original
three had simply returned each time, and Taffy seemed hesi-
tatingly to agree. She suggested that maybe the subsequent personalities had only seemed different because the roles they had
to play were different.

I realized that the three alters in the movie—Eve White, Eve
Black, and Jane—were the first ones that both Taffy and Don had

experienced. Neither my daughter nor my husband had known the childhood alters, just as neither had known Taffy's mother, the Freckle Girl; she had disappeared during Taffy's infancy. I also knew that my parents and psychiatrists had protected both Taffy and Don from exposure to the alters during the early fifties.

But Don continued discussing theories, unaware of the information that the recall had given me. Taffy, who had listened to me describing many of the recall experiences as they happened, seemed to be allowing Don to speak his mind—like a good therapist. Agreeing in order to elicit more feelings and observations. Listening more than talking. Inserting suggestions at the right moment. And caring.

Suddenly, I sensed the deep emotions expressed in their voices as they talked about my former alters. I expected that from Taffy, because she had named all of the alters who had emerged since Jane. But I was amazed to hear these feelings expressed in Don's voice, even though he simultaneously denied a great deal.

"I never really noticed much," he said. "Chris was moody all right. I *knew* that. And whenever that happened, you could be sure that nothing would go right. I guess I just blamed it on all those funerals. Every time somebody died—and in our big families, somebody was always dying—well, every time I'd just say to myself, 'Look out. Here we go again.'"

His words sent a sickening ache deep within me. This poor, distant man really had *not* noticed much. Not in nearly twenty years. While I was living in that hazy land of inner anonymity, he had also been existing in a world of his own. *But how?* How could nine or ten different women have passed in and out of his marriage without Don noticing?

Then I looked at Taffy. Her smooth, round face was glistening with tears that masked a serene smile. In that expression, I saw hints of the child who had grown up too soon, but also the mother who had begun honing her maternal skills before she became a teenager. She had made Don's detachment possible. She had drawn a circle around my alters' lives and had been their protectress. She, the child, had spared Don, the adult. That's why he had barely known *the others,* only acknowledging my alters when to do so met his needs, but otherwise ignoring them as

steadily as he had attempted to shut me out. And Bobby had been
at least partially spared, too. He lacked any real feelings about
most of my alters because he had been protected by Don, Taffy,
and the alters themselves. Bobby was not even told about my
disorder until he was thirteen.

Then there was me. While Taffy protected my alters, they
protected me. Taffy's circle of protection was concentric to the
one they had drawn, decades before, around the unconscious *me*.
And, somehow, these circles of love had left me to the peacefulness of my inner hideaway. That's why I only knew *the others*
as the result of my mind's recall—a motion picture not much
different from what we had just watched. A secondhand familiarity.

Only Taffy was the true witness. She alone had been the adult
alters' confidante, their friend over morning coffee. She alone had
cried with them and laughed in concert with their joys. She alone
had discussed their diary entries to help each one find meaning
in the chaos. The truth was startling. At that moment, my daughter knew me better than I knew myself.

Needless to say, I played a lousy game of cards that night, and
later, when I went to bed, I tossed in confusion. Were Taffy and
Don's theories correct? Had the same three alters returned each
time? Evidence in my mind said no, there were many. But I really
didn't know. My knowledge was not rooted in experience; it had
all seeped into my mind like glucose from a bottle plugged into a
vein. Yet in the recall and in more recent memories extending
deeper into my consciousness, the alters *had* all seemed different. Just as whatever I felt to be *self* during all those years had
seemed different each time, too.

It took me days to sort out my feelings. By the end of November, I penned one of the most probing entries in that year's diary:

> Some uneasy thoughts have crept into my mind recently.
> Am I *one*? Have I not always been *one* after a resolution? More
> importantly, how do I know that I'm *one*, and what is the
> difference this time?
>
> The answer to the first two questions is *yes*, of course. But
> this time, there is a difference. There are feelings of being
> alone, of emptiness and a definite fear. After the earlier

resolutions, I knew *they* were gone—or no longer present—but I always had a secure feeling. I think I felt that way because, unconsciously, I knew *they* were *available.* All my life I had accepted their existences, without realizing it.

Now, I know *they* are not ladies-in-waiting. Instead, they were created as maids of burden.

And now my fear stems from the unknown. I don't know what to expect of my own emotions. Before, I knew what would happen in a crisis. But I no longer have this knowledge. I don't really know myself, and this is what's frightening. I am not alone, as far as my friends and loved ones are concerned. I am only alone within—desperately alone within.

The question is: what fills this void in others who have never had more than one personality? If I can find that answer, then I can know that *the others* will not return.

I have begun to question if I were ever meant to be a solitary being. Yet now I am alone and there is nothing I can do about it. Sometimes this realization produces near panic. Yet this must be *normal* because I lived with the others for nearly half a century. To suddenly be different naturally requires adjustment. But am I normal now, or was I normal then?

Believing that we spiral up to perfection through many levels of life, who is to say I may not be on a lesser level now than before? I could be regressing and curbing my own progress in the scheme of things.[2]

At my next therapy session, Dr. Tsitos's comment was like a knife slicing through fog: "What I hear you saying, Chris, is that all your life you've been seeking recognition. Do you agree?"

I envisioned my alters' various and desperate attempts for public attention over the years, and I agreed. But I also sensed that, for most of those decades, the original personality—this now confused *I*—had basked in a rare, continuous inner attentiveness. It was as if my own eyes had been consciousness-blind eyes during the disorder, yet had been encircled in that shared unconsciousness by nearly two dozen pairs of other, ever-watchful eyes. Yet how had this been possible?

When I explained this to my therapist, he said, "Writing the book with Elen may help you answer such questions. But only if, during the process, *you* also become an interesting *person*, rather than merely a person who has an interesting *illness*. Remember: This writing can be good therapy, but it can also enhance good growth as an individual. If both occur, then the illness will no longer be necessary."

"But how can I grow when you won't let me work?" I protested, reminding him that I had, once again, turned down a job offer—this time, a managerial position with the Franklin Simon chain.

"By writing a book and getting well, you've already got two full-time jobs," he responded. "With whatever time each week that you have left, you need to find new ways to express yourself. To entertain yourself. To enhance yourself. Solid personality growth takes time."

"That's just it," I said. "I'm not certain I know myself *well* enough to write this book."

"Then become a detective in your own mind," he said. "Probe your memories like a gumshoe spying on secret files. And get out of your routine. Find anyone who knew you and discover what they have to say about who you were." Suddenly, a wise smile flashed across his face. "The recall has probably given you all the clues you need. Now it's up to you to discover meaning within the mystery of who the *real* Chris Sizemore is."

In subsequent months, I followed Dr. Tsitos's advice. The clues in my mind did lead to answers about myself. But they told me more than that. This sleuthing began to unravel mysteries about my family as well. Particularly about Don.

At birth, the eldest son in the Sizemore family was given no name—only the initials D.G. And apparently, these initials bore no meaning. They were not an abbreviation for a traditional family name such as David Graham or Daniel Gordon. They were more like serial prefixes on a piece of farm machinery. And in 1923, the practical purpose for bringing children into the world of raising flue-cured tobacco on a small North Carolina farm was to have more workers.

By the time my D.G. started first grade, he was already accustomed to following his mother into the fields along Bear Creek.

She chopped weeds with a full-size hoe, and he with a hoe whose handle had been cut to fit the boy's swing. Mother and son did a man's job. While they labored as a team, a bond developed between them that would last until her death. But the pair did not have to labor alone for long. One by one, other children grew, until their arms fit D.G.'s hoe. Each time, this new child took his or her place, and D.G. received a new hoe with a slightly longer handle. And so it went. A farm family's love was defined by work. But what about the fun and games that usually define a childhood?

"Oh, we got to play, whenever Mother got too winded or too weak in the sun, and every day after lunch," Don recalled once, while courting my alter named Jane. "Plus, any winter night was ours, too, as long as the wood was chopped and the dishes washed and the babies put to bed."

"And what did you play?" Jane asked, though I now remember.

"Well, lunchtime meant we could swim off the heat of the day in Bear Creek," he said, a boyish smile spreading across his thirty-year-old face. "And we got breaks. When Mother slumped under a shade tree and fanned her sunburnt face with her hat, that meant we could kick rocks down the road, or play ball with the homemade bat and wad of twine which we kept hidden in the woods, or make whistles out of reeds, or cut slingshots from crooks on trees rooted closest to the creek."

He said that his father, who worked timber in the winter, also joined the family in the fields. "And his constant reminder was, 'If you're farming, you work thirteen months a year.'"

Though I've searched my mind as thoroughly as I could, this brief exchange with Jane in 1953 seems to have been the only time Don ever talked about his early years. That era now seemed as much a mystery as my own life had been. And even then, young D.G. seemed to have been an enigma to most people. A kind, dependable young man, yes. But one to be reckoned with. "Nobody crossed D.G.," one of his relatives would subsequently tell the Bell Lady. "If he said something, the family accepted it as so."

In Bonlee High School, D.G. was on the basketball and baseball teams. Shop was his favorite class, and the shop teacher left

D.G. with a maxim the boy never forgot: "If you have a craft, you can always get work with your hands."

But these high school years were not an escape from work. D.G. continued to shoulder the burden of his chores at home, second only to his mother's, and he drove a school bus over that section of the county. Each month, he brought cash from his twelve-dollar check and slipped it into his mother's apron pocket while she fixed supper at the Warm Morning wood stove. He said nothing in the giving, and she said nothing in the receipt. This mother and son talked through actions.

Upon graduation in 1942, D.G. worked for nearly a year as a lumberjack on his father's crew. At nights, the son did chores for his mother, or, when the season came, he played baseball. For him, it had become a mesmerizing sport. Not even the threat of World War II dimmed his passion—or that of other farm boys in the region—for the most American of games. Baseball seemed a natural pastime while waiting for the draft. These boys played on mud lots and pastures near Burlington and Asheboro. They polished their skills and were fiercely competitive. And they had a special incentive: Pat Murray, a scout for the Brooklyn Dodgers, frequented these games in central North Carolina.

Over the years, D.G. had not allowed himself many dreams about fortunes off the farm, but the mere possibility of catching Murray's eye triggered D.G.'s hopes. The boy from Bear Creek threw himself, brimmed with scrappiness, into every game. After all, the Dodgers had garnered the National League pennant in 1941. Their star was on the rise. Maybe even the New York Yankees would fall next season, and some Tar Heel could be the next rookie to get his break in that World Series?

But D.G. did not become that rookie. Sliding into second base during a night game—the mud lot lit by headlamps on cars that the players had parked around the field—he ripped his shoulder muscles. Weeks later, when these hidden wounds healed, his strength to field a ball was only half of what it had been.

"We've got no place to run to," he told a high school pal, Kenneth Moore, "and I don't like walking." Moore agreed, and the two of them volunteered for the U.S. Navy. On the "buddy system," they went through boot camp at the Great Lakes Naval Training Station on Lake Michigan; then they were stationed on the coast of Rhode Island. From this last post both were assigned to the *USS Bremerton,* a heavy cruiser manned by seventeen hundred crewmen and officers. It was a population nearly as large as the Tar Heel county that Kenneth and D.G. had left. But the men on the electrical engineering crew of the 71st China Forces did not call Seaman First Class Sizemore by the initials D.G. At the suggestion of his shipmates, D.G. named himself Don.

Still, the *Bremerton* was not Bear Creek. "There's no place on a ship for a baseball diamond, and I got awful lonesome for playing ball," Don told Jane after the war. "But I never got what you call 'homesick.'" At that point, I remember that he looked at Jane as if he were going to say more. But he checked himself and added, "Always too much work to get homesick on a ship." Even then, talking to Don was like listening to edited tape on radio news. He rarely elaborated. His style was John Cameron Swayze's.

Without baseball, Seaman Sizemore had a tough time relaxing during his first weeks aboard ship. He didn't smoke cigarettes, even though he had grown the tobacco used in them. And he didn't play cards, because his mother had taught that gambling was a sin. So the farm boy couldn't enjoy these time-honored pastimes at sea. Or could he? Within a few months, he had gained the reputation as a man who didn't waste money. One who *saved* money and would lend it. That ensured him a place at any card game. But he went a step further. After lights out, Don routinely lit and held stick matches while the other seamen played poker. He was keeping an eye on his money. He was enjoying the company of men, and he was doing his part. It was his way of honoring principles in the face of reality.

The first time they crossed the equator, en route to Trinidad from Philadelphia, where they had commissioned the cruiser, Don and the other new seamen were subjected to an ancient rite. His head was drenched with a mixture of sulphur, vinegar, and worse. With this as a base, the veteran sailors broke raw eggs on Don's head while he crawled across—and struggled to keep his nose an inch above—the swaying deck. When he was weakened from that ordeal, he had to ride the *sallee*—a long stick made from rags that had been rolled tight, then towed alongside the ship until the seawater had hardened the rags.

But childhood on the farm had toughened Don. His instincts

allowed him to endure when others faltered. Employing an earthy stoicism, he outlasted all the others and proved himself seaworthy. And that tropical triumph won friendships. In return, these new friends became his role models—particularly the veteran crewmen. "We had some salty guys on our ship," he recalled with fondness. "Some had gone down with ships, as many as three different times, and I vowed to be just like them." However, the *USS Bremerton* saw no action during his duty in the Pacific, and its crew was never put to a battle's test.

Near the war's end, Don was a petty officer, third class, and had earned enough points for an honorable discharge. So along with war brides, he became a military passenger on the *USS Breckinridge,* an old cargo vessel that had been converted into a troopship for the return voyage to San Francisco.

These were the few glimpses of my husband's past that I could discover as a detective within my own mind. Although they were only bits and pieces of conversations he had had with my alters, these insights gave me reasons to understand some character traits that had enabled him to endure my illness. They explained why he had been dependable and hardworking. Why he had not abandoned me or the children. He didn't like walking. He abided by principles. He triumphed over ordeals. But the stoicism that made these traits possible was closely linked to a detachment. What other man could hold lighted matches while others had fun?

Yet I identified with Don's youthful baseball dreams, never encouraged toward fame, dreams cut short by history. I understood the sense of identity that had motivated him to name himself. And I empathized with his disappointment at missing a chance for heroics. But I identified most particularly with a vow he had made, and later told to Jane.

"When the war ended, I was on liberty in Shanghai, and the *Breckinridge* was scheduled to sail in two days for home," he told her one night while they were riding around Augusta in his '51 Ford. "But Shanghai was on its knees. Dead bodies were scattered like tree limbs after a storm. People had just starved to death. It was horrible. I had never seen so many people so poor. Particularly the children. And wherever sailors went, the children seemed to come from nowhere. Begging and pulling at our uniforms, they trailed us wherever we went. I'll never forget their eyes. All those pitiful eyes . . ."

Jane sensed that he stopped without completing the story, but they had not been dating long. At this point in their relationship, they were just a quiet, handsome couple who increasingly spent more time together. They had not yet discussed engagement or marriage. In fact, it was rare when Don talked openly, as he was now doing. So Jane was puzzled. Should she say something to get him to continue? "It must have been painful to see," she finally murmured.

"It was so little, and helpless. Its legs looked like a newborn colt's."

"What?"

"The tiniest of the dead babies."

"You mean babies starved to death, too?"

"Along the roadside there were more babies than anything," he said. His eyes were so filled with tears that he had to pull the car to curbside. "And right there in Shanghai, I made up my mind. I vowed it: I would never get married until I could make enough money to take care of my children."

Was this the first moment that Jane had been attracted to him? My heart did not know for certain, and that missing link troubled me. A woman should remember that first attraction, should be able to feel it again and again. But I could not.

Dr. Tsitos had told me to develop personal interests. To grow by finding outlets for expression. But it was Harriet Henderson who provided the means, just as she had for my alters. She and I began painting together on Sundays at her apartment. These were marvelous, enlightening afternoons. But I soon understood that Harriet's friendship had first been forged with my alters, so I had to define my own place in this relationship, and I had to know how she had felt about the others. One day, I decided to start the process by questioning Harriet about the past.

"What was I like when we first met?" I asked while we were both doing routine work painting backgrounds on canvases.

"You were just darling. A vivacious, blue-eyed, black-haired, lithe-figured, bouncy little girl," she said, recalling her first impressions in 1965. I had been thirty-eight at the time, and Harriet in her forties.

"And what about my behavior?"

"You had mood swings, but none were ever directed at me," she said. "And I didn't realize you had a problem until you told me." Harriet had been the first person outside the family with whom my alters had talked in detail about multiple personality disorder. "But even then, I didn't quite believe you," she added. "I just knew that you were very vulnerable, that you desperately needed support, and all the love and help you could get. I was willing to give it."

"After you were told, could you see that the others had been a part of me?"

"Then and now," she said. "Of course, I didn't know about multiple personality then, but they were all there in you. And they still are. As you paint or talk, I can still pick out those aspects in you."

"But were they *real* to you then?" I interjected. "Was I real to you no matter which personality was out?"

"Oh, sure," she said, laughter sparkling in her soft voice. "I got along with every one of them." She explained that it was like having lots of friends wrapped into one, and both of us laughed.

"But if you enjoyed them so much then, do you *miss* any of them now?"

"They haven't gone anywhere, Chris. They're all still right here. They're *in* you," she emphasized. "It's like death. When people die, they don't cease to exist. They make a transition. But feelings like grief create problems for the people left behind, be· cause we, the living, are only aware of that transition. The dead know they're still here. We just don't."

"That's wonderful!" I exclaimed, suddenly glimpsing what wholeness might mean in my life. "Then you're saying that *this* life—reality—is an illusion, too?"

"It's *all* an illusion. Like magic," Harriet responded, an air of wisdom as luminous as her deeply colored eyes surrounding her. "But we have to work our way out of the illusion in order to see our true being. And that's what you're doing now."

"Is that why you've recommended painting for me?"

"Absolutely," she said. "I don't think there's anything that takes you out of yourself like painting. I go on a trip when I paint. Everything around me is gone. I don't hear a thing. And that's what I think you need, Chris. Working with these brushes and oils and canvas, you'll find yourself. You'll see."

During the last months of 1974, I took my friend's advice and started working my way out of the illusions. The means in this dead of winter was to do spring cleaning and redecorating with a vengeance. I was determined to rid our apartment of my alters' influences and to establish my own tastes in our home. But I had no idea what a herculean task it would be.

For example, I had discovered in my artwork that I liked soft colors, but this preference was in sharp contrast to the way that the Purple Lady had decorated our master bedroom. It had white curtains with purple flowers as big as my head. The bedspread was hideously adorned with these same purple blossoms, and enormous purple pillows were scattered about the bed like giant grapes on white bread. But the space under the bed and the closets was worse.

The double closet contained the most outlandish array of clothes imaginable. So did boxes under the bed. There were dozens of white pants that had been paired off with wild blouses, all worn by the Strawberry Girl. If there was a strawberry motif to be found in an outfit, she had purchased it. One white, sleeveless tank top had huge red strawberries all over it. And there were a few flamboyant pant suits that the Purple Lady had habitually worn. But there were also drab suits and dresses from the Turtle Lady's era, and several stylish suits and cocktail dresses that the Retrace Lady had bought in sizes I could no longer wear. It was chaos, like bargain racks in the specialty shops where my alters had worked. It was surreal. And everything was jammed so tightly on the bars that anything removed had to be ironed before it could be worn. There was barely room enough for Don's clothes, and I had no outfit to call *mine.* So my first task was obvious. I boxed away virtually all *their* clothes, leaving only those I could tolerate and that fit me.

Other rooms in the apartment were similarly cluttered with my alters' collections. I packed away boxes of bells, turtles, and decks of cards that had been strung out on shelf after shelf like souvenirs in a roadside novelty shop. I winnowed their paintings from the hallways and room walls, where they had been hung in helter-skelter competitiveness like a sidewalk art show. In the process, I realized that my alters had turned our family's apartment into a museum in honor of their eclectic lives. The more alters that had surfaced in my life, the less space there had been for my family. Just before the unification, therefore, our apartment had become nearly as crowded as my mind.

In the cleaning process, however, I realized that Bobby's room had been spared. His was the only haven in the apartment that my alters had not overrun with their things. It was obvious that they had loved him and that they had wanted him to have as normal a life as possible. His shelves were neatly arranged, displaying books about religion, philosophy, and the American Civil War. All his clothes in the closet and bureau were hung or stacked in a tidy, orderly manner. The walls had been painted royal blue and yellow, and bumper stickers lined one wall from floor to ceiling. A giant STOP sign rested on the floor just inside his door. Obviously, he was a healthy, protected fifteen-year-old, and that assurance became one of my few comforts.

Given our limited finances at the time, all I could do beyond restoring some order, neatness, and space to the apartment was to begin saving money to paint the most abhorrent walls in soft colors and wash down other areas. I bought some houseplants and generally attempted to bring simplicity to each room. And in the process, I began focusing on my personal appearance as well.

At 179 pounds and a height of just over 5', I was no longer the lithe, winsome woman whom Harriet had met ten years earlier. Having no clothes of my own and no money to shop for a wardrobe that suited my tastes, I had to try on what had belonged to my alters in order to discover what fitted my overweight body and suited my fancy. But I hated what I saw in the mirror. I was obese and ugly. And there weren't many size-eighteen dresses in the lot. So I launched the first of what would be many diets in subsequent years, and this one had a goal of trimming down to a size twelve.

By the beginning of 1975, I had lost nearly thirty pounds. I was thrilled at being able to pull a dress away from my skin and wad inches of material as proof of my diet's success. It was solid, graspable evidence that I was becoming my own person.

* * *

"You're young and smart," Bobby said one morning while I drove him to school. "Why don't you go to college like Aunt Becky and Aunt Tiny?"

"I just might," I said, fighting back tears. It was the first direct sign that my son was accepting me. "But do you think I could make it?" I asked. Having dropped out of high school because multiplicity had made studying so difficult, I was terrified at the prospect of becoming a student again.

"Sure," Bobby said. "You've changed." At the school, he patted my hand and reminded me that he wanted something other than hamburgers for supper. Then he bounced out of the car and ran blissfully toward the school entrance.

On the way home, I decided to take Bobby's advice. A professor at Piedmont Technical College had invited me, through my twin sisters, to talk to the Human Services Program in Greenwood, South Carolina. That seemed like a perfect opportunity to get a feel for what college might be like and to test myself. I had never given a speech, never spoken to strangers about MPD, and had never revealed publicly my identity as *Eve*. This seemed like the perfect chance.

But that Thursday did not turn out to be an informal chat with a few college students, as I had been led to believe. Instead, the classroom and corridor were jammed with people, including newspaper and television reporters. My brief remarks, focusing only on my present life and that of the three alters who had become famous in the fifties, were followed by scores of questions. To my surprise, I was not afraid. It seemed natural that I should be there and natural that I should be fielding questions about my experiences. I don't know where these skills came from. Like Athena from Zeus's forehead, I rose to the occasion.

And the media took note. "For one of the world's most widely publicized multiple personality cases, life offers new challenges and excitement, but with a unique serenity and happiness born of acceptance," wrote Tom Harrison, one of the newspaper reporters at the event. "Mrs. Chris Sizemore now speaks with considerable confidence as well as first-hand knowledge on the subject. . . ."[3]

The only apprehension I felt was when several questions

focused on my future and, more specifically, on how my family had coped with the disorder. I related only positive details, because it *was* true that my family had given enormous love over the years. It was also true, however, that family members in Virginia had no idea I was being interviewed by reporters. So while I could be candid about the disorder, I owed it to them to discuss how far that candor went before revealing our private lives.

The other painful question concerned a relapse of the disorder. "What are the chances in the future that, under severe stress, one of the other personalities may come back?" asked Charles Moore, another print reporter.

"It is altogether possible," I responded, and a chill ran down my spine, "[but] I have been told by my therapist that it is not likely. So, I will just assume that it won't happen. Hopefully."[4] Yet I did not know. After decades of hiding, this going public had happened too fast. I had not planned it. I had brought no prepared text and had not anticipated questions or how I would answer them. Yet something about the experience convinced me that my life had changed. That evening I wrote in my diary, "Today is Taffy's twenty-seventh birthday, and a milestone in my life. I revealed my true identity for the first time, and the rest is now history."[5]

When I returned to Fairfax, the family gathered for a meeting. Everyone seemed pleased to see how happy the unexpected event had made me, but all of us were fearful. We had hidden too long. Each of us had learned complex ways of denying the Eve legacy. And given this, how could we deal with reporters' calls? By consensus, Bobby, Don, and Tommy developed what they believed to be acceptable, but protective, answers to probing questions.

"It's been rough, but I have one of a kind," Don said he would tell reporters asking about our marriage. "It wasn't easy, but never boring."

Bobby, displaying his humor, said, "I'll tell them, 'I'm like anybody else—anybody, that is, who has three or four mothers running around.'"

I laughed with them, but I knew that pat answers would not get us through this. Taffy seemed to agree. Once the joking diminished, she said, "I'm not sure I can handle this." Our living room became deathly quiet. Taffy's opinions held a formidable position in our lives. We had depended upon her for so much and so long.

"Are you saying it was a mistake to go public?" I asked.

"Not for you, Mother," she responded. "You've got to make a life your way. I love you too much. I won't hinder that." Her smooth cheeks began quivering. "But Tommy and I can't afford stress. Not right now."

The South Carolina press coverage in January 1975 did not spark other calls from the media, and the family's hesitancy made me proceed with caution. We had a reprieve, but I had been smitten. The Piedmont event had made me feel good about myself in ways that nothing else had. I was propelled by extraordinary energy. I resumed my work on the apartment, and the following week I learned from the building manager that a unit across the hall from ours was coming available. She said it would be painted and repaired before its new occupants moved in. I immediately asked for it, even though I had not discussed the decision with Don. I needed this move. At no expense to us, it would be a fresh start. I could settle our family in a redecorated apartment that would be free of my former alters' influences. Finally, I would be the only lady of the house.

In the midst of making preparations to change apartments, I also secured the services of a Washington attorney, Denver H. Graham, to investigate how *The Three Faces of Eve* had been handled. My previous counsel had been unable to solve the legal problems, and I was determined to put all this behind me so that my book with Elen, and now possibly my lecturing, could proceed without a hitch. In addition, I had gained new insight into my story's professional value, as first told in Thigpen and Cleckley's book. In February, the *American Psychologist* published a list of "psychological classics" through 1970. From a survey of 5,672 different books and articles cited in eight major psychology texts in use during the early seventies, only eight were deemed "classics," and only two of these classics were cited in all the textbooks. This pair of leading classics was *Sexual Behavior in the Human Male* by A. C. Kinsey, W. B. Pomeroy, and C. E. Martini and the *The Three Faces of Eve.*[6] This fact made

me realize that, despite the notoriety my family had suffered, my
case history had made a valid contribution to the world. But this
realization also convinced me that telling my full story now mattered more than ever.

Yet this same month I would discover that this telling would
not be simple. While Taffy and Bobby were helping me rummage
through closets and boxes for the move, I encountered some of
their deepest feelings about the previous "mothers" among my
alters. I was piling lots of my alters' clothes and belongings for
the trash when I suddenly noticed that Taffy's back had stiffened.

"If you're throwing these away, may I go through them?" she
asked, a coolness in both her voice and manner.

"Sure. You can have anything," I said, not feeling any attach-
ment to the musty items.

Taffy examined the discarded pieces one by one, the way a
mother carefully fingers through her children's old baby clothes.
Occasionally, she and Bobby discussed how one of my alters had
looked in these outfits, or when the clothing had been purchased.
I tried not to listen. I had the strange feeling that my children's
affectionate memories were not really being shared for my
benefit.

At one point, Taffy gasped and held up an old black Bible.
"How could you throw this away?" she moaned. "It belonged to
my *real* mother."

Bobby had also been squirreling aside several items that had
belonged to the Purple Lady, his favorite among my alters, and he
joined Taffy in objecting. "You just can't do this," he said. "These
things meant a lot to them. The others *always* protected and
saved whatever had belonged to the ones who came before
them. So what gives you the right to throw them away now?"

I was astonished. I felt like a stepmother to my own children.
Yet, at the same time, I knew that I needed this rude awakening.
It was obvious that each of my alters had been a different person
to my children and that the other "mothers" had been real
enough to implant deep feelings and memories in both my children's lives.

"You keep whatever you want," I assured my children. "I'm
not trying to destroy the past. I'm just struggling to make room
for the present, to make a place for myself in your lives."

"And you *are* our mother now. We're glad you're here," Bobby said, a softer tone in his voice. "I didn't mean to hurt you. I just thought you should know."

Taffy clutched the Bible to herself and added, "I'm sensitive right now. About maternal things in particular."

"It's all right," I said. "I understand."

"But you don't," she said. "I need my mother's Bible for a purpose. A special one. You see, I'm pregnant." Her announcement immediately dispelled the tensions in the room. We hugged and cried and marveled at how life begets life.

The fact that Taffy was bringing new life into our family enhanced an unusual sense of wonder within me. The ordinary seemed fascinating. A leaf twisting in the wind could seize my imagination. Even in my familiar surroundings, I was like a preschooler on vacation. Early in 1975, this freshness found expression in my paintings and writings:

> I saw a robin this morning, the indication that spring is around the corner. And it isn't just the season; it's in my heart as well. I can see all my life taking form for the first time.
>
> After each resolution this thing I call *self* felt that it would be the last. But in a month or two I would begin to doubt and flounder like a lost ship at sea. But I'm really going to make it this time. I have had upsets but no setbacks. I have been depressed but no apathy. I have known fear but no terror, and I have had doubts but no regression.
>
> This brings me to myself. I have self-knowledge and self-control. I am trying to be self-revealing but have some selfishness. I have some self-fulfillment and am working on self-improvement. But above all, I have self-identity. And all of these have come in six, short months because Dr. Tsitos, Dr. Ham and my family have helped me face the *real* me. I could not have done this alone.
>
> And I know that no matter how things go with the book, the lectures or the legal problems, I shall not be moved. Just being alive is exciting. I don't have to be involved. I can enjoy it as a spectator.[7]

Combined with this sense of wonder was a resurgence of re-call and abreactions. Maybe the physical contact with my alters' belongings evoked this new flood of memories? Maybe the odors or my touch of old silks and cottons and wools or simply envi-sioning the eras implied in each article's design triggered this resurgence? Or possibly it was self-hypnosis? But whatever the cause, this flooding of my mind was far more profound than the earlier experiences. It was erratic rather than chronological. And there were more abreactions than before, as though my uncon-scious mind was now giving me the deeper pains that had not been part of the earlier memories.

And with this resurgence came feelings.

Guilt and sorrow, grief, depression, anger, and doubts erupted within me like wildfires across parched grassy plains. And the reality of these feelings was overwhelming. As I abreacted the surgeries, the childhood burn, and other crises in my alters' lives, I was no longer a mere visitor who observed the past from a protected distance. I felt unmistakably that *I was in the past.* The people and objects, the settings and colors, were not illusive. They were so real that I was terrified of touching them. But there was one common aspect to the earlier recall and abreactions: They were momentary, only spots of time, vivid but fragmentary immersions in the past.

However, there was one major difference that brought bal-ance. Interspersed with the pain were marvelous moments of joy. As if riding on a carousel, I revisited tender, charming moments of my childhood. Christmases and idle moments of quiet playing. In the Strother Place's attic I held my foil ball and changed dresses on my favorite doll. I peered into the wooden toy box that Daddy had made. I snuggled in the quilt that Mother had stitched and pondered the rich colors in the stained-glass win-dow. Yet none of these moments lasted, and their evanescence angered me.

"If the unconscious can recall an instance, such as these I have described, and then forbid us entrance to the full knowl-edge, then I wonder how much we *really* know but are not men-tally conditioned to interpret into awareness?" I wrote in the midst of this frustration. "I repeat: we are what we think."[8]

4

L ooking back on the spring of
1975, I now appreciate the extent to which Dr. Tsitos became a
pioneer in the treatment of MPD, in part because of the follow-up
therapy he began with me in March. He understood that I was a
neophyte in the world of reality. He had compassion for the fragile balance I was maintaining between the conscious and unconscious aspects of my existence. And he possessed the skills
necessary to help me. Wise and intuitive, he employed techniques as a therapist that were years ahead of published research.
Like Dr. Wilbur, who had successfully treated Sybil earlier in the
seventies, Dr. Tsitos knew that he was ushering me through uncharted territories of the psyche and that there were few guidelines for either of us.

In fact, all the time he was working through the unification
process with me, there had been few pertinent resources in print
to which Dr. Tsitos could turn. But he persisted, and during the
subsequent eight-month period his therapy took me far beyond
the reported stages for most patients, again with the notable exception of Sybil. However, the question that he refrained from
asking in my presence, but that he must have pondered, became
apparent in March 1975: *Where do we go from here?*

Not to professional literature, that was clear—and would be
confirmed in September 1975 by one of the era's experts on the
disorder. "The state of research into the field is primitive," said
Dr. Arnold M. Ludwig, who was then department chairman for

psychiatry at the University of Kentucky Medical School. "And for a very good reason, namely, the appearance of these patients is relatively rare." He noted that at that point there had been "only about 100 documented multiple personality disorders recorded since the illness was first identified."[1] And I would subsequently understand that none of those patients had reached as far into the integration process as I did during the winter of 1975.

So there were even fewer precedents on which Dr. Tsitos could draw for conducting what is now called *postunification treatment* of MPD. Other than the work of therapists such as Drs. Wilbur and Ludwig—preceded in 1905 by the inconclusive efforts of Morton A. Prince, M.D., and in the fifties by therapy for me from Drs. Thigpen and Cleckley—there had been no research of consequence about how a therapist, after helping an MPD patient through unification, should guide that patient in crossing the narrow bridge from multiplicity to normalcy.[2]

Thus, I began the journey along that unexplored bridge. Consciously, I felt great, even though I experienced an acute awareness of the unknown. This feeling was overwhelming, but not dominated by darkness and regression. Instead, I consciously saw only light, hope, and the seemingly endless possibilities that normalcy offered, once I had completed the overall integration process. But I now understand that my unconscious mind, not solidly existing in either multiplicity or normalcy, remained troubled. Behind my conscious efforts to lose weight, bring order to our family life, and plan a career for my future, I was unwittingly vacillating back and forth on that bridge. Some days Dr. Tsitos's counsel and my daughter's encouragements beckoned me toward deeper commitment to the realm of normalcy; but most days I was living with, or by, memories that beckoned from that other realm. My alters were like the Furies, except that they were silent in their screams. I consciously heard no voices. And yet their soundless invitations for me to return to the unconscious were no less effective.

Something was bound to happen.

"People must recover the 'lost' aspects of their personalities, lost under a pile of inhibitions, if they are to become integrated in any effective sense," wrote Rollo May in a book published this same year.[3] I had been attempting that, particularly in my relationships as wife and mother. I began putting everything I had into our marriage, but Don didn't seem interested in responding. I studied cookbooks, prepared different types of meals, and served them by candlelight, but he turned on the television and watched the evening news. I experimented with new hairstyles and makeup, but he wouldn't comment unless prodded to do so by Taffy or Bobby. Fortunately for me, however, the children's reactions were different.

"All of it is behind you. It's over," Taffy kept reassuring me. "Just know that you're all right and that you can now do with your life what you want." She seemed so confident—in most ways, more confident than I at the time. And she regularly reinforced the contract she had mentally signed the previous summer, loving me even though she had no idea who I was or who I would become. Her words were simple and genuine: "You'll never be alone, Mother. I'll always be here for you."

But I also sensed conflict in my daughter. During the months prior to my unification and throughout my subsequent ordeals of recalls and abreactions, Taffy had taken care of me on a daily basis. She and her family sacrificed a great deal for my health. But now that she was convinced of my recovery, Taffy seemed to be struggling to restore balance. She still remained in constant contact with me by phone, despite the difficulties of her pregnancy, but she no longer came to our apartment every day. Instead, she, Tommy, and our grandson, Jimmy, began visiting only on weekends. It was a reverse cutting of the umbilical cord. My daughter was trying to give up looking after me, the mother. But as inevitable as this change was, neither of us found it easy.

Looking back, I think Taffy withdrew as much for Bobby's sake as she did for herself and me. Families of mental patients have to do this. It's essential for well family members to support one another as readily as they do the person who is ill. Otherwise, emotional problems can pass like viruses from one to the other. Thus, Taffy seemed to recognize that Bobby, who would turn sixteen in May, needed to be needed, too. And it worked.

Gradually, Bobby started talking to me with more ease. On morning car rides when I took him to school or in the evenings before bedtime, he became more cheerful and demonstrative. Always a respectful child, with dark blue, penetrating eyes, Bobby seemed to come into his own in proportion to the confidence he was gaining about my health. He began to exhibit trust, and one day he wanted to talk about his "other mothers."

He didn't remember the mother of his birth, the Bell Lady, and he had vague recollections of my subsequent alters, such as the Card Girl, the Banana-split Girl, and the Turtle Lady. But he had definite opinions about the last three, and the most negative were directed at the Strawberry Girl. The worst incident, he said, was the day in 1974 that he found her watching a western on the television in his bedroom. None of the others had violated his privacy, so this intrusion surprised him.

"Mom, what are you doing?" he asked, uncertain which personality he was addressing.

"I'm ready to ride herd," a childish voice responded. "Wanna play cowboy, too?" Then the Strawberry Girl began riding an imaginary horse around the bed, her hands tugging at invisible reins and her body rocking up and down as if her unseen mount were trotting.

Since Taffy had warned Bobby about the Strawberry Girl's regressions, he was able to guess which personality it was. So he bristled. "I'm too old to play cowboy, and that goes double for you."

"Oh, yeah?" she quipped, "You just watch me." Then she jumped from the floor to the bed and whipped the air with her right hand as if she were stinging the imaginary horse's haunches into a gallop.

"Just get out!" Bobby yelled, and the Strawberry Girl rode a clean jump off the bed. He pointed her toward the door. But she persisted, begging him to play, too. He had no choice. He pushed that mother out the door and locked it behind her.

"Did any of the others mistreat you?" I asked.

"Oh, no," he said. "That was it. I just told the Purple Lady about it, and she set the Strawberry Girl straight."

"And the Purple Lady *was* good to you, wasn't she?"

"Sure," he said. "We had good times. Got along. Did things together. I could always count on her. She took care of me."

Suddenly, I felt compelled to know. "What if you had been given a choice?" I asked. "What if, before last summer, somebody had said, 'Bobby, you can have one of the personalities come out and stay forever—but you have to choose.' Would you have chosen Purple Lady?"

"Sure. We had great times."

"But I'm not Purple Lady."

"I know, Mom," he said. "You're one person now. But we're starting to have good times, too."

I hugged my son and asked, "Is that enough?"

"It's normal, Mom. No more changes. No more personalities. That's all I've ever wanted."

However, I wasn't so certain that I could guarantee him normalcy. Not just yet. My heart knew that something was wrong, and the first signs were familiar and disconcerting.

I had headaches. Severe pressure headaches like those when a new alter had surfaced in previous years. But I didn't heed them. I dismissed the headaches as connected with concern over Taffy's discomfort during the early months of her pregnancy. Yet that perplexed me, too. I didn't understand Taffy's irritableness or morning sickness or the fact that she routinely went back to bed each day after getting Tommy off to work. But why didn't I understand? I had regained memories of how pregnancy affected my body, but somehow I could not relate Taffy's very real and normal discomforts to my alters' experiences. It was as if my feelings and memories had once again slipped out of sync.

"I have to correct my thinking," I wrote on the day after the headaches began. "Nothing is going to send me back to that world of confusion and frustration. I can't help anyone when I am not balanced myself. But when I really know this, then why am I so afraid?"[4]

Three days later, I felt calm, lucid,[2] and relaxed—strong enough, in fact, that I prepared our family's income-tax forms in one night. Don, who had come home that evening in a good mood, made coffee and worked with me. As much as tax work can be, it was fun. Midway through, however, I took a break from the piles of receipts and calculations and went to the bathroom. Whimsically, I weighed myself on the scales. The dial indicated that I had lost sixteen pounds since January, and I was ecstatic.

But that joy was immediately dispelled by a sudden hunger

that seemed to jolt me. I knew that feeling. I had experienced it in late February, one evening when Don and Bobby, opting for a ball game, had left me alone in the apartment. About nine o'clock, a similar hunger seized me. It seemed so unbearable that I decided to take a sleeping pill and lie down on the couch. But about an hour later, I awakened—or came to myself?—and I wasn't on the couch. Instead, I was seated at the dining table and was using both hands to cram nuts into my mouth. Like a starving person. At the time, I found it humorous and had subsequently forgotten that incident until, standing on the bath scales during the break, I remembered it vividly. That also frightened me. Was something happening to my short-term memory?

On March 5, I had a similar experience. After returning home from taking Bobby to school, I felt chilled, as if I were suddenly coming down with a severe virus. But remembering what had happened with the sleeping pill, I was afraid to take any medication. So I pulled a heavy robe over my clothes, wrapped up in a blanket, stretched out on the couch, and fell asleep while watching the *Today* show. I knew I was asleep because I was dreaming. In the dream, I was driving home from Taffy's house. The road was narrow and winding through a dense forest. A heavy fog blurred the windshield. Somehow I lost control of the car and it left the road. When it halted, the trees seemed to press on the car's roof with such force that I could feel the pressure on my head.

However, about an hour after first curling up on the couch in the living room, I awakened to find myself on the bed in our master bedroom. And I did not feel as though I had just awakened *from* this dream, as one normally does when consciously remembering a dream. Instead, I just remembered the dream as if it were separate from the memory of awakening.

Four days later, I started to alter one of the Purple Lady's pant suits, which I had kept in the closet but could not wear because I had lost so much weight. But that Sunday afternoon I realized that, since the previous summer, I had been unable to sew. That depressed me and I procrastinated doing the work. By Monday night, however, I prodded myself into a second attempt. I had to fix the pant suit. Otherwise, there wouldn't be enough outfits for me to wear on the South Carolina trip that Elen and I had scheduled. Excitement about working on the book seemed motivation enough, so I went to get the pant suit. But I discovered that it had already been altered. I knew that *I* hadn't done it. Obviously, Don or Bobby had not, and no one else had been in the apartment overnight.

"Perhaps I am walking in my sleep, or perhaps I'm not," I wrote during this period. I couldn't be certain. I knew that sleepwalking was a form of dissociation, but how could I be *working* in my sleep? I had no idea. So I resolved to focus on what I understood about my own will: "My psyche knows *me* and realizes that I *will not* allow a transition through headaches. *Will no longer* accept, 'with my eyes open,' this method of coping. And it has used sleep before to pass from one personality to the other—but never in the beginning of a formation. I won't allow this either. Yet I'm not sure how to prevent it. There *has* to be a way."[5]

Given the peculiarity of these incidents, I was brimming with details to tell Dr. Tsitos at my monthly session in mid-March, and I did so during the first minutes of my appointment. As I talked, light from his office windows seemed to hurt my eyes. When I finished describing the incidents, I held my breath. I didn't want to hear bad news.

But he said calmly, "It's to be expected," and showed no fascination about what I had recounted. Clearly, he had expected such episodes, and he continued persuasively, as if I should have anticipated them, too, "You're in an interim stage of integration, and you know what's going on. You acknowledge that these are 'the old ways of coping,' and you're right. These are forms of dissociation, and in the future there may be many more of them. But they signal no relapse. They're reactive, not active." And when he saw that I remained hesitant, he added, "It's more like an alcoholic who, in early treatment, returns to drinking."

"But what do I do?" I felt so helpless. I thought about Taffy's confidence and Bobby's desire for normalcy. I didn't want more dissociation, any more than I wanted a relapse of MPD.

"Just acknowledge it. Tell me about every incident. And tell your family. Assure us that *you* know the incidents are happening. And reach out for help. Ask the family to call your attention to such states," he said, then paused to make certain I was listening. "Dissociation thrives on deceit. So, if you or they deny such behavior, then you are failing to face the truth."

"But I can't tell them," I responded. "Bobby's not ready to understand, Taffy is having a difficult time with the pregnancy, and Don will just say, 'Here we go again!' I can't burden the children any longer, and I can't take that negative stuff from Don. Not now. He keeps reminding me that I have tried many times to get well, and that each one has been a failure. So, no. I've got to keep this from them."

"And that's the next rule," Dr. Tsitos said, continuing in a steady voice. "Don't panic." He smiled and I laughed, realizing how he had seen through my reaction. "These temporary states are unimportant. You know what they are. *You're* in control now. Dissociation can no longer hurt you."

"But how can you be so sure?"

"I'm certain that you're getting stronger and that you *do not* want a relapse of MPD," he responded. "You are my certainty. As long as you take responsibility for meeting your needs, you will call forth the character traits you need, rather than using 'the old way' to create new characters."

Listening, my mind had spun off in its own direction. "Of course," I said, "that's it." The insight made me gleeful. "It is so clear to me now that my dissociation was *not* evolutionary. The same three personalities did not return each time. Each was a different entity. Each was created individually, and each disappeared the same way. I am right, aren't I? And the reason that some of them had similar characteristics was because they were derived from *me.* I don't know why it has taken me so long to see that."

"And what exactly do you see?"

"That as marvelously special as each one was," I responded, hesitating, my voice clouding with emotion, "none of them was *normal.* Each had distinctive emotional problems, and yet all were part of some larger problem. *My* MPD."

"Yes, Mrs. Sizemore," Dr. Tsitos said, "you and I have witnessed the experience of a lifetime: a neurosis within a neurosis. And now you understand that, too."

"Then why didn't you tell me this before?"

"Your psyche is healing itself. That's why. And so far, it has presented all the right insights at just the right moments."

That assurance, which he had repeated so often, always gave me renewed confidence. And trepidation. But occasionally some humor as well. "So I shouldn't ask you when all of this began?" I interjected, smiling.

"You don't yet remember, do you?" he said. "But you're going to see your father next week. Talk to him. Ask for his memories about your first year, and see how much of what he says is familiar to you. That way, when I see you in April, we can work through those memories. His and yours."

I left my therapist's Annandale office that day with such happiness and anticipation. The Little River Turnpike never looked so vibrant. Adrenaline surged through my bloodstream, and memories floated smoothly into my consciousness like music from stereo headphones. I couldn't wait to talk to Dad. He had always been my confidant. He would remember. He *had* to.

One night, however, my mind took me home. Before going to bed, I had been concentrating on early childhood memories to prepare for the talks with Dad. But after retiring, I began dreaming about the attic in the Strother Place, an eighteenth-century plantation house we had rented in South Carolina during the Great Depression. It was the period when my alters had been the ones I remember as the Run-away Girl, the Innocent Girl, and the Hiding Girl.[6]

But the girl in my dream seemed to be *me*. Dressed in my blue pongee dress, worn only on Sundays, I felt as though this attic were the safest place in the world. No one else in the family had wanted it, because the attic was separated from the rest of the house. A haven unto itself. And in my dream, I blithely lost myself to lone playfulness.

As the dream progressed, this trip back in time began to feel even more enjoyable. The room seemed so familiar and its shapes distinctly different from what I remembered seeing when awake. Flat, somehow. And incomplete. But all my childhood things were there. The small bed covered with a multicolored quilt that Mother had given for my playroom. And the braided rug she had made from colored roping of old clothes that had been torn and then stripped together. Near the window was the wooden toy box, a gift of Dad's craftsmanship. Its side boards of various timbers ran in peculiarly smooth angles to the box's edges, as if to emphasize the specialness of the homemade toys it protected.

But the stained-glass window was the dominant feature. It seemed to glow in the moonlight so that green and amber and blue hues mingled in the light as it was refracted through the window's design: a distinct pair of hexagonal panes, framed by three triangles on top and bottom and by a long octagon on either side.

Brightened by this multitude of colors in the quilt and rug and window, however, the rest of the room appeared somber. The surfaces of its wooden walls, ceiling, and floor were darkened by age. Even the porcelain doorknob had yellowed. But the darkness did not disturb me. It actually seemed to balance the room, giving it a richer presence of warmth and peace.

Suddenly, I felt as if I were awakening but didn't want to. At that moment, I realized I was no longer that little girl. Immediately, she floated like a spirit toward the corner created by the attic's eave, but then she turned. Our eyes met. I could feel myself looking away, but she did not. She seemed so lighthearted, as if suspended in air just inches above the floor, my doll tucked casually under her left arm. Picture perfect. Then the girl smiled at me without altering the smooth, straight line formed by her lips, and the scene began dimming.

I got up from the bed and rushed through the Fairfax apartment for my easel, paints, brushes, and a clean canvas. I was no longer asleep, though I had no feeling that I had awakened. I was not back in the Strother Place attic because all that I could see were the rooms and furnishings of our Virginia apartment. Yet that attic's presence seemed to permeate me. Once I began painting, however, the attic and the girl reappeared. Not in my mind but on the canvas. I could not paint fast enough, and I felt wonderful.

But later, as I brushed on the last touches, I felt utter exhaustion. Muscles in my shoulders and arms and back ached as if I were succumbing to a severe flu. So I left everything and stumbled back to bed. Nestled under the covers, I felt a sense of relief pass through me, and that's when I decided to name the painting "Blithe Spirit." Just then, I could almost see my father, Acie Costner, the dear, long-suffering man who was in a nursing home at the time. But this was no dream or vision. It was pure imagination, and I was deeply comforted by it. I imagined him sitting in his wheelchair and feeling equally alone in the night. Then I remembered something he had said decades before. The words had been counsel that Dad had given to my former husband, Ralph, when the family decided to send me to Dr. Thigpen in 1951.

"Remember this," Dad had said, "my daughter may be sick, but she is *not* crazy. I know my Christine." Comforted and at peace, I sank deeper into sleep.

Awakening before Don and Bobby the next morning, I rushed back to the canvas. But I was disappointed in how the painting looked. It seemed flat, simple, and the colors either too bright or too muted. I was devastated, and I wanted no one to see it. Just then, I heard Don in the bath, and I decided to hide this thing. Fast. I spotted the gap between the antique organ and a living-room wall. It was perfect. So I quickly slid the canvas in that gap and went to the kitchen to make coffee. As far as I was concerned "Blithe Spirit" could stay sandwiched there forever.

The talk with my father never came to pass.

On Monday, while Elen and I were preparing to leave for South Carolina that Wednesday, the call came that Dad had suffered a heart attack. Five days later, he went into coronary shock and died in thirty-five minutes. It was 2:05 P.M., March 22, when I lost the one man in this world who had loved me the longest. And with him, I believed, departed the last pure link to my childhood that I had been seeking so desperately.

When it was clear to us at Dad's bedside that we were witnessing the moment of his passing, I prayed silently, "Lord, as he crosses to the other side, please, make the bridge short, sunny and wide."[7] It was no idle coincidence that I envisioned a bridge. My psyche seemed to understand something elemental, as if I possessed a peculiar familiarity with the journey Dad's soul was now taking. He had touched my life as no other could. And his passing would leave me so alone. The eldest of my generation. The next in line. The next to die?

How, I kept wondering, *will I endure even more aloneness than before?*

During the next three months, I wrote no thoughts or memories or details of events in the diary. My life had become as silent as four in the morning, and the stillness was profound. Dad's full name had been *Doctor* Acie Costner, and I felt as though the physician of my being had perished. He had been such a frail man, yet so sturdy. Like a diviner whose rough hands are sensitive enough to follow pulses from a tree branch in order to find underground water, Dad's instincts had been unexplainably true. They were his strength. But left with only his absence and my memories, I experienced sorrow's great depths.

Yet I felt inadequate to express such enormous emotions. On occasion, I would catch myself talking too loudly or repeating myself. At other times, words simply did not come to mind, leaving me speechless and numb. Gradually, the sessions with Dr. Tsitos made a difference. As he had previously done with guilt, my therapist struggled to help me cope with grief and the meaning of death. At home, Taffy reinforced this therapy. All of us understood how crucial this follow-up was: Seeing death had somehow been connected with the previous emergences of virtually all my alters, beginning with my first memories of encounters with blood and death at the age of two. And at least Dr. Tsitos knew, prior to Dad's death, how vulnerable I had become in terms of dissociation. So the emergence of yet another alter was a distinct possibility.

The children dealt with my grief by giving. One afternoon after school, Bobby and four boys from Fairfax High dropped by the apartment. My son acted casual to his friends, but I knew the importance of this surprise visit. I served the boys cookies and milk. We chatted, the boys joked, then they left. But when Bobby reached the door, he stopped and winked at me. It was a secret gift. Though a sophomore in high school, he had never brought friends home before. The wall of secrecy around my mental illness had forced us to invite no one into our home. This was the first time, and in so doing, he was reaching out, as if to say, "Everything's fine. This death won't be like the others."

Taffy was equally sensitive. On April 4, my forty-eighth birthday, she pulled me aside from the family meal, handed me a small box, and said, "This *is* your first birthday as an adult, right?"

Choked with emotion, I could only nod. I had thought that no one understood the day's significance for me, but I should have expected it of my daughter. When I opened the box, it contained an orange daisy pin with green leaves. Not the most expensive gift I've ever received, but the most precious. To this day, that pin remains in a velvet box among my treasured possessions.

Another day in April, while I was having lunch with Taffy in Fredericksburg, she mentioned that a nice dress shop was having a great sale. "And there's not an outfit in your closet that you've shopped for or bought," she added. "Don't you think it's time you had a dress of your own?"

In the shop, she helped me select several choices in my new size, twelve, then she held up another. "The Purple Lady would have loved this." It was an attractive chiffon and, of course, purple. At first I disliked it, for that reason alone, but then I remembered my conversation with Bobby.

"I'll take it," I said. And I'll never forget the details. The sale price was thirty dollars. When I got home, I tried it on dozens of times in front of our bedroom mirror. Then I carefully hung it in a special place in my closet. It was enough just to have it. A dress of my own. But I vowed not to wear it until I was certain that I would stay well.

At the April session with Dr. Tsitos, he related my grief to what death had recurringly meant to me. And he observed, "Through the years, you were most troubled when you equated each alter's disappearance with death. Is that right?"

I resisted responding. The very sound of the word *death* upset me. Finally, however, I unleashed a burst of feelings: "Those *were* deaths, because my alters were alive. I have worn their clothes. I have read their wills. Their memorabilia is packed away in our apartment. And my children loved some of them deeply. Isn't that sufficient proof of their lives? What's more, if I'm the only person who created them, then why am I not *solely* responsible for their deaths? That's why I keep saying, 'I killed them.' And I will not permit another one to emerge, because I'll have to kill her, too. I intend to survive."

"Chris, are you saying there is another?"

"No," I said. "In spite of everything, I am unmistakably alone."

We did not settle the issues of death, grief, and guilt that day, or in many subsequent sessions. But Dr. Tsitos remained patient and diligent. Gradually, he guided me toward—but stopped short of forcing me to accept—a personal awareness of how grief and guilt, sorrow and loneliness, are acceptable and necessary life experiences. "These feelings actually have more to do with life than with death," he noted. The goal, for example, was that I could learn *to express* guilt or anger or grief rather than creating an alter to be my surrogate in coping with, or in expressing, such emotions. As before, my therapist's method was to prepare me adequately, but then to allow the next step to be mine. At my own pace. At my own level of understanding.

Thirteen years later, a leading MPD clinician in the eighties, Richard P. Kluft, M.D., would describe the crucial phase of this therapy as guiding patients in "abandoning autohypnotic evasions":

> The MPD patients' dissociation-proneness is a given. Consequently, it is critical for unified patients to learn about this propensity, fully appreciate its potential pitfalls, and achieve mastery over it. Some therapists attempt to turn this capacity into a skill and [to] teach constructive hypnotic coping skills and autohypnosis. Others help patients to evolve nondissociative alternatives using psychodynamic and cognitive-behavorial approaches. *The crucial issue is* not so much the technique that is applied as it is *the effort to help patients achieve active mastery of,* rather than helplessness before or evasive use of, *their dissociative talents.*[8]

If my dissociative talents produced Andréa de Cosná, then she proved to be my weakest creation. Mute, unable to drive a car, and claiming to be thirty-two years old, this new alter emerged and disappeared in a period of about six weeks. But unlike most of the previous ones, Andréa had no interest in *things.* New clothes did not start appearing in my closet, and no collections began cluttering our apartment. Nor was I afflicted with amnesia. I was constantly aware of her presence, but she didn't seem to think in words. I only knew her name because she occasionally signed it on notes or poems, written in her distinctively left-handed script. It was as though she had sprung from the right side of my brain and existed as living *images* of the grief I still harbored following my father's death.

I did not acknowledge my coexistence with her until June 26,

when Taffy and Tiny followed Dr. Tsitos's instructions and confronted me with the changes of behavior that they observed
while we vacationed in Nags Head, North Carolina.[9] A day earlier,
I had driven Bobby to take his written exam and road tests for a
driver's license. But I later learned about his surprise encounter
with Andréa.

"While I took the test, you left," he told me. "Remember?"

I said that I did, but I could see the disappointment in his
eyes, so I asked, "You tell me what you saw."

"I passed everything, got my license, and came back to the
car. You were sitting in the passenger seat and eating an ice-
cream cone. I scooted behind the steering wheel and said, 'Hey,
Mom. I got my license!' But you just looked at me. Then you took
the napkin from around the cone and handed it to me. On it was
a note: 'Hi. I'm Andréa.'"

Given my family's subsequent confirmation that they had seen
Andréa, too, my initial reaction was deep disappointment in myself, confusion, and utter disgust. "The whole struggle was for
nothing," I muttered. "I just don't know why I'm so weak that I
can't face my problems the way other people do. Am I doomed
to hide my real feelings through an endless string of these
women in my mind?" But my deeper anguish was that, for the
first time, *I* could see the suffering which my alters inflicted on
my family. Always before, the unconscious mind had shielded me
from that reality.

Later, in a long-distance phone conversation, Dr. Tsitos
agreed to see me as soon as I returned to Virginia. But as the days
on the beach progressed, I delayed going home. I had to sort out
what was happening. First of all, I realized that Andréa was the
only alter with whom I had *consciously* coexisted since the day,
nearly forty-six years earlier, when my mother had cut her arm
and I had watched the little Red-headed Girl run to get Dad. All
the intervening alters were now clear in my memory, but I had
not shared consciousness with them. Certainly not as I was now
doing with Andréa.

Also, Andréa seemed trapped—partly in consciousness with
me, but mostly beyond my awareness in whatever zone of the
mind there is that links consciousness with unconsciousness. Was
this why she seemed to have few thoughts, other than what she

wrote as notes or poems? All I knew was that Andréa remained as mute within my consciousness as she was during the infrequent times when she made herself known to the family. The only good effect of this was that I was spared voices within the mind that had deeply troubled the other alters.

Shortly after I returned to Fairfax in late July, Andréa disappeared. Like the small French village of Cosne from which she apparently took her name, Andréa de Cosná seemed to have been a dot on the map of my life. Dr. Tsitos termed her a "fragmentation," and placed little importance on her fleeting existence.

But I have never forgotten her. She helped to bear my greatest sorrow. And years later, I understood that she had not departed without making a contribution to my life. She did not leave behind things and memories and many life events, as the others had done. That was not her design. In her muteness, she was a deeper sort, and her legacy to me was more precious. A line from one of her poems affirmed, "God gave me a message without a word to say." Alone once again, I gradually discovered that message: Feelings were now linked to memories. This meant that as I would subsequently recall moments from the *others'* lives, I no longer divided those feelings into three parts. For example, I knew sorrow in its wholeness.

This ultimately convinced me that Andréa was no setback. She accomplished her task. Coexisting with her, I had felt raging emotions. Not directed at others such as family or friends. These feelings were directed exclusively at myself. They expanded my sense of self. I had been prepared for the possibility that someone like Andréa might emerge. And when she did, I had not retreated. Instead, I had accepted that I created her, and I had refused to yield ultimate control of my life to her.

But what did Andréa's existence imply about clinical unification? As important as such therapy is, didn't the "slippage" that allowed this "fragmentation" to emerge indicate that complete integration might somehow be out of a clinician's reach? Did this mean that the patient had to take some final step alone?

Though nearly another full year would pass before I got some answers, I at least understood that Andréa had demonstrated the limits of multiplicity to me. Without her, I would never have known *firsthand* how severely MPD can limit a patient's life. But

I would later realize that by initially appearing to limit my healing process, she had actually expanded it. Rollo May explains this paradox succinctly:

> Creativity itself requires limits, for the creative act arises out of the struggle of human beings with, and against, that which limits them. . . . [And] consciousness itself is born out of the awareness of these limits. . . .
>
> It is not by accident that the Hebrew myth that marks the beginning of human consciousness, Adam and Eve in the Garden of Eden, is portrayed in the context of a rebellion. Consciousness is born in the struggle against a limit, called there a prohibition. Going beyond the limit set by Yahweh is then punished by the acquiring of other limits which operate inwardly in the human being—anxiety, the feeling of alienation and guilt. But valuable qualities also come out of this experience of rebellion—the sense of responsibility and ultimately the possibility, born out of loneliness, of human love. Confronting limits for the human personality actually turns out to be *expansive. Limiting and expanding* thus go together.[10]

I returned from Nags Head with unstoppable determination. "My life *must* change," I said to Taffy. "I've tried enough approaches to get your dad's attention that I could write an advice column, 'The Lonely Heart's Checklist: Thirty Ways *Not* to Save a Marriage.' But it's hopeless. We can't go on like this. Either we start loving one another again, or I'm out."

"Then tell him," she responded. "You've tried in the past, but you've always stopped short. Always kept your true feelings hidden. So just tell him. Tell Daddy everything and give him a chance to sort it all out. There's a mountain of silence between you two, and it won't be torn down overnight."

So when my husband came home from work, I took Taffy's advice. Some of it, anyway. Bolstered by newfound depths of emotion, I hurled my deepest feelings in laundry-list fashion. Straight at him. One-two-three. An avalanche of hurt and concern about our marriage gushed out of my mouth before Don could get comfortable in a kitchen chair.

He was obviously stunned. Then he retaliated. "Well, what about me? I made it possible for you to go to the beach because you weren't feeling well. But you stayed weeks longer than you said. There's been nobody here to look after me. Nobody to cook or clean or wash clothes. A man can't work all day, then scrub all night on an empty stomach."

"Wifely duties don't make a family," I interrupted, halting his timeworn rebuttal. "We go nowhere together, and I need to go places. The world is new to me. Don't you understand? And there are larger issues to iron out than who washes and starches and presses the shirts. I want to talk issues."

He didn't answer. He just walked out of the kitchen, went to the television set in the living room, and turned on the evening news.

"I'm not finished," I snapped, following him and turning off the set. "Tonight, the headline story is our marriage."

He sat resolutely in his favorite chair and said, "Well, I'm finished, and that's it."

"Oh, no. This time, we'll talk this thing through or go hoarse trying."

"I've said my piece, Chris. And I won't say something more that I'll regret."

"Fine. Then listen to me, Don Sizemore. WE . . . ARE . . . VEGETATING. I'm forty-eight, you're fifty-two, and we're both smothering to death in this marriage. You don't even *like* me. And I don't blame you, because I haven't liked myself, either. I am doing nothing *important* with my life. And you're not even doing the *unimportant* things with me."

"I work all day and come home at night. What else is there?"

"There's life outside these walls, Don, and I've never seen it. None of us has. We've hidden behind my mental illness so long that the world has passed us by. Well, I want to flag that world down and put us back on board. I want us to do things. To go places. The whole family. But also just you and me. Is that too much to ask?"

He hurled his billfold on the coffee table. "Lord God, woman, just open that thing. We don't have a nickel. Haven't had in years. The way things are, we couldn't afford to watch a crowd wait for a bus."

"So we start by stopping. And the first thing we stop paying is rent—"

"—and doctor bills?"

"Those, too. It's a fact that my illness has caused our financial woes for decades, and I am dreadfully sorry about that. But I promise you: This time next year, those psychiatry bills will dwindle to nothing. And in case you haven't noticed, I haven't spent a frivolous dollar in a year. I've just been fighting to be normal. And thank God, I finally am. Not well, mind you. But normal just the same. I'm mad and it feels good. I'm longing, really hurting, and I'm just damn glad to be feeling something. So let's start living. Let's plan a normal home, a normal marriage, some affection now and then, and normal quarrels as needed. You're my husband. Start *living* with me."

He looked into my eyes with sadness and admiration—a mixture that startled us both. Then, just as quickly, he looked away. "We can't buy a house," he said. "We've lost three. There are no savings, so I don't have a shot at a down payment, and I can't tolerate buying and losing another one."

"You've got the homeplace. Why not borrow against it or rent it out to somebody?"

"No renter or banker will touch Mother's house," he said. "I can't do that to her memory."

"Then move us there," I responded. "By the time you find a job in Chatham County and borrow money to fix that house up, I'll be out of therapy. I promise you."

"And just how would I, an electrician, earn a living back home? Fixing radios and toasters and an occasional heater switch in a tobacco barn?"

I didn't want to hear it, but he was right. I slumped into the blue brocade couch. All I knew was that Don was a decent man, we were miserable, and I didn't have a clue. "Then we're stuck here."

"We are and I accept that," he said. "I gave up dreams a long time ago."

"But do you love me, Don?"

There was no malice in his voice as he answered, "You started this, so you answer. Can you honestly *say* you love me?"

"All I can say is I just don't know anymore."

A few days later, I was crying in the bedroom. Partly for the
mess our lives were in. And partly for myself. I was ready to make
choices but had not an inkling how to do it alone. That's when I
realized how deeply I missed my alters' helpfulness. No twenty-
four-hour period now was like those before the unification, when
my alters had left notes on the blackboard or had spoken advice
in my head, all to help me plan and cope. Being one person simply meant that I now had to do all the planning and coping by
myself.

And normal days seemed so long. I could fix Don's breakfast,
see that Bobby got ready for his day, then I could clean the apartment, do the laundry, and check on Taffy by telephone. But by
ten in the morning, what else was there to do? Dr. Tsitos still
insisted that I wasn't ready to get a job. And when he did allow
me, what could I do? Manage another ladies' specialty shop and
earn a hundred dollars a week? That wasn't going to free us of
debt. That's part of how we had fallen into such a crisis. So how
about college? But I knew that was out. We didn't have the
money to send Bobby, and he would be ready to enroll in just
two years. Then what about some new career? Sure. I had already
tried writing and lecturing and painting, but where had those
projects gotten me? Nowhere. It was as though once I got well,
then the *specialness* about me had disappeared right alongside
my alters. All I had been trained for was to be sick. And the emotional problems that now kept me in therapy—painful as they
were—seemed so boringly normal that I often wondered how
Dr. Tsitos stayed awake during my sessions.

But I was also crying because I now understood what life
would be like without Dad. Just then, Don entered the room. I
tried to hide my tears, but he had seen them. He came to the bed
and sat beside me.

"Why are you crying, honey? You're not still mad, are you?"

I looked into my husband's quiet eyes. "No. I'm not angry. I'm
just feeling sorry for myself. Without Dad, I just don't have anybody anymore that I can tell my secrets to."

"You have me," Don said, and took my trembling hands in his.

"That's right," I responded. "I do." And I leaned my head on
his shoulder.

*   *   *

In retrospect, our life and relationship as it is today as well as my public career and my selected privacy are all rooted in that simple, poignant exchange. It had taken nearly twenty-two years of struggles before our marriage could reach that single moment when Don and I shared the same feelings at the same time about anything basic. We didn't say words like *I love you.* We didn't solve all the problems and start over. In fact, my follow-up therapy with Dr. Tsitos would continue for another two years, and some problems in our marriage continue into the present. But my husband became my friend that day. Affection finally had its basis. As a couple, we had a good beginning.

A month later, there would be another important beginning for our family. Our second grandchild would be born to Taffy and Tommy. And that September event became particularly significant because of what my daughter did. "Mother, I can't name my child Eve," Taffy said at the hospital, "but I can name her Christi, after you." I held the baby girl, felt the bond between Taffy and me extended into this precious new life, and I prayed that little Christi would grow to love her mother as much as Taffy had loved me. But I also prayed that my namesake would *never* know in me another Nan. And if that prayer was answered, Christi would become the first of our family to know me only as a normal woman. One woman. A typical grandmother.

But Christi was born during the most atypical period in our family's experience. Her fresh hope came amid events that stormed with such magnitude into our lives that I now wonder how they could have happened so rapidly and how we all survived.

I could not have imagined what I was setting into motion that August when I entered paintings in a community show at the library of George Mason University. I just wanted a break. If I could get fifty dollars a painting, then that was money I could bring home to help Don. But as the exhibit opened, buyers were not attracted by either the paintings from the "Eve" collection (those done by my alters) or the few I had finished since the previous summer. All were simply signed Chris, and none was selling. So I telephoned the *Fairfax Journal* and told them who I was. By this time, the several stories that had appeared about me in southern newspapers had resulted only in local distribution, so I had no reason to fear this one. I simply hoped some publicity might sell my paintings.

Fairfax Journal reporter Peggy Longmire interviewed me, and her article was published September 4. But my paintings didn't sell that day, either. Harriet Henderson consoled me by promising to secure a place for some of the collection in an up-coming Georgetown exhibit. However, a storm of events inter-vened. Prompted by Longmire's story, the *Washington Post* sent Donnel Nunes, a reporter and a GWU journalism instructor, and Gerald Martineau, a staff photographer, to do a feature on the long-lost Eve. The news angle was not that I was a painter but that there had been many more sets of alters in my life since the famous set of three in the fifties. I had not revealed this in any of the previous appearances or interviews.

Ten days later, when their detailed feature ran on that D.C. daily's front page, the Associated Press released a national version of the *Post*'s story, accompanied by a photo of Bobby embracing me. Within a few weeks, I began receiving clippings from across the country,[11] and my public life began.

Our Fairfax apartment fell under an immediate media siege. Through the mail and by telephone, more than one hundred in-quiries came from writers, book publishers, reporters, and pro-ducers. The postmarks hailed from Hollywood and New York City, as well as from distant places like Sweden and Norway. Sci-entific publications such as the American Medical Association's *Today's Health* wanted interviews, as did popular magazines in-cluding the *Ladies' Home Journal.* In addition, there were offers for representation from lecture bureaus and literary agents, plus some purchase requests for my paintings. By all indications, each of the creative forms that I had pursued for so long as an MPD patient suddenly seemed viable for a career.[12] But I had un-finished business to face.

Correspondence from Denver H. Graham arrived five days after the *Post* story broke. While it confirmed that my Washing-ton attorney was expediting legal efforts, begun a year earlier, to recover all rights to my story from my former psychiatrists in Georgia, Graham's letter also indicated that the psychiatrists had not yet approved the wording of, or signed, a formal release. They had only agreed in principle not to block my literary efforts.[13] Being an optimist, I inferred that my legal hassles would soon end. But the negative implications were chilling. If there was in fact a 1953 agreement in which my former alters (while still under psychiatric care) had assigned to Drs. Thigpen and Cleckley "all worldwide rights forever" to my story, then the current offers could prove meaningless.

The most immediate threat was to any *movie* offers for my story—as indicated in Dr. Thigpen's next letter. He cautioned my attorney that my alters *had* executed a contract with Twentieth Century-Fox in the fifties. That agreement, Dr. Thigpen predicted, probably would not prohibit my writing an autobiography: but he warned that the Fox contract could irrevocably bar that story from being purchased for any subsequent film purposes.[14] And indeed there was a movie proposal among the current deluge of offers. A producer wanted to do a sequel to *The Three Faces of Eve.* But I declined for reasons that I explained to another *Washington Post* reporter in early October: "The man said this could be revved up and really be sensational. But I didn't want that. My life is so different from that."[15] And I meant it. I was determined that, legal difficulties or not, my story would not be sensationalized. And if either that determination or the film agreement my alters had signed while I was not legally competent meant that Hollywood would not make a movie of my full story, then so be it.

At this juncture, however, an editor at Doubleday & Company, Inc., sent not only a contract and an advance to Elen and me but also the publishing house's assurances that its staff would intervene as agent and publicist for the book. My cousin and I would be free of concerns about rights and media inquiries. All we had to do was get the story on paper—provided that I also received releases from my former psychiatrists. Thirteen days later, my attorney informed Doubleday that he possessed a certified psychiatric opinion that attested "that Mrs. Sizemore was not . . . legally competent to execute any valid release or contract during the period of time she was under the care of Drs. Thigpen and Cleckley." By December 1, the last snag in that endeavor was removed when my attorney received a letter from Dr. Thigpen, affirming that both he and Dr. Cleckley would "be glad to sign releases."[16]

It was a remarkable moment. After twenty-one years of legal impediments, I finally had an editor, with the means to do so, who was committed to publishing my true story. And in retrospect, it's amazing how far my share of Doubleday's advance went. At $6,250, it was more than I had earned managing ladies' specialty shops for an entire year. And when the manuscript was completed, I was to get the same amount again. Over twelve thousand dollars. That obviously did not make us rich in the seventies, but we needed every cent.

Enough was set aside so that Bobby, then a junior in high school, could finish his first year in college. Then Don and I paid off as many debts as possible. With the remainder, I bought gifts for every member of the family, and still there was money left over. So I started a house fund. Since my medical bills had caused us to lose three others, I was determined that my story would help buy the fourth. And I bought two gifts for myself: a white lace and chiffon negligee and a pair of white satin slippers. But I hid these alongside the purple dress I had bought in the spring. They were special. I would not wear them, I decided, until the publicity tour for the book.

By Christmastime, all the family responded to the changes in our lives by giving gifts reflecting their new perspectives of me. My grandson, Jimmy, gave me a small wooden sculpture of the letters spelling *Eve,* and my husband's gift was a gold necklace and heart in which *Eve* had been inscribed. It was the first jewelry Don had ever given me. I cherished these gifts. They represented a milestone. My family was celebrating the fact that, after decades of hiding, there was no longer any need for secrecy. They could love and acknowledge me for all I had been, was, or might become.

And to a person who had lived within multiplicity, this full acceptance mattered. To the family and, through the book in progress, ultimately to the world, it was okay that I had been Eve and now I was me. The truth was my Christmas. And as I watched my family laughing, exchanging gifts with one another, and appearing so relaxed, I realized that Andréa de Cosná had been a convincing persuader. Seemingly trapped between conscious and unconscious realms, her muteness had hurled me toward normalcy. I had heeded the wordless message that God gave her. I had a voice for a purpose, and the time had come to speak out.

5

*B*ut I didn't get to speak out. Not immediately, anyway. At the beginning of 1976, Doubleday's publicists postponed most of my appearances but assured the media that Elen and I were completing the book and that, after its publication in 1977, I would certainly be available for interviews.

When reporters persisted, they were referred to Dr. Tsitos, who cautioned them that I was still under psychiatric care. But some reporters inferred that I had gone public only to decline subsequent interviews because, in fact, I was not cured of MPD. Responding to such skeptics, Dr. Tsitos explained, as he had previously done with the *Washington Post,* that "it made a great deal of difference to Mrs. Sizemore to get rid of that deceit. You know, [the deceit] made her feel very guilty because of what it did to her family."[1]

In retrospect, I see that this standard tactic in the book industry—scheduling all publicity to coincide with book publication so that it serves to sell more books—also functioned as a protective reprieve for my immediate family. After the *Post* stories and my brief appearance on the *Mike Douglas* show, the family tried to make me believe they were taking everything in stride. But I knew differently. Underneath their composure, some were shaken. Don and Taffy—who had painful memories of earlier media reactions to the three Eves' stories in the fifties—were understandably wary. Both highly value privacy, and neither wanted to risk more hurt from the book-in-progress or from media stories that did not use pseudonyms. Only Bobby seemed optimistic. Openly fascinated with the belief that his mother was a new celebrity, he seemed ready for me to take on the world.

My keenest insight into the family's uneasiness came during a filming session by CBS's *60 Minutes* crew in January. During the filming, our neighbors in Fairfax gathered on lawns and sidewalks while the cameramen and technicians worked for three days. Our apartment became a chaotic fishbowl. The crew moved furniture in and out of rooms. The glare of TV lights was distracting. And cameras seemed to probe the innermost thoughts behind our answers to Morley Safer's questions.

But Safer himself could not have been more helpful and sympathetic. The debonair correspondent taught each of us how to sit on our jacket tails in order to keep our collars straight, and he periodically stopped the cameras to coach one of us whose posture had slumped or whose mannerisms had marred a take.

My family rose to the occasion. Everyone readily responded to questions about their lives with an MPD patient. Giving short, truthful answers that worked well for television, they recounted incidents that vividly demonstrated the difficulties I had endured. But I realized that each of them stopped short of revealing what *they* had endured.

Clearly, they needed a reprieve in order to heal from past crises as much as I needed it for follow-up therapy. They had to see more consistency, and some semblance of what they considered as normal from me as a mother and a wife before they could convincingly face the public—if, in fact, they ever chose to do so again.

This was particularly true of Don. Sometime after the CBS filming, he would reveal to friends glimpses of what he had suppressed for decades during my illness.

"I had no problem with the TV people," Don said. "I told them, 'I can see that Chris is well. She's got so much energy now, and things around here finally feel sort of normal.' But I couldn't tell strangers that doctors have promised me so many times before, 'Your wife is cured,' only to find out that no doctor really knew the score."

"Are you saying that you're still afraid I'm not well?" I asked, shocked not only at his candor outside our family but also at the implications of what he was saying.

Don addressed our friends: "It's just hard to forget that, for years, Chris could just change at any minute. Whether doctors said she was cured or not. So being told again that she's well doesn't make my fears go away. Not overnight, anyway. A man remembers, and it was always there with me. Every morning when I left for work, I never knew what I'd find when I got home."

He paused, then added, "And I couldn't tell a soul. Not for twenty-three years. That's what made it so hard. Back in the fifties, people just didn't talk about mental illness, and Thigpen had warned us that we didn't dare. So we were stuck. But even later, when things started loosening up in the sixties, I still couldn't talk. I had shut up for so long that it was just easier to stick to the job. What choice did I have? No man at work had problems like mine. Over lunch or while we were bowling or at union meetings, those guys would talk about their wives running up bills on three or four credit cards. Or kids getting into trouble. But how was I going to slip into talk such as that with a line like, 'Yeah, I know troubles, too. My wife is three people right now'?"

As I listened, I realized that there had been no one for Don. While therapy sessions over the years had enabled me to express feelings and to get hope and encouragement, Don kept everything inside. Like a Humphrey Bogart character, he had endured my illness with a lean determination and a tight lip.

It was equally clear why Don had not gone with me to psychiatrists: He never really trusted them. Yes, he paid for the sessions. And, yes, he listened to instructions that the doctors sent. But Don didn't believe that talking about problems helped solve anything. Actions always spoke louder to him than words. And, until the CBS interviews, he had always acted as though talk outside the family were threatening. His initial comment about the *Post* article had been: "My God, Chris. Once the public gets ahold of a thing like this, there's no end to it."

"So how can you talk about it now?" I asked, and silence encompassed the room. Our friends looked at Don, but he looked at me.

"Because it's not much of a secret anymore," he responded. "And because you finally seem different, Chris. You've started saying that you no longer want to go to doctors. That you don't need them. And that *is* different. You've never said that before. Not since the beginning." Then he added, "And I guess, day by day, it's getting easier for me to rouse up and go to work."

"But are you certain that the healing will last this time?" I asked. "You know that, after going public, there's no place for us to escape another failure."

"Then if we don't make it, girl, we don't make it," Don said. "We'll just have to start over again."

"When the drama and the unusual aspects of MPD are put aside," Richard P. Kluft, M.D., would observe in 1988, "the therapist remains confronted with a suffering human being [who continues] to face problems in living and adjustment." And he notes that, at this stage in an MPD patient's integration, both patient and therapist usually experience a letdown, as if subsequent therapy seems anticlimactic. This is one reason, according to Kluft, that many patients begin struggling with the desire to end the therapy altogether.[2]

But as much as I wanted therapy to end, I wasn't ready. Normalcy in a family's life is not created quickly, and I had no idea how to sustain what ours had achieved in the few hectic months since Andréa had disappeared. In addition, my proneness for dissociation had not vanished along with my alters. In short, I was well and famous but facing everyday problems with few normal experiences on which to base my decisions or behavior. Years later, Dr. Kluft would succinctly describe this by observing that "the cure of multiple personality disorder leaves the patient afflicted with *single personality disorder,* the state in which most patients seek psychotherapy."[3]

And for me, the basic issue had come down to *acceptance.* Erik Erikson describes this type of circumstance in any mental patient's life as the acceptance of one's own life history and the people in it as "something that had to be" and for which there are no substitutes.[4] It's an intriguing concept—particularly when applied to an MPD patient's pursuit of integration. My going public had forced the issue of acceptance. By so doing, I had claimed the uniqueness of my life history. I had claimed all my alters and my family members as persons for whom there are no substitutes. But in the wake of making these claims publicly, I had to act on this self-acceptance. I had to secure my place in the family and, to a larger degree, in society at large. But acting on self-acceptance, I was to discover, is not easy.

In monthly sessions during the spring of 1976, Dr. Tsitos reinforced my struggles by encouraging me to be patient, to live one day at a time and to prepare for whatever future the book might bring. He specifically encouraged me to make our home life comfortable and normal for the family and to discover ways in which I could refine mastery over dissociation. Exploring positive uses of dissociation, he said, could help me achieve greater acceptance of the negative ways in which the disorder had affected our lives.

So I concentrated on my role as a housewife, and Bobby was the first to notice. Periodically, he complimented me on the orderliness and neatness I was maintaining in our apartment. And he loved the evening meals. "All right!" he would say with an enthusiasm about food that only boys seem to muster, "we've got homemade iced tea, homemade rolls, steak, and potatoes. Now this is *no* Swanson Salisbury special!" And Taffy, always making certain to bolster my confidence, regularly offered tips about menus or household management.

But as important as these domestic differences were, I was striving to do more than merely be a good housewife. I was trying to redirect my energies away from what had been a lifetime of *continual expectancy.* For years I had shopped for at least three alters at a time. I had routinely kept on hand their favorite foods and clothes. I had cooked and planned and lived as if, at any moment, the guests in my mind would simply return. And when they had, I had lived and eaten for three. At one point, this even meant experiencing three menstrual cycles each month—a phenomenon that had necessitated the hysterectomy. But in order to ensure normalcy in 1976, it was crucial for me to operate under a new sense of expectancy. I had to manage our household as if, at any moment, *real people,* such as reporters or the family's friends, might drop in. I had to expect the expectable.

Yet mastering dissociation proved more difficult than keeping up with the laundry or making suppers that pleased my family. I could fit household tasks into a schedule. But I could not regiment my unconscious mind so easily. And Dr. Tsitos had cautioned that my mind would continue "to process material" in ways far more subtle than the earlier recalls and abreactions. Integration—I would learn—is a gradual, extended process whose means vary with each MPD patient.

In one sense, everyone functions from the unconscious level. But I harbored suspicions about what my unconscious mind had effected in the past, so it was a struggle to trust my unconscious self again. I had to search for concrete and positive ways in which to regain that trust. Gradually, trust evolved as I pursued creative projects such as writing or painting in a dissociative state—mostly at night—the way I had painted "Blithe Spirit" the previous year. Interestingly enough, a producer for *60 Minutes* had motivated me.

On one of the filming days, the CBS crew moved the organ in our living room, and the producer discovered "Blithe Spirit." I was mortified. But he seemed to love the painting, and despite my protests, he insisted on filming it. I was astonished. How could he like what appeared to be my worst painting when so many others in the collection demonstrated better techniques and more relevance to a report on MPD?

"It's fresh," he said. "This little child in the attic is totally different from the others. Like Grandma Moses's primitives, it may be your uniqueness as a painter."

My uniqueness? The words thrilled me. I had been struggling to paint as competently as my alters had. But I never seemed capable of duplicating their styles and techniques, much less establishing my own as an artist. Yet this producer was saying that I had already done so. Using his words, then, I renamed the painting "The Attic Child," and launched a series of similar paintings.

But I quickly discovered a problem with the *means* by which I had done the first one. As positive as working in a dissociative state had been for producing "The Attic Child," I had little conscious control over when such creative sessions occurred or what I produced. These creative impulses simply arose from my unconscious mind while I was asleep, but the following mornings what I discovered were not paintings but *poetry.*

From February through April, I wrote dozens of poems in my sleep. Or more accurately, I both slept and also worked. Like the classic sleepwalker whose dissociation is far more normal than MPD, I would get up in a dissociative state during the night, pen a poem on a sheet of paper, then return to bed, only to awaken feeling refreshed in the morning from what seemed to have been an exceptionally good night's rest.

And what excited me more than the poems was the fact that no alter had written them. The handwriting was my own, and the writing style remained constant, week after week. Moreover, when I read the handwritten poems and typed them each day, their images and themes were unmistakably my thoughts and concerns. These facts assured me that this dissociation was not another relapse of MPD. It was merely a behavior not unlike sleepwalking, except that this *sleepwalking* was productive, positive, and seemingly purposeful.[5]

For example, one of these poems, "The Black Tambourine," confirmed what Dr. Tsitos had predicted: that my mind was continuing to process material, continuing to reconsider what multiplicity had meant and what normalcy was meaning.

The poem's opening stanza describes a dancer: "She moved in slow form to the sad mourner's beat,/Red velvet fell in soft folds at her feet./ Rivers of sorrow and triumph found their way/Where truth cleansed the mind in the midst of decay."

The next stanza indicates that the woman in red velvet is a figurative image of my unconscious self prior to the unification (and before Andréa de Cosná emerged): "Revealing her pain with a banshee's scream,/ She swayed to the sound of the black tambourine./ She created satellites, repeatedly three,/ But destroyed them all that she might be free./ Her frail body writhed to the wail of her song,/ A murderess she, twenty-one strong."

However, unlike my conscious perspectives before the unification, the last two stanzas indicate that I unconsciously understood how my alters had survived their disappearances, even though I was still clinging at the time to the conscious belief that my alters had "died":

She treasured the dead, as dew on a flower.
Her soul tore her thoughts in this reckoning hour.

Her eyes wide with tears, her moans soon connecting
The past and the present, their heartbreak reflecting.
Her hair swirled around, her feet set a new pace,
She rejected that life, there'd be no other face.
The black tambourine was the Grim Reaper's call,
Now they dance to its rhythm, they dance one and all.

This dance celebration of healing was a strong image for me. During the remainder of that and subsequent years, I would paint scenes of my alters in various rituals, including the lone dancer with the black tambourine as well as trios of ballet dancers, celebrating hand in hand. Unlike "The Attic Child," these dance paintings were done as conscious creativity, but their forms repeatedly drew upon images from the unconscious sleepwriting. My friend Harriet had been right. Nothing takes one outside one's self like painting. And in so doing, my mind was once again learning to heal itself.

During this same period, Don demonstrated more confidence in my wellness. For Easter he bought a gorgeous pot of hyacinths as a surprise gift, and I understood their significance. It had been years since he last brought flowers home for me. It wasn't Don's style to court. But after nearly twenty-three years of marriage, he seemed to be wooing me again. Tentatively, to be sure. But wooing nonetheless. On my forty-ninth birthday, his gift was a pair of earrings, inscribed with the name *Eve*, to match the necklace he had given for Christmas. And this generosity and confidence spilled over. Prior to Bobby's seventeenth birthday, Don gave him a van. Like the ebb and flow of tides, healing was pushing deeper into the tensions in our home. And as my family relaxed more, I began relaxing, too. For the first time in decades, I began sleeping without a night-light.

At a speaking engagement that spring in York, Pennsylvania, my son sat proudly on stage while I addressed high school and adult vocational students from psychology classes. Bobby seemed to listen intently to what I said, and in the question-and-answer session, he responded with ease and spontaneity.

Years later, my son would point to this trip as a milestone. "Going home that night," he recalled, "I had a real sense of confidence about you being able to handle public speaking and appearances. And that's when I decided you were going to make it.

You were self-assured. You had a plan. And you were going to stick to it."

"But was that also when you decided that I was well?" I asked.

"No," Bobby said, "I believed in that before the York trip. I had seen it in your eyes. With the other personalities, there had been a beaming vibrancy in their eyes, a starelike look that I could pick up immediately. But with you, there was a normal, relaxed look in your eyes."

This sense of relaxation came, in part, from a form of self-hypnosis or *autohypnosis* that Dr. Tsitos had taught me before Andréa's emergence. As with other aspects of dissociation in MPD, autohypnosis was a skill I needed to master because I had been its unwitting victim during various stages of the disorder.

However, my therapist was not recommending any of the meditation forms that were popular in the mid-seventies. He was not suggesting that I seek, as with Transcendental Meditation, "to transcend" normal consciousness in order to arrive at a state of "pure awareness." Nor was he suggesting that I repeatedly meditate until I was left "with the awareness of nothing, or pure consciousness," as Claudio Naranjo and Robert Ornstein had proposed.[6] In contrast, Dr. Tsitos's technique simply called for me to relax my head, then my shoulders and arms and hands, all the while imagining the one place in the world where I most wanted to be. As relaxation gradually moved down my body, I would experience a response such as sleep or relief from anxiety and stress.

In a sense, I was simply *willing one thing,* because using my therapist's technique I found myself, with increasing frequency, imagining the same locale: the Strother Place attic. And this singleminded will produced an effect similar to an out-of-body experience, except that I knew I was traveling only in my mind when I revisited that attic from my childhood. These childhood images seemed intensely real and rich in memories. But the effect was momentary. The images would soon fade, and my mind would slip out of the trance. Invariably, however, I would return to consciousness with an image to paint.

And paint I did. Beginning with a few that spring, these images have enabled me over the years to produce scores of install-ments in "The Attic Child" series. And after the first months, autohypnosis became less important, then unnecessary al-together. But those initial, deliberate searches of my unconscious mind also accomplished another step in the healing process as they resulted in a shuttle of unconscious images onto painted canvases. I found new delight in my unconscious mind. I re-gained an intimacy with the early years of my childhood. And unwittingly, I prepared myself for a stage of MPD integration that is beyond the clinician's reach.

This final stage of MPD integration was related to a series of recurrent dreams. Both Don and my cousin Elen observed me during the early weeks of this phase, and she has written elo-quently in *I'm Eve* about their memories. But none of us fully understood at the time the healing implications of these dreams—some of which focused on my memories before the age of two.[7]

Many MPD authorities still question such phenomena. But Dr. Kluft confirms that "dreams often monitor integration," and he suggests that such dreams by MPD patients appear to be "some sort of healing process in which the mind may or may not be assuming a new configuration." Yet he cautions that published research about such healing dreams has been minimal through 1988 and that, consequently, few professional explanations are available.[8]

I have no explanations, either. I only know what I experi-enced. The recurring dreams began intensely in May 1976. At first I experienced them several times each night while I slept and sometimes while napping during the day. Often, my physical reactions to these dreams were so violent at night that I would awaken Don. During waking hours, I also experienced regres-sions into childlike states. And these dream experiences persisted for nearly ten months, with the dream patterns remaining the same during the first few months, except that the frequency of the dreaming gradually decreased.

In each sequence, I saw all of my former alters, ranging in ages from a toddler to Andréa, my last adult alter. And they were always in a templelike structure made of marble and tall columns.

Dr. Thigpen, Dr. Tsitos, and I were also in these early dreams. And each sequence always began with my alters appearing ominously, one by one in the order in which they had existed, only to turn on me and attack as a group. Dr. Thigpen, laughing at me, encouraged the alters. But before they could do harm, Dr. Tsitos would intervene and stop the attacks by calling me into another templelike room.

There was never a view outside that first room. But the second room always had a view of lush trees and flowers and a green lawn juxtaposed against the somberness of a child-size white casket displayed on a dais in the center of the room. Each time, while Dr. Tsitos was encouraging me to give up my vigil beside the casket, to leave the second room and to enter the beauty outside, my alters would enter. But their second procession would always be calm, orderly, and in a straight line, and one of them would always remove the casket from the dais. Then they would follow the casket-bearer down a stairway that led from the room, and they would disappear.

This moment in the dreams invariably made me weep, disavow any responsibility for the death of whoever was in the casket, and chase after my alters. But on reaching their point of exit from the room, I would always be shocked to find only a long drop at the end, no stairs, no way to proceed.

However, Dr. Tsitos would comfort me each time by saying, "Don't be concerned. Just enjoy the scenery. The steps will grow." When I would look outside once again, steps would rise from the ground and extend to the room's floor. "It's all right. Go ahead," he would say, and I would start down the steps, descending three at a time. But at this point in each sequence, I would always stop, look back at Dr. Tsitos, then awaken. For some reason, I could never reach the ground. . . .

As the frequency of these dreams decreased, my confidence increased. Despite the lack of resolution in these dreams, other aspects of my life were clearly reaching culmination. In June, Elen and I finished the manuscript and hand-delivered it to Doubleday's Manhattan office. A month later, the publisher accepted the work and predicted that it would be a very successful book.[9] Claiming my own history had not brought rejection. I was stunned and elated.

Two months later, the same thing happened. In the mid-seventies, most Americans viewed *60 Minutes* as unimpeachable. It was consistently one of the highest-rated shows on television. So when the televised news magazine aired our family's interview on their first show of the fall season, it placed a solid stamp of approval on my life and family and work as a painter. For days friends and family and even strangers telephoned to congratulate us. There were no rejections. Only acceptance. Overwhelming acceptance. It all seemed so wondrous I could hardly believe that good things were finally happening.

A month later, I was sitting in the green room of the *Mike Douglas* show talking to Andy Griffith. Here we were, Eve and the sheriff of Mayberry, chatting as if we had known one another for years. And this camaraderie did not stop once the show began. When we were seated together onstage, Mike Douglas could barely get a word in. Andy Griffith seemed more interested in my story than in his own reason for being on the show.

But then the actor shocked me.

In the midst of my answering questions about dissociation, Andy Griffith interrupted. "I've never admitted this publicly," he said, looking straight into the camera, "but if this southern lady can admit *her* dissociation, I can certainly talk about mine. I'm a sleepwalker, too."

It was another healing moment for me. And a remarkable one. I don't know why this legendary television star demonstrated such compassion and empathy, but I remain in his debt. His public confession made mine easier, and that was exactly the boost I needed. I had been scheduled for a lecture tour of South Carolina, and until this encouragement, I had toyed with the idea of canceling. Instead, I departed with renewed hope and confidence, and what I discovered in my native state during the subsequent week-long tour was the public's fascination with my story. And their *need* for a mental patient to speak out.

During stops in Anderson, Greenwood, Greenville, Conway, and Spartanburg, audience attendance was between five hundred and a thousand persons per lecture. But neither my sponsor, the Mental Health Association of South Carolina, nor I had anticipated such crowds. I was being paid twenty-five dollars per lecture, plus expenses, and a few communities had declined to participate because they feared that ticket sales would not cover the costs. I had prepared no more than a five-minute speech, expecting a question-and-answer session to fill out the hour at each appearance.

The audiences' questions proved more than sufficient, with some sessions running overtime. And it was from one of these audience responses that I finally gained the sense of security to make a commitment: *I could do this as a career because the public welcomed it, and some received hope from it.*

As Andy Griffith had done earlier, one man made the difference at my last lecture. He was tall and well-dressed. He introduced himself to me and the audience as an attorney. And he looked very distinguished, as if his were a responsible position in that beach community. But when the man spoke, his voice was humble.

"For twelve years now I have not gotten therapy because I was afraid of the stigma," he said. "I have tried to work my own problems out. My wife and I have done so in secret. We were scared to do otherwise." Then he looked directly at me. "But because you're here tonight, ma'am, I can admit to myself that I am mentally ill. And because of your courage, I can now say, 'I will get help.' We can't do it alone anymore."[10]

When he finished, the whole audience seemed to be crying. I was weeping, too. Not only because of what he had said, but also because of what his words meant to me. This lawyer's public admission was sufficient proof that telling my story publicly *could* make a difference.

In addition, the entire MHA tour convinced me that I was finally learning how to use the dominant qualities of my former alters. The *Eve White*, or mother-image, types could never have spoken before such enormous audiences. But the *Eve Black*, or party-girl, types, would have loved it. Unfortunately, those party girls could not have coped with the intellectual rigors of such public scrutiny. Only the *Jane*, or intellectual, types among my alters could have done that. However, like the mother-image types, my intellectual alters would not have had the courage to do so. But unlike either the *Eve Black* or the *Jane* types, only my *Eve White*–type alters could have felt and expressed compassion in public. . . .

*   *   *

My mind's stage was set, therefore, for the night I said good-bye to all my former alters. It was early in 1977 and two-thirty in the morning when I awakened, knowing that I had just had the most important dream of my life.

At first I thought it was another of the dream sequences. But I quickly realized that this one was different. Dr. Thigpen and Dr. Tsitos were not in it, and more peculiarly, neither was I. The only people in this dream were my alters. And the templelike room that they entered was more beautiful than in the earlier dreams. This time it was in perfect balance. Its walls and the positioning of its columns and the angling of its steps leading down from the columns all formed concentric, semicircular lines. Like computer-generated graphics, which would become popular in the eighties, the symmetry of this room was so flawless that every line and shape seemed alive. In motion, yet motionless.

And these sisters of my mind were beautiful, too. Each entered from the same door and proceeded in a curving line down a few steps to the center of the room. When they stopped, the line they formed was also concentric to the walls and columns and steps, and my alters were in the exact order in which they had lived. Each wore a long white Grecian gown with an empress-style waist from which white satin ribbons flowed, and each had her hair done up on top. Even the children.

Then they turned, joined hands, and smiled serenely, as if all were aware that I was watching. But no one spoke. Their communication seemed spiritual. In a moment, Eve Black moved. She had been in line between the children and adults, but she left the line and went into a small niche amid the columns behind them. When she returned, she was bearing a small white casket. It was tiny, the size of a matchbox, and it fit easily in her cupped hands.

But Eve Black did not return to her place in line. Instead, still carefully bearing the tiny casket, she stopped in front of the youngest alter. They all joined hands once again, and Eve Black led them out through the exit. Their disappearance was orderly, rituallike, and final. The beautiful circular room fell silent, and my vision of it clouded, as if a veil had fallen between the dream and me, the dreamer. That's when I awakened.

After that night, I have never felt or seen my alters again. Not consciously, or in any knowable unconscious manner. That dream was MPD's last drama in my life. Indeed, since that experience I simply remember them. When I close my eyes and think back, I can only see them or remember their actions or words the same way I recall Don's or Taffy's or Bobby's from years gone by.

Ironically, however, by experiencing—and believing in—my alters' disappearance on this unconscious level, I was finally able to accept that they and I are one. Not fully understand it, mind you, but accept it, because this dream was as tangible as the concentric shapes in its beautiful room. My mind could *hold* to it. And I could trust that our existences now formed a balance that made their stories my life.

That spring I slept with ease. When problems arose, perspective came more readily. Family tensions resolved more naturally. And lines smoothed in my face until I appeared years younger than my fiftieth birthday in April would have warranted. It was as if inner peace were working its way outward in my life and affecting everyone around me.

Levity began to characterize my conversations with Don. We laughed more. For the first time in our marriage, he would call from work. Just to chat. Or we occasionally went out to eat. Just the two of us. Then, encouraged by this easy talk and the diminishing tensions in our lives, we began making plans. He agreed that our friend Mickey Stewart, a northern Virginia realtor, should find a house for us. And Don asked if he could use his vacation to accompany me on Doubleday's author tour for the book. I realized that this string of national appearances would be our first trip alone as a couple since our honeymoon, twenty-four years earlier. So I agreed, secretly hoping that maybe the tour could be like a second honeymoon.

It was all so simple and cautious and gentle, this furtive courting that my husband was doing. In the way that some fortunate middle-aged couples discover, my husband was reaching out to me. And my heart was responding. No, none of this was miraculously erasing hurts from the past for either of us. But it *was* rekindling some of what we had lost.

One night I remembered the last time Don had been like this.

And just remembering comforted me, because these had once been Jane's memories, but now I honestly felt as though they were mine.

It was the summer of 1953, and we were dating in Augusta, Georgia. The city's lawns and trees and flowers were lush and beautiful that year, and our favorite times were Saturday nights at the municipal auditorium. We attended concerts by Fred Waring's Pennsylvanians and Les Brown's Band of Renown. But our most memorable moment also occurred there, while attending the Horace Heidt Talent Contest. The young singer who won that contest went on to become the popular recording artist Brenda Lee.

During the event, Don and I had been holding hands and not saying much. But at intermission, he held up my left hand and whispered nonchalantly, "Those sure are pretty, nice-looking hands, Chris. What size ring do you wear?"

I didn't think it sounded like the opening line for a proposal. After all, we were seated in an audience of several hundred people. So I played along. "Six," I said. "Is this for a friendship ring?"

"That's not what I had in mind."

When I looked at him, his expression was cautious and gentle. "Then just exactly what do you have in mind?" I asked.

"We could start with a diamond," he said, then looked at me with such anticipation in his eyes that I knew: no kneeling, no promises of love, no words about dreams for the future. No, Don Sizemore had said all he was going to. "We could start with a diamond" was his solid proposal of marriage. I would get no other.

Casual but unalterable, then, was how our life together had begun. And that was where we were returning. Don had loved me in sickness. And though I had changed so many times since, he was again offering the same. In health, just as he had in sickness.

By July 15, 1977, we needed this confidence in one another. It was the publication date for *I'm Eve*, and we were standing in the green room of the *Phil Donahue* show. In fifteen minutes, Don and I would be Donahue's only guests for an hour of "live" television.

Trying to ease our nervousness, Don whispered, "I'd rather be squirrel hunting."

"Well, you're not," I whispered back. "This time you're on the other end of the gun." Though I was joking, I did have a bad feeling about the circumstances. Dr. Tsitos, who was scheduled to appear with me on the show, had telephoned from Virginia. He was ill. So the staff insisted that Don take my therapist's place. He agreed, but I could see that the prospect did not please him.

Then, minutes before airtime, Phil Donahue entered and greeted us. After some affable exchanges, however, the host looked coolly into my eyes and said, "Suppose I say to you, 'I don't believe this.' What will you do to prove it on the air?"

It was baptism by fire. His words momentarily banished the thrill of Don and me traveling together around the nation to tell our story. This would be no second honeymoon. *This* was reality.

"I won't do anything," I responded, not knowing what my resistance would provoke. "I didn't come here to prove anything."

The host nodded, reached for his note cards, and pointed us toward the studio. But he never did pose that question before the audience or on-camera. Instead, Donahue conducted an aggressive and insightful interview. I was just beginning to relax when he began asking Don about our sex life during my years of multiplicity.

"Suppose you were in the mood for making love, Don, but she wasn't," Donahue said. "Or she wasn't a personality who considered herself your wife. Then what did you do? Just let it all hang out?"

I choked. Neither Donahue nor the millions of Americans watching could know how Don and I had struggled simply to reach the fragile bond we were finally sharing. What, I wondered, would this do to us?

But my husband responded very quietly, and with dignity: "Whichever one was 'out' was my wife." His expression and tone of voice were the same as when he had said, years before, "We could start with a diamond." And just as final. His response seemed to have a tremendous effect on both Donahue and the audience. Thereafter, the interview became more relaxed. Donahue shifted his approach and asked Don which alter my husband had liked the best.

"I fell in love with, and I married, Jane," Don said, "so I guess I liked her the best." However, he looked across the table and shot a capricious glance in my direction, then added, "But I'm getting used to *that* one now." The audience laughed, and their questions flowed steadily until the show went off the air.

Three days later, Don and I were in Manhattan for the *Today* show. It was one of Jane Pauley's first appearances as the show's cohost. She impressed me. Here was a bright and attractive and very composed woman working shoulder to shoulder with men. Why had I not understood this before? After the show, as Don and I toured Doubleday's Park Avenue offices, I saw the same thing. Scores of fashionable, intelligent, and successful women were holding responsible leadership positions in what was then the nation's largest trade publishing house. Again I was impressed, but also perplexed. While I had spent decades as a housewife or an underpaid manager of dress shops, other women had solidly launched themselves into the world. Now, they were making a difference. But why had it taken me more than half my life to realize that, just maybe, I could do the same?

Later that afternoon, I told yet another seemingly successful woman, who wrote for the New York *Daily News,* "I don't think I feel special." My mind was still pondering how I compared to these successful women. But I caught myself. The spotlight was, after all, on me. I had a job to do. So I added, "I feel average, though. And that's a very good feeling."[11]

By the time Don and I returned to Fairfax that weekend before having to resume the tour the following week, a myriad of thoughts preoccupied me. Limousine rides and box seats to see Yul Brynner in *The King and I* on Broadway, champagne and fresh flowers in our hotel suites at both the Whitehall in Chicago and the Barclay in New York—these were the touches of success that I had never dared to dream about. Yet they had been ours all week. And more was to come. *Ladies' Home Journal* was running excerpts from the book, the Associated Press was releasing a feature interview of me, and *Kirkus Reviews* had described *I'm Eve* favorably, noting that "without the neat puzzle-solving or slick suspense of *Sybil,* this remains a compelling, unsettling document that tempers the forty years of nightmare with common sense and dignity."[12]

Despite all this excitement, however, my self-image seemed

terribly low as I curled in our bed and tried to nap on Saturday. Of course, I had loved the attentions from reporters and photographers and television cameras during the tour's first week. And being interviewed by the best had gone smoother than I expected. But then, I had plenty of experience. I had been answering tough questions in psychotherapy for over twenty years, and few reporters could match an analyst's probing.

Why, then, did I not feel fulfilled?

One of the reasons became apparent the following week. At the Brown Palace Hotel in Denver, the manager asked me to sign their register of famous guests. So alongside the signatures of Calamity Jane, Theodore Roosevelt, and "Wild Bill" Hickok, I entered mine. Later that week, Don and I had lunch in Beverly Hills with *Los Angeles Times* columnist Dave Smith at the Brown Derby. As we all sat in a booth underneath photos of Judy Garland and Mickey Rooney, the writer interviewed us. But the piece that he subsequently published began:

> One expects her to look different. No, not like Joanne Woodward, not exactly . . .
>
> Then how? Somehow sort of fevered and electric, poised for flight or attack, or maybe a bit muffled and distant as if monitoring the conversation with one ear, the other listening covertly to the eerie, mad music of a Theremin that plays continually, sinuously from a strange landscape inside her mind.
>
> It is impossible to meet this woman as if she were just anybody's Cousin Alice. She is quite literally a legend, for good or ill, assured of a place alongside Lilith, Medea, Juana la Loca, Lady Macbeth and Lucia di Lammermoor.
>
> She's Eve. . . .[13]

What could I say? I admired Dave Smith's imagination and his skill as a wordsmith. And I understood that his intentions were good. It had been obvious during the interview that he had read *I'm Eve* and seemed to have tracked my story well. In fact, the rest of his article proved to be one of the best ever published about my life. In particular, I appreciated the way he described my husband: "It doesn't take long before one is regarding [Don]

Sizemore, just as much as his celebrated wife, as some kind of walking miracle—of survival, devotion, commitment."[14]

Like much of the tour, however, Smith's introduction made it clear that the media's fascination with my former mental *illness* could impede my speaking to the public about mental *health.* And if I couldn't speak about a mental patient getting well, how was I ever going to turn this living legend of mine into a real life? In contrast, my earlier lectures had demonstrated that, apart from the media, the public was keenly interested in hearing about mental health.

Years later, Rosalynn Carter would express similar concerns about this era. When President Jimmy Carter had begun his administration in January, one of his earliest efforts toward social reform was the creation of the President's Commission on Mental Health. He named the First Lady as its honorary chairman, and during the remainder of 1977 she tirelessly conducted hearings on the needs of the mentally ill. But after the first few public events, media attention waned.

"And when I asked a member of the White House press corps about it," the First Lady recalls, "he said, 'Well, Mrs. Carter, mental health is not a *sexy* issue.'"[15] And essentially, my book tour confirmed the correspondent's opinion. The media was attracted to my former illness, but not to mental wellness.

During subsequent days on the West Coast, therefore, Don and I took some breaks from interviews and appearances. Even though we spent the rest of our time being treated like celebrities, we gradually felt more comfortable during the private moments of anonymity.

After one particularly strenuous day of interviews, Don and I decided to go to Disneyland. And en route to the park, we passed the studios of Twentieth Century-Fox, where portions of *The Three Faces of Eve* had been filmed. Twenty years earlier, Jane had longed to be here, but Dr. Thigpen would not allow it. However, now that Don and I were here, somehow this glamorous Hollywood spot had lost its allure. We didn't even stop.

At Disneyland we walked hand in hand for hours and enjoyed feeling like strangers to this paradise. As afternoon became evening, I begged Don to stay for the Parade of Lights. He consented, but I could see that he was tiring. Still, we kept walking and holding hands. Disneyland's marvels seem endless, and this fantasy world about us somehow felt more real than the new luxury in which we were temporarily living. Suddenly, I felt Don's weight bearing down on me. When I looked up, his eyes were closed. He was walking but was fast sleep.

As I guided him to a bench, I had to laugh. One of the reasons he had accompanied me on the book tour was his fear that something might happen to me under all the stress. Yet he turned out to be the only one of us who dissociated.

After more interviews and shows in San Francisco, we went home to Fairfax once again. Don's vacation was over, and I was not scheduled to resume the book tour until later in August. But we realized that a decision had to be made. The book was succeeding. The Literary Guild had announced it as a featured alternate selection for August. By mid-month, my photo and the book's review were given cover-page treatment in the *Los Angeles Times Book Review* and *The Atlanta Journal and Constitution Magazine*. The following day, the *San Francisco Examiner* began running a seven-part series of excerpts from the book. And by August 19, *I'm Eve* had hit the B. Dalton bestseller list.

Clearly, I would have to continue promoting the book, but just as clearly, Don would not want me to travel alone. Since MPD first resurfaced in my life shortly after our marriage in 1953, he had not allowed me to go anywhere without some friend or member of my family at my side. But after having seen so many professional women standing alone in the business world, my perspective had changed. The question was: Had Don's?

In addition, the first reviews of *I'm Eve* started arriving, and they demonstrated an ambivalent view of the book. *The New York Times* categorized all the books and magazine articles about my life as "one of the longest-running public neuroses of our time," but concluded that *I'm Eve* presented "a valuable mine of material on the genesis of mental illness and the mystery of personality, of the enemies we have within who sometimes seize control of our behavior." The *Pittsburgh Press* was more succinct: "This is a gripping factual story, surely stranger than fiction."[16]

From the West Coast, reviews were also mixed. "By the end

of the book, we have learned more than we ever wanted to about Eve," determined the *Los Angeles Times,* "but her story is a revealing reminder of the often alarming powers of the mind." The *Seattle Times* was a bit more empathetic: "Her abnormality is not freakish but human. Her problems are not fantastic but unusual. . . ."[17]

Even though Dr. Tsitos had prepared me for harsher criticism, it was difficult not to take these standard reviewers' barbs personally. After all, the book had been written as part of my therapy. So I had a great deal to discuss during our next session. We first talked about the book itself, since he had just finished reading it. Then we covered the initial reviews and some incidents from the tour's first two weeks.

Finally, he reminded me that *I'm Eve* was not my life. It was merely my life's story. And he suggested that, even though writing it with my cousin had been solid therapy for me, reading it might not always be a therapeutic experience for its readers or reviewers.

"In a sense, once a book is published," he added, "it has its own life. Its venturing into the world means that the book has ceased to be *your* therapy. Instead, it has become merely a product for others to accept or reject. And since you're not a publisher or editor or bookseller or reviewer, isn't all of that really separate from you?"

I agreed but described how low my self-image had fallen after the first week of interviews and appearances. He responded by asking how the tour made me feel. He sought out specifics about what I found to be depressing. Or what made me fearful. And I answered these questions in detail. Then he asked what I had enjoyed.

My response was immediate. "Strangely enough, I feel most comfortable on 'live' television shows with studio audiences, or when I'm fielding questions after a lecture." Then I added, whimsically, "You know, I lived a long time with many *eyes* constantly watching me. So an audience is second nature. Like old times."

"But could playing to an audience cause you to dissociate under stress?"

"I don't think so," I responded. "Talking to real people is all I've ever wanted to do."

"Where does the tour take you next?" he asked in a confident tone.

"I can't tell you," I said, pausing. "It's a secret this time, Doctor, because I need to go alone. Do you think I can?"

"If you're not ready, it's time we found out," he said, and smiled.

"But it's more than that," I said. "I've lived half a century, and I still don't know if I can look after myself."

"I see. Then is this something you may want to discuss with the family?"

"Probably."

"And what if they say no?"

"Then I'll just have to convince them," I said. "I *have* to do this."

"Because you think that traveling alone will help change your self-image?"

"If you had *never* been alone, Doctor, then suddenly you saw a chance to be on your own, wouldn't you try it?"

"Fair enough," he said, and encouraged me as I left to face my family. When I reached the office door, he added: "Have a great time. And send me newspaper clippings."

My family gave their blessings, even though I didn't tell them where Doubleday was sending me. In some ways, it was their most courageous moment on my behalf. They let me be myself.

And I can't describe the preciousness of that trip. Carrying my airline tickets and my luggage. Choosing hotels and restaurants, and paying the tabs. Dealing competently with strangers, and feeling good about being anonymous. Finding my way around Toronto. Sightseeing. Meeting appointments and coping alone with the stress of a television interview. Then catching a flight to New York City. Hailing a cab. Checking into a hotel. Being recognized. And the next morning, trying to fool the panel on *To Tell the Truth*. Or later, selecting when I would fly back to Washington.

All of these were experiences as new to me as life itself had been just three years earlier. And for the first time, saying "I'm Chris Costner Sizemore" finally meant something. Just to me.

*   *   *

When I returned home, reviews from southern newspapers began arriving in the mail, and they portrayed a strikingly different perspective of *I'm Eve.* "There is a surprise by-product in the story," noted the *Chattanooga Times.* "In tracing Chris's early history as a child, the two authors—double first cousins—developed a cultural 'roots' for those of us born in the southeastern coastal states. The sense of family, their beliefs and customs all shine forth. One only needs to change the names." And a Memphis writer affirmed that, "in the vein of *Sybil* and *The Bell Jar, I'm Eve* treats mental illness openly and unashamedly. . . ."[18] These blurbs hung in my mind for weeks. They gave me encouragement that, at least to some, my message had gotten through.

Late that September, Don and I bought a house in Herndon, Virginia. And Bobby, who had graduated from Fairfax High School in June, entered as a freshman at George Mason University. Nearby, in Fredericksburg, Virginia, Taffy and Tommy had also purchased a home. Our family was putting down roots. After decades of chaos, we were securely establishing our lives.

It meant a great deal to me that money from *I'm Eve* had helped us to lead normal lives again. In a sense, I was paying the first installments on debts to those who had sacrificed so much for me. And the benefits were immediate. I felt intensely proud to find Don relaxing in the den or building a fire in the hearth or working productively on the lawn. He had lost these pleasures when my doctor bills had forced us to sell our last house and reside thereafter in apartments.

But I was also doing something crucial for myself. I was ensuring my independence and my haven. For the first time in our married life, I could feel good about telling our neighbors who I was. Don and I were free to attend neighborhood parties or backyard barbecues. And I could walk across the lawn in the mornings, greet the woman next door, and, if she asked, feel free to join her for coffee and chats about happenings in our family's life. This home in Herndon was our first to have no secrets locked in its closets.

On the contrary, I could display the secrets. The house was

large enough that I could hang all the important paintings my alters had done, plus new ones as I finished them. And there were plenty of nooks and shelves in which to arrange all my alters' collections of bells and cards and turtles and such. All of me had a place in Herndon.

Once we settled in, I resumed my work. In October I received a copy of *Viva,* an international magazine whose November and December issues were running more excerpts from *I'm Eve.* At the time, its English edition was distributed abroad to nearly a dozen nations.[19] A few days later, I was seated beside Ben Bradlee, the widely respected editor of the *Washington Post,* at the National Press Club's annual book fair. We were autographing our respective books and casually chatting. I commented that, as different as my life certainly had been from his, we shared at least one rare experience in common. Each of us had been portrayed in popular and Oscar-winning motion pictures—his being *All the President's Men,* which was a box-office hit that same year.

"But you forget that we shared something else," Bradlee said. "I did you a good turn by placing your story on the *Post*'s front page in 1975."

"And why did you?" I asked, not fully realizing until then that any *one* person made such decisions at a major newspaper.

"Because you were courageous, and that deserved recognition and good placement," he said. "Now, you do me one."

"Sure."

He pointed to his stack of books, which had not sold as quickly as mine, and said, "Help me sell my books."

I did. But I also came away from that event with an important insight. Behind even the toughest, most sophisticated, and most seasoned journalists like Ben Bradlee, there is another self. A human one. And despite some of the difficulties I had encountered with the media, I was determined to overcome such stumbling blocks in the future.

I had a message. These people were bearers of messages to the public, but news was their turf. If I was to communicate beyond reporters and reach the public, I first had to communicate with, and relate to, the journalists themselves. Person to person. But how?

*   *   *

Not knowing exactly, I retreated. But just once. I was too uncertain about how long-lived my career as either a writer or a lecturer might be, so I responded to a newspaper ad for the position of dress specialty-shop manager. And when I arrived at the store, I was delighted to find that the interviewer had been my supervisor some years before. He knew I was a good manager, so I expected little trouble in securing the job.

"But, Mrs. Sizemore, you're a famous person now," he said. "You don't really want to do this kind of work."

"Oh, but I do," I responded, stunned at his reaction.

"Then we'll call you," he said, and excused himself, saying that he had to finish monthly reports.

Back on the parking lot as I slid into my car, I noticed that he did not take the HELP WANTED sign from the window. And in subsequent weeks, he did not call. Neither did a number of other employers from whom I sought a job. It quickly became clear that as normal as my life had become, some basics had unalterably changed. Some people, no matter how much I succeeded, would still view me only as a former mental patient.

PART II

Can a Former Mental Patient Live a "Normal" Life?

$$6$$

I was not idle long. Early in 1978, new opportunities for *I'm Eve* surfaced not only in America but also in Europe, Asia, and the United Kingdom. Spurred in part by the *Viva* excerpts, Norwegian, Swedish, and Japanese publishers bought rights to the book. And Jove, a Manhattan paperback publisher, planned to release its mass-market edition in America during the summer.

But one of these publishers wanted me as well as my book. In late January, I received confirmation from Victor Gollancz Ltd. that the venerable London firm would be publishing their edition in April, under the simple title of *Eve.* And they asked if Don and I would come that spring to promote the book in England and Scotland. I was ecstatic. My Great-grandmother McClure had emigrated from Scotland to North Carolina, so it felt like agreeing to a homecoming when I wrote that Don and I would gladly make the trip.[1]

Our correspondence must have passed in the crossing, because two subsequent letters from London contained extraordinary news. The first indicated keen interest from BBC television in interviewing me, and the second confirmed that the National Film Theatre would be showing *The Three Faces of Eve* as a special event during its spring season in London. But to my surprise, this division of the British Film institute was also inviting me to address them.[2]

It was an overwhelming prospect that my life story and book

would finally be linked with Twentieth Century-Fox's movie. And in such a glamorous way. As if there were real justice in both art and life. Provided one waited twenty-one years . . .

Even though the success of *I'm Eve* promised a financial security that our family had never known, it was also becoming clear that success does not fill spiritual needs. And I had felt a spiritual vacuum expanding within me that winter.

I began searching my soul. My parents had been Methodists, and our son, Bobby, and I had become active members of the Herndon United Methodist Church, though Don and I had not been regularly involved with any church in years. And my personal views about religion were complicated because my alters had belonged to various denominations: Episcopal, Holiness, Christian Science, etc. At best, then, my soul had a tolerant bent, but with no particular confidence in any doctrine. I only knew that I believed in God and that I owed my wellness to God's mysterious workings in my life. But neither health nor faith had answered my basic question: *Why me?* Why had I been the victim of a rare disorder and decades of suffering?

Without answers or any real commitment to a particular dogma, I remained open to new sources of insight. One came in February from David W. Stevens, an astrological counselor in Ohio. He completed a chart based on my exact date and time of birth, then he responded to the question of *Why me?* by indicating, "The difficulties you have experienced in the past, Chris, are responsible for the greater awareness you now possess and enjoy." He also cited a Christian assurance for the astrological finding in my chart that suffering had not been punishment. To my surprise, I took comfort in what I read in that Scripture:

> As [Jesus] went along, he saw a man who had been blind from birth. His disciples asked him, "Rabbi, who sinned, this man or his parents, for him to have been born blind?"
> "Neither he nor his parents sinned," Jesus answered, "he was born blind so that the work of God might be displayed in him."[3]

But was it possible that I been mentally ill so that, ultimately, God might be displayed in me? It didn't seem plausible. And yet something about me continued to have an effect on people. Thousands of letters continued to arrive each month. Some via Doubleday. Others sent by magazines and newspapers that had published interviews with me. But even more letters came through mental-health associations where I had visited, and virtually all made some comment about how my story had given them hope. More specifically, when individuals came up to me after a lecture, an unusual number touched me and often said, nervously, "I just wanted to see if you were *real.*"

It was an unsettling irony. While I seemed to be giving hope to others, I lacked the essentials of spiritual strength in my own life. I was well, succeeding, and basically at peace in my mind. Yet I was far from feeling peaceful in my soul.

On March 3, Dr. Tsitos and I talked casually for a while. I was making my monthly visit, just as I had been doing since June 4, 1973.[4] Finally, I said what I had postponed admitting until the last moment: "I don't feel like I need to come back anymore, Doctor Tsitos."

"You haven't *needed* to come for quite a while," he said, and smiled.

Feeling a sense of relief, I joked, "Then why have I been paying you all this money? For nothing?"

At that, we both laughed. It was a celebration for wellness. Then he added in a serious tone, "I just didn't want you to feel as though I were rejecting you. *You* had to make the decision to end therapy. I couldn't. You harbored too many negative feelings about the way, years ago, that Doctor Thigpen ended your therapy."

As usual, Dr. Tsitos was correct. I needed confirmation that it was all right for me to end the therapy. On my own terms. It had taken me twenty-one years to find in him a therapist who could help me get well. And during the next five years, his psychotherapy had enabled me to probe my mind and find its problems. Then it had allowed my mind to heal itself within the reassurance of his reasonable advice and counseling. But any therapy should end when the sessions no longer provide what the patient needs, and psychotherapy could not probe my soul. That search is a solo flight. And such spiritual searchings might take as long as psychotherapy had in order for me to find inner peace. But approaching my fifty-first birthday, I had to start this journey.

Dr. Tsitos agreed to consider our professional relationship as open-ended—meaning that, should I have psychological problems in the future, we could resume the therapy sessions immediately. Otherwise, he said I seemed solidly capable of handling everything on my own.

And there was a great deal to handle. Shortly, Don and I were scheduled to fly to London. Correspondence was piling up, and my lecture schedule had become unusually demanding.[5] Then, two weeks before I was to address the National Film Theatre following their showing of *The Three Faces of Eve,* Doubleday told me that Twentieth Century-Fox had purchased a six-month option for the motion picture/television rights to *I'm Eve.* I was elated. The option meant new hope that film audiences might someday be able to view my *complete* life story; not just the illness, but the wellness, too.

This option also made me believe that my legal concerns had finally come to an end. Why else would Twentieth Century-Fox secure an option in a story that—according to the documents that Dr. Thigpen had held over me all these years—my alters had already sold to them "forever." My assumption was that the option meant the studio executives were finally acknowledging the fact that I had not been legally competent to sign such a sweeping waiver of rights in 1956 and were recognizing my rightful claim.[7] Whatever the studio's motives, I believed in March 1978 that the legal questions had been resolved, and I was delighted.

My family also shared in this enthusiasm. In particular, I had never seen our children and grandchildren as excited as during those final weeks of preparation before Don and I departed for England. My ending therapy. The possibility of a new movie. A profile of me running in the March issue of *The Saturday Evening Post.* And a glamorous trip abroad. It was as though I had been transformed in my family's eyes. No longer was I simply a mother who *used to surprise them* with my unusual sickness. Instead, I had become a woman who now surprised them with accomplishments beyond any of our imaginations.

* * *

British nationalism was still in peak form when we arrived in London late that April, one year after Queen Elizabeth II's Silver Jubilee celebration. The manager of Durrant's Hotel, for example, was very courteous when he escorted Don and me to our room; but the dapper Briton made a point of reminding me, "Our hotel, madam, is *older* than your country."

The next day, I went across George Street from Durrant's to the Wallace Collection. It boasted a distinguished array of fine art and, during the month, was featuring an exhibit of four of the *Eve* paintings: Retrace Lady's "Journey into Darkness" and "The Garden of Eve," Card Girl's "The Human Candle," and Bell Lady's "Splitting." This was the first time my alters' work had been viewed outside the United States.

While I stood there alone, quietly relishing the experience, two Englishmen entered the sedate gallery and stopped to one side of the four paintings. The businessmen, apparently using their lunch hour for a stroll through the display, were unaware of who I was.

The taller gentleman seemed puzzled by "The Human Candle," its bold colors portraying a human figure covered from head to toe in melting wax. "Some chap has a bloody problem," he quipped, and without another comment, the pair strolled into the other exhibit areas. *If he only knew,* I thought.

During these first four days in London, I would experience no chaotic, American-style news conferences. On the contrary, Gollancz had arranged for four or five orderly, polite interviews each day. These included appearances on several popular BBC radio shows, plus in-depth interviews with major newspapers such as the *Daily Mail* and *The Times,* as well as with *Psychology Today.* All of it seemed as civilized as croquet, which impressed me.

And then there was BBC television, where I would discover that British broadcasting maintains almost courtly traditions. On Friday, the *host* of *Nationwide* met Don and me at the entrance to TV Centre and escorted us inside. Similarly, everyone we met at the government-sponsored studios was cordial, warm, and personable. In fact, the atmosphere seemed more like a genteel cocktail party than what I had previously known as television production. To the British, it seems, TV information need not be a bitter pill to swallow, since the shows where I appeared were not "talk shows" but news programs.

However, journalism in England is not without its rough edges, as two tabloid newspaper headlines demonstrated. One banner head stated, ADAM COMES TO ENGLAND AND BRINGS EVE, which displeased Don the moment he saw it on a newsstand. And another was offensive to me because of its insensitive allusion to the mastectomy that former president Gerald Ford's wife had suffered and had spoken about openly in the United States as a means of dispelling the stigma associated with that procedure. However, the British headline and its subhead printed in large bold type were AMERICA'S FIRST LADY OF SUFFERING COMES TO ENGLAND: CHRIS SIZEMORE WINS OVER BETTY FORD.

Maybe some British journalists were flippant about suffering because, in fact, citizens of the Isles have survived a variety of sufferings over a long and predominantly honorable history? And for me, the epitome of this darker British legacy is Mary, Queen of Scots. That weekend, I visited the controversial queen's tomb in Westminster Abbey, because I had read a great deal about her. From the age of two, as an infant monarch, she became embroiled in conflicts that resulted in three unhappy marriages. At one time, she was immensely powerful, holding claims to the thrones of Scotland, France, and England. But she was also accused of treason, blasphemy, and even murder, making her one of the most infamous women of the English Renaissance. And the price exacted upon her life was nearly twenty years of subjection and exile, then imprisonment, and finally execution. The once-celebrated beauty was stripped to her waist before a gallows' throng, and then beheaded.

So on May Day, as I stood near her effigy, I wept. I mourned this queen who, despite her royal birth, had not been able to escape suffering. And I mourned my own lost years, which had been, in part, a result of the film that would be shown in my honor in just twenty-four hours. My life was coming full circle. A rite of passage accompanied by joys. And by long-held sorrows, too.

Jane, my former alter, had described it best. "I feel I have really lost something," she explained to Dr. Thigpen on October 20, 1953—the day after Eve White and Eve Black had disappeared, leaving Jane seemingly "cured" of MPD and believing that *her* life had come full circle. "[But] to other people it might seem another way." She could only describe the experience in a metaphor—it did not seem real to her: "Suppose a screen had been put up in front of you. Now for a year you have two sisters. They are behind this screen, but you know they are there. You are aware of them working, playing, living, though all the time the screen hides them. You know where they go, and in a sense you go with them, though you are then behind the screen. . . ."[8]

And to my alters, this "screen" was a constant. They were always aware of it. And of what existence is like on the other side of it. But as my ritual dream had demonstrated in early 1977, this perception of the "screen" may distinguish one stage of wellness from the complex patterns of illness in some MPD patients. When my alters were not in a state of temporary resolution in the disorder, they were constantly aware of the "screen." In contrast, I no longer see it in my mind.

But neither did Jane. Temporarily. So, continuing her metaphor, she tried to explain this to Dr. Thigpen: "All of a sudden the screen is not there. And they are nowhere." Then she added in a changed, depressive voice. ". . . Something is missing. It is amazing how suddenly it came to me that they weren't there any longer. I knew clearly that they were gone. . . . I just wish I had known that it was the last time I would be with them. . . ."[9]

I have subsequently learned that if an MPD patient loses sight of the "screen" but still cannot identify where the alters are, then the patient may have reached some form of MPD resolution—as Jane did—but the patient probably has not achieved unification. For that, he or she must also be able *to claim the knowledge of where the alters are.*

But the problem with making, and accepting, that claim lies in how many MPD patients perceive "switching." When my alters "switched," allowing a different alter to surface in my body, they had to pass through a darkness each time. And the worse the disorder got, the blacker this darkness became. But during periods of the disorder's resolution, such as Jane was describing, the darkness grew lighter until it seemed like a translucent screen.

And in my case, my alters were most keenly reminded of this darkness whenever they viewed a body at a funeral. Somehow, they associated "switching" through the darkened "screen" as a passage akin to death. And with good reason. They knew existence behind the "screen."

There, time is not important. Time and reality, as normally perceived, are illusions. Instead of a scheduled life, alters behind the "screen" seem to exist only in a process, and that process consists only of learning and knowing and feeling in a seemingly infinite span. Devoid, even, of the knowledge of time.

So, viewing the effigy of Mary, Queen of Scots, I felt a strange kinship, as if time did not separate us. As if she were, at that very moment, dwelling within the process from which I was excluded and about which I harbored only distant intimations. It was a peculiar feeling, and one that I have subsequently heard expressed only by some MPD patients or by persons who claim to have had near-death experiences.

If my visit to Westminster Abbey was surreal, then the next evening was its solid opposite. I wore a black sequined dress, and Don wore a black silk suit, white shirt, and black tie. For once in my life, I genuinely felt like a celebrity. And this feeling was enhanced as our cab approached the theater, where police held back lines of people and a red carpet extended from the entrance to the curb. I imagined the scene to be every bit as splendid as the original premiere of *The Three Faces of Eve.*

Keith Lucas, the British Film Institute's director, met us at the curb and escorted us along the red carpet into the theater. We were seated on the ground level's back row, the first two seats off the aisle. Minutes before the showing, I was handed a "programme note" that included an October 19, 1957, review of the movie, and I read it with particular fascination because October 19 had been the date Jane chose as her birthday. The review from *The Manchester Guardian* stated:

> In its very different way, "The Three Faces of Eve" is also a true record which succeeds in being entertainment. It may seem odd to describe as entertainment an account of a complicated case-history of medical psychology, but so well is

the story put together and so well is it acted—especially by
Joanne Woodward and Lee J. Cobb—that it is, indeed,
enthralling.

As to the veracity of its story, that may be discovered not
only from the manner of the film itself—in which extreme
improbabilities are related with a convincing quietness—but
also by comparing the film with the account of the same case-
history which has been written (and published) by the doctors
in the case. The story is one of multiple personality—of the
pathetic little housewife, Mrs. Eve White, who turned at times
into the sybaritic, nymphomaniac Eve Black and who
eventually developed yet another personality, that of the
thoroughly sensible, self-reliant and likable Jane; and in the
end, Jane totally ousted both the other two and reigned
happily and alone.[10]

Then the review startled me by referring to an even earlier
film, about which I knew nothing, even though the reviewer
seemed to believe that both films were based on the same material: my case history.

The same true story had already been exploited in another
film, "Lizzie," in which Eleanor Parker played the triple role of
the patients: the difference between the two films is precisely
that between a typical essay in Hollywood melodramatics and
a real attempt to do justice to an extraordinary subject.

When, however, all is said and done, the chief distinction of
"The Three Faces of Eve" is provided by Joanne Woodward,
who, never with much help and sometimes with no help at all
from make-up and tricks of the camera, really does succeed in
altering, from moment to moment, from Eve White to Eve
Black to Jane—and often back again.[11]

The review failed to mention Nunnally Johnson, the legendary director and screenwriter who had contributed so much to
the making of *The Three Faces of Eve*. But as the lights went
down in the theater, I remembered the man. Late in 1957, he had
sent a packet of miniature stills, used by Fox's publicity depart-

ment, and Jane had treasured them. They had been her only glimpse into the film that was otherwise forbidden to her.

Watching the film as the guest of honor, however, I could feel what seemed to be decades of resentment and pain exorcising themselves from my heart. And I could not stop crying. Even though I struggled to muffle my sobs so as not to bother the people seated around us, the tears flowed throughout the entire movie.

Later, when the house lights came back on, Keith Lucas placed a microphone onstage and invited me forward. That's when I realized why Don and I had been given the last seats in the theater. Not only had that given us privacy to view the film, but it necessitated that I walk the full length of the aisle in order to reach the stage. Only the British, I thought as I walked, could plan with such thoughtfulness and yet such ceremony.

Reaching the microphone, I was stunned as the audience stood. It was a spontaneous, decorous response. Then, politely at first but followed quickly by enthusiastic cheers, this audience of strangers gave me a standing ovation. They honored me before I could say a word.

It was the single most glorious moment of my life.

On the flight back to America, four days later, Don and I could not stop talking about the wonderful time we'd had. Virtually everyone we met had treated us with a level of respect and affection that I had never known before. The audience at the National Film Theatre had given us an evening that lingered like a sweet dream. Then, going to Scotland had made both of us feel young again. Don had played golf at St. Andrews Old Course, and I had purchased an item made from the McClure tartan.

But I was also bringing back two intriguing insights. One had come from a television reporter in Edinburgh. He reminded me that Robert Louis Stevenson had spent some of his childhood in that city, and the reporter said that *The Strange Case of Dr. Jekyll and Mr. Hyde,* the first popular account of a person with dual personality, had been based on an actual barber in Edinburgh.

"Was the barber a McClure?" I asked, whimsically.

"It's just a legend, as far as I can determine," the reporter said. "But since you're a McClure, we may be starting a modern legend of our own."

The other insight came from a prominent British psychiatrist who had attended the National Film Theatre showing. "Eve Black saved you," he said, after we had discussed my case for a few minutes. "She ensured your sanity because she refused to let Doctor Thigpen administer electroconvulsive therapy."

"I'd never thought about it like that," I said.

"Of course," he continued, "had that happened to your mind, it's very possible that a part of your psyche might have been damaged—making your integrated state today an impossibility."

Back in Herndon, the pace of our lives did not slacken, even though I felt unusually fatigued following our trans-Atlantic trip. Nearly a thousand letters had come during our absence, including inquiries from a Los Angeles screenwriter, William Wood, who indicated that he had already begun work on a television script. Apparently, Twentieth Century-Fox had arranged with CBS to produce *Eve* as a made-for-television movie, and the network had assigned Wood as the project's writer. I took this to mean that the studio actually planned to exercise its option and to purchase the motion picture/television rights to *I'm Eve*. But a few weeks later, Wood wrote that the *Eve* script was being delayed because CBS had switched him to another assignment.[12]

This delay, though common in movie production, was my first inkling that Twentieth Century-Fox might not be as eager for a sequel to *The Three Faces of Eve* as I had imagined. And I began to speculate. Had they bought the option, with its built-in renewal, simply to prevent me from challenging their 1956 agreement and subsequently selling the rights elsewhere? If so, was their lure of a possible purchase actually a ploy to bar the story of *I'm Eve* from ever becoming a movie?

I resumed doing as many lectures as I could fit into each week, but I also tried to schedule regular, weekly sessions at home for my painting, because I had agreed to participate in a major exhibition at year's end in Houston, Texas. And invitations to speak were coming more often.

Earlier in the year, I had already added statements of advocacy for the mentally ill to my speeches.[13] But in mid-May, I appeared on the same program in Duluth, Minnesota, with Walter "Fritz" Mondale, then vice-president of the United States. He explained some of the progress that had been achieved during what was then the first year of hearings by the Presidential Commission on Mental Health. What impressed me was the depth of involvement that the commission's honorary chairman, Rosalynn Carter, had sustained. The commission's monthly hearings had become valuable forums for registering the needs and problems of mental patients across America. And as a result of the First Lady's leadership, I subsequently emphasized such advocacy even more in my lectures.

"I know what First Lady Rosalynn Carter is saying. The stigma of mental illness exists because some people are afraid and because everyone wants to be accepted," a local newspaper quoted me as having said, later in 1978. "People suffering from stigma can't function to their potential, and everyone can lose—the individual, the family, employers and society. . . ."[14]

But I was becoming involved so quickly in so many endeavors that I failed to recognize one key pitfall of career women who are also wives and mothers: I was not maintaining that delicate balance between work and family. For several weeks, I came home to find Don working quietly, sometimes sullenly, in the garden. And I unwittingly misread what I saw. I assumed that Don was happy because this was the first summer that he had been able to garden since Bobby, now twenty, had been a toddler. During all the intervening years, we had either been forced to move before Don could harvest his garden or we had lived in apartments with no garden privileges.

So, convinced that Don was cheerfully occupying himself with the garden and his full-time job while I pursued my work, I increasingly made all the decisions about my travels and appointments without consulting him. It seemed reasonable enough. After all, he had not asked me if he could buy a new Rototiller or if he could plow up the portion of our backyard that he had selected as a garden plot. Nor had he ever consulted with me about his profession as an electrician or his membership in a union.

However, our differences surfaced one morning, typically enough, while we did something totally unrelated to our unspoken problem: waiting on a slow teller at a drive-in bank. Suddenly, the woman irritated me, and I snapped at her. While she and I yelled at one another through the microphones and speakers, Don took her side of the argument and attempted to intervene.

"Mind your *own* business," I said, shifting my anger from the teller to my husband.

"How you act *is* my business, Chris," he said, then waited until I drove away from the bank before admonishing me for having been rude to the teller.

"Oh, no," I retorted, struggling to drive and argue with equal proficiency, "we're not arguing over what happened back there. This one's been brewing for a long time. So, just tell me, Don: What is it, exactly, that you don't like about me?"

"You don't do what I tell you anymore," he said.

Knowing Don's style of arguing, I realized that he had made his point. All of it. But I wasn't convinced that *this* was his only complaint. "And just why should a fifty-one-year-old woman snap to, every time her husband issues an order?"

"Because," he said, his voice softening, "for most of those years, you *depended* upon me. Good or bad, I made all of the decisions. I had to. You couldn't."

"I couldn't because I was sick."

"But you're not sick anymore," he said. "You're just damned independent."

"And you can't stand that, can you?"

"I didn't bargain for it," he said, "and I have no idea where it will end."

"But why does *my* independence have to end?" I asked, opting for a shortcut home. "Yours never has." This argument promised to be long.

"Because," he said, "I always knew that when you got independent, you'd leave me."

I was stunned. Hurt. And so lost in my thoughts that I could not immediately respond. Naively, I had believed that the successes and triumphs that we had shared these last twelve months had somehow erased our doubts about one another. My God, our silver wedding anniversary was approaching in December. "Well, you're wrong," I finally said. "I'm not going anywhere, Don Sizemore. And try as you will, you can't run me off."

"I wasn't trying to," he said, "and I don't know how we got into this argument in the first place."

"You didn't *like* my independence."

"Oh, yeah," he said, but with a lilt in his voice. "Well, I still don't. But that's no cause for breaking up."

"I said *that* was out of the question for me. And it better be for you."

"If I didn't leave when you were sick, Chris," he responded, "I'm certainly not packing now that you're well."

"You just don't want to miss a thing," I joked, and he laughed.

"No," he said, "life with you has never been simple." Then he patted my hand on the steering wheel, and said, "I guess I just love you more than I thought."

"Independence and all?"

It was a rhetorical question, and my husband didn't answer. He had had his say for the day. But looking back, it was a breakthrough moment just the same. Thereafter, we began sharing our true feelings, either in arguments or in calmer conversation. And we put to rest the issue of who made decisions. When possible, we discussed concerns. Otherwise, we made our different ways in the world. Adults living distinctly different adult lives.

But we also buried my *sickly wife role* that day. It was a step long overdue, and Don needed to be relieved of it as much as I did. He had singly shouldered the burdens of all our decision making for too many years, and such unbalanced responsibility had taken its toll. However, just as Dr. Tsitos had waited until I was ready to end therapy, Don had wisely waited until I was ready to assert myself. Then, gradually, my husband took comfort in having a wife who no longer depended on him to make all the choices. He found new joys in having me as an equal partner. And he learned how to let me go, knowing that I would always come back.

That is, Don gradually did these things.

Around Memorial Day, our family spent two weeks in Chatham County, North Carolina, at the house and on the farm where Don had been raised. After having discussed, and often argued about, what to do with the Sizemore homeplace, we finally began fixing up the house and furnishing it for weekend and

holiday use. And everyone worked. My sisters and their husbands—Tiny, Luther, Becky, and George—pitched in. So did
Bobby, Taffy, Tommy, and the grandchildren. Don's sister Christine and her husband, J. T. Brown, who lived on the adjoining
farm, would come down in the evenings. On Saturday, my cousin
Elen and her husband, Bob, joined us.

In a sense, it was like the old-fashioned work parties I remembered from childhood—barn-raisings or corn-shuckings, quilting
parties and roofings—most of which ended with lively gossip and
storytelling. Porch talk. Family and neighbors leaning in cane-bot-
tomed chairs or lounging on the porch floor in the cool of the
evenings.

So, as we labored, the older ones of us were actually striving
to revive something in ourselves. We had been raised to work at
tasks that made us sweat. *That addictive bond between southerners and the land.* But in adulthood our lives had changed, so it
had been years since any of us had worked until our bodies were
spent and our clothes damp and limber.

During the first few days, men cleaned the old well, serviced
the pump, and made the cistern functional again. The grandchildren cleared the lawn of debris, and we women scrubbed the
floors and walls and ceilings in the house, then hung curtains and
arranged the furniture until the place, by week's end, took on a
certain coziness.

But it was Don who seemed to benefit most. Night after night,
his contributions to the porch talk seemed to blossom with a
treasure of boyhood memories. Telling legends about warts, and
how to catch frogs in the woods without ever touching them.
Recounting how Bear Creek boys extracted bearings from bro-
ken-down tractors, then used these "steelies" as marbles. Or hot
afternoons when they raced by pushing used tires or old buggy
wheels down the dusty ruts in the dirt roads. Or icy, snow-quiet
Sundays when they went "winter swimming," which meant jumping from the crib rafters, fifteen feet above the floor, into bins
overflowing with dried corn shucks.

Having the grandchildren as listeners seemed to spur Don's
memories. He showed nine-year-old Jimmy how to make a "bean
shooter"—notching a maple fork, cutting an inner tube, then
carefully wrapping string to bed the ends of the inner tube inside

the maple notches. It was just one of the many homemade toys—
the only toys—that we adults had to play with as children in the
heart of the Great Depression. And Don seemed to remember
how to make them all. A sharp Barlow knife could fashion green
hickory, baling twine, and dried dogwood limbs into a bow and
arrows, with carefully carved ash used to make the arrows'
points. The trunks of dogwood trees, skillfully turned on glass
cutters, made baseball bats. But the most craftsmanship was required to make a baseball, and he described that process in detail.

By the end of our vacation, the homeplace was at least functional and clean. And so were our hearts and minds. We had created a place to come to, and more than a few memories. Plus the
beginnings of some family traditions. We particularly needed the
latter. Over the years, with my role in their lives perpetually
changing alongside the changes of personality, we actually had
very few family customs. There hadn't been sufficient continuity
to establish them on weekends and holidays and family vacations.

However, as I enjoyed the fourth summer of my wellness, I
was determined that the business of family traditions would continue.

In July, Jove published the mass-market edition of *I'm Eve,*
which remained active and in print for a decade. That same
month Shokichi Kawaguchi—the Tokyo translator who had produced Japanese texts for both *The Three Faces of Eve* and *The
Final Face of Eve*—wrote that he was now translating *I'm Eve*
and that Kodansha would be publishing the edition before year's
end.[15] Though I never met this affable man, he had endeared
himself to me in the early seventies by sending the most charming letters, written in fractured but respectful English, as he labored over his translation of *The Final Face of Eve.* In one of
those letters, he described me as "the most unusual character in
this century."[16] How could I *not* like him?

But as Taffy and I discussed his letter, I realized another importance that he had held in my life, and I immediately responded, "You are the *only* person, other than my family [and
doctors] and one girl friend, who knew my real identity. The only
person with whom I established a friendly relationship prior to

my becoming a public figure. It is significant that I trusted you, and that you honored that trust."[17]

As much as I had enjoyed our family's closeness at the Sizemore homeplace, the vacation's aftermath found me suffering from guilt. Four years earlier, during the first weeks following the unification, I had felt similar guilt about MPD's effect upon my family.

What was new, however, was that I now had money. We weren't rich, but I had a great deal more than ever before. So throughout the earlier months of 1978, I had been showering my family with gifts. New golf clubs for Don to use in Scotland. A used car for Bobby. And for the grandchildren, special mementos from virtually everywhere I traveled. Shopping uplifted my spirits; giving made me happy. And, for a while, at least, this seemed to lessen my guilt.

But Taffy had resisted excessive gifts from me, and during a trip to Williamsburg, Virginia, she finally confronted me. We were in a store displaying expensive merchandise, and I was eagerly recommending what I could buy for her. Suddenly, my daughter simply took me by the arm and escorted me outside.

At first I was furious. But as we walked along the sidewalks in the restored historical section of the city, Taffy explained. "Mother, you don't *owe* me anything," she said.

"But I do, darling," I protested, my voice quivering from both disappointment and a tenacious trace of anger. All I could envision were the years of her childhood that she had sacrificed for my well-being. "You've done so much for me," I added, "and I'm finally in a position to make it all up to you. Now what's wrong with that?"

"I just don't want you buying me things."

"And why not?" I asked, puzzled that Taffy was acting so stubborn about something as wonderful as being given gifts. "Don't you see that I must *do* something with what I have? And who better to do for than my family?"

"Do for yourself, Mother. Or for Dad or Bobby," she responded. "But you don't have to *buy* me. All you have to do is love me."

My daughter—who had known me before I knew myself—

once again recognized what I was doing before I understood my own feelings and actions. Money is no substitute for love, and only love can dispel guilt. Yet it was a hard lesson to learn.

I honored her wishes that day. But it would take me a while to accept the cold reality that no matter how guilty I felt, I could not make up for the sacrifices that others had made for me. Giving *things* had become habitual. All my alters had done it. As if to say in the giving, *Who I* am *is too uncertain for me to give of* myself, *so please accept this object; its value is a* known quantity, *which is something I may never be.*

But Taffy did not simply saddle me with her refusal. Instead, through the remainder of that summer, she and I began having lunch at least once a week. Just the two of us. And while sampling various restaurant fares, we learned to laugh together. We discovered that we liked the same foods. And we began the slow process of, once again, reversing roles. This time, however, I was becoming the mother and she the daughter. And through these discussions, I gradually came to appreciate others' sacrifices and to love my family and friends because of what *they* had given.

By the time that autumn came, I found myself under more pressure than ever. I had not planned to promote the paperback edition of *I'm Eve,* but it evoked a surprising number of requests for radio and newspaper interviews. Fitting these into my schedule meant less time to prepare for lectures, plus deep cuts into the work sessions I had allotted for painting. And I could least afford this loss in painting time, because the Houston exhibition was less than three months away.

As a result, I attempted to be a superwoman. Between September and early December, I made myself available at any time to any reporter who sought an interview, but I also hid away to paint as productively as possible. I canned the late produce from Don's garden harvest, and mindful of Taffy's advice during the summer, I cultivated more special times to spend with the family. But I also ended up making more trips for lectures and television appearances than I had originally planned. In short, I struggled to be all things to all people. And more specifically, I was wedded to my appointment book, to list making, and to an intense desire to be perfect.

My first sign of trouble was that the closer I came to the date when my collection had to be shipped to Texas, the more exhausted I became I couldn't quit thinking at night, and often my thoughts were repetitive. But there were no headaches or recurring dreams or blackouts, no sense of having lost time—the usual MPD symptoms that I knew to consider as warnings—so I didn't call Dr. Tsitos. I had to deal with pressure. *Alone.* Otherwise, I could not sustain my work. So I decided that insomnia was the result of feeling so compelled to work that my mind simply could not shut down.

Despite all the pressures, by December 7, when I viewed my collection of paintings at the Fine Arts & Collectors Gallery in Houston, it appeared that I had succeeded. Among the paintings on exhibit were more than a dozen that I had completed during the previous eleven months.[18] And the gallery's patrons seemed to like my work. Many of their comments during the gala reception confirmed that they recognized key contrasts in my style, perceptions, and technique as compared to the paintings my alters had done. All of the daytime experiences in Houston, then, felt like solid vindication for SuperChris. But alone in the hotel room each night, I remained unable to sleep.

By the flight back to Washington, I felt utterly exhausted but also justified in the choices I had made under pressure. At home in Herndon, euphoria was added to the feelings of exhaustion and self-vindication when Doubleday informed me that Twentieth Century-Fox had renewed its option on *I'm Eve.*

I believed that, because the option's final expiration date was May 23, 1979,[19] the decades of frustration over my life story's film rights would simply end in six months. At that time, the studio would either have to purchase the rights or release me from any further obligation. In either case, I could finally close the book on Eve's legal quagmire. Two days later, however, I would unwittingly suffer from a new nightmare, the legal implications of which, instead of being civil, were criminal.

Looking back on this period, what I should have done was sleep for a week. But I couldn't. I had been planning special ways to make Christmas 1978 our family's most festive. In addition, Taffy, Tommy, and Bobby were arranging for a party to honor

Don and me on our silver wedding anniversary. So I returned from Houston with only four days to prepare for the arrival of sixty-five couples. My children were preparing the food, beverages, and entertainment. But the party was to be in our house.

So I went to the Giant Food Store near our neighborhood. I shopped there regularly. The clerks knew me. On this trip, I intended to buy cleaning supplies, toilet paper, napkins, air fresheners, Kleenex—all the items that guests might need but that I didn't keep in quantities sufficient for over a hundred people in one night. Once inside the store, however, I stopped at the magazine rack. That's the last memory I have of that day until, sometime later, when the store's security guard was searching my purse.

The woman retrieved a tube of acne cream and a multipack of chewing gum. Both had Giant Food Store stickers on them, but they were not in a sack and there was no receipt as proof that I had purchased them.

"My God!" she exclaimed. "Why, Mrs. Sizemore? Why did you do it? Surely you're not hurting for money. And for things like this that you don't even need?"

Only then did I realize that I was being accused of shoplifting. "I don't know," I responded. "It's all so strange. I don't even remember doing it."

"What?" she said, her face registering disbelief. "Why *don't* you remember?"

"I must be sick," I said, not exactly in response to her question.

"You mean sick like, uh, before?"

"I just don't know," I repeated, then asked if she would telephone Dr. Tsitos for me.

"I'll let you call him," she said, and then took me to the office telephone. When he answered, I explained what had apparently happened, then I asked if he would talk to the security guard.

Based upon her responses in the phone conversation with him, I could discern that Dr. Tsitos was confirming my identity, then assuring her that I was his patient. Then he apparently asked what I had taken—"Merchandise worth less than five dollars"—and if the store intended to press charges against me.

"We've already taken a picture of her," the security guard said. "And we've recorded the incident. So I can't just drop it."

When the woman hung up the telephone, she looked at me for a moment but said nothing. Her expression remained one of disbelief, but there was pity and confusion in her eyes. "I'll have to discuss this with the manager," she finally said. "In the meantime, is there someone who can come for you?"

I gave her our home phone number, she dialed it, and I listened as she explained to the person who answered, "Is this the Sizemore residence? Well, I'm Merle Davidson, security guard at Giant's, and we'll need for you to come down here. Your mother has been caught shoplifting."

The words seemed to freeze me in the chair, because Bobby had answered our phone. My son had just been told that his mother had committed a crime. It was the most humiliating moment of my life, and yet I still had no idea how the shoplifting itself had happened.

"Do you want to speak with your son?" the woman asked, interrupting my thoughts.

"I should."

But when I picked up the receiver and said, "Bobby?" his voice was the saddest I have ever heard it.

"Mom, what happened?"

"I think I had a change."

"Oh, God, no," he said. "This can't be."

For a moment, neither of us spoke. Then Bobby assured me that Don and he would come for me.

Dr. Tsitos's preliminary diagnosis was that I had experienced a fugue state but not a change of personality. I understood the distinction because he and I had previously worked through instances of fugue states, based on my childhood memories. Later, however, I would discover an irony related to this diagnosis. While in Houston, I had discussed the differences between MPD and such fugue states during a newspaper interview. And the article based on that interview would, coincidentally, be published the same day as my apprehension for shoplifting. "One experiencing a fugue state," the Houston article quotes me as having said, "may appear 'normal' but is in actuality assuming an identity quite different from the real one."[20]

Dr. Tsitos assured me that while the ramifications of shoplifting were serious, the fugue state itself had probably been in-duced by stress. Nothing more. And though such a state is dissociative, he did not view the incident as evidence of a relapse into MPD. He said that my inability to recall what had happened during the shoplifting, and the uncharacteristic nature of my actions, were typical of a fugue state. He also suggested that my recovery from this dissociation had most likely occurred before I got to his office, and he predicted that I would probably not suffer a recurrence.

Basically, then, he downplayed the psychological importance of what I had experienced. But neither of us underestimated what the criminal aspects of my actions might do to my life, my family, or my career. A decade later, Bess Myerson would suffer public humiliation and media exposure as the result of a similar shoplifting incident, which came during an enormously stressful period in her life. But in 1978, I could only imagine what my fate held. And the best that I could foresee seemed horrible.

Don paced the floor, though he periodically stopped and stared at nothing in particular. And he has a way of putting his hand on his forehead, then moving it slowly down his face until it rests under his chin. He made this gesture several times. Then he sat beside me on the couch and touched my hand, as if to reassure me that everything would be all right.

I was not so sure. In less than forty-eight hours, we were scheduled to entertain family and friends. But our twenty-five years of marriage seemed to be disturbingly close to where it had begun: with me as the wife with a mysterious mind, and Don as the perplexed husband. Yet this time I could be tried, convicted, and jailed, and there would be no happy ending after that. My career would be finished.

Minutes later, the telephone rang and my entire body jerked. Don answered it, then listened with little comment. When he placed the receiver back in its cradle, he said, "Baby, that was Miss Davidson at the store. She said the store manager has decided not to press charges."

So our anniversary party began as a bittersweet occasion for me while guests arrived that Saturday evening. Neither they nor our grandchildren knew about Monday's shame, and Bobby,

Taffy, and Tommy acted as though they had believed Dr. Tsitos. As though the fugue state was something to dismiss and forget. But I struggled between tears of joy, which might be expected, and tears of deep sorrow, which I could explain to no one. Would any of our family's celebrations ever be untainted? Would we never have peace?

Friends and family complimented me on my white silk gown. And everyone seemed astonished to see Don wearing a handsome black tuxedo. He smiled, his smooth face remarkably free of wrinkles or burdens, and he moved from room to room like a man who had never been happier in his life. Later, with everyone gathered around us, Don and I cut a tiered wedding cake while cameras flashed and guests joked. Don's boss, Jim Loy, proposed the champagne toast. Then Don and I exchanged gifts: a silver golf tee for him and a white-gold necklace bearing an opal for me. It appeared to be the perfect anniversary party. Except that my heart was broken.

Moments later, I spotted Merle Davidson in the crowd of friends and family. I had invited the security guard to our party, but suddenly lost my breath as she walked toward me.

"I brought you something," she said, and handed an envelope. Without opening it, I thanked her then excused myself, clutching the envelope tight against my gown. I weaved through the press of guests until I reached a bathroom. Everyone seemed happy but me. Inside, however, my bittersweet mood changed. I opened the envelope to find that the security guard had torn up my mug shot and the shoplifting report. All the pieces of both the photograph and the store's report to the police were my gift.

At that moment, I understood the remarkable truth for my life in the famous line uttered by Blanche DuBois in the final scene of *A Streetcar Named Desire.* As the doctor who has come to take her to a psychiatric hospital draws her up gently and supports her exit with his arm, leading her through the portieres of her sister's New Orleans apartment, Blanche holds on tightly and says: "Whoever you are—I have always depended on the kindness of strangers."[21]

For had Merle Davidson not shown me that moment of kindness, that forgiveness beyond professional duty, then there probably would have been no subsequent career for me. Not as an advocate. Or a writer. Or as an artist. In many ways, then, I am in her debt for the rest of this story.

7

*S*hould I have remained anon-
*ymous, as "Sybil" had done? Should I have delayed releasing
the manuscript for* I'm Eve*? Or at least, should I have avoided a
"public" life until after completing the follow-up therapy for
MPD?* In spite of Dr. Tsitos's assurances that the fugue-state experience was not a relapse of MPD, these and other questions
haunted me during the early weeks of 1979. I didn't have the
answers. And I knew of no one else who would truly understand
my concerns. No one, perhaps, but Sybil herself.

To ensure anonymity, Sybil communicated with the outside
world only through her therapist, Cornelia Wilbur, M.D. But I
was certain that Sybil would see me, so I telephoned Dr. Wilbur
and asked her to arrange a meeting.

"Sybil sees no one," the therapist responded, without hesitation. "Not even you, Chris. And I am sorry, for your sake, but
that's the way it is."

Realizing, then, that nothing could be done about my past and
that I only had the present in which to live life, I pushed aside
some of my self-doubt. Running from life was no longer an option. This time, many people depended on me. Some even
seemed to draw strength from my efforts as a lecturer, painter,
and writer. Admittedly, I also had detractors who seemed eager
for my downfall, as if my failure would somehow justify their
prejudices about the incurable nature of all mental illnesses. But
no matter how others viewed my life, I had to make the choices.

I was at a crossroads. And I opted to remain in the public lane instead of veering back onto the private one.

My motivation, as I would subsequently understand, was rooted in a personal need to expand the definition of *integration.* For decades I had viewed integration merely as an end to MPD rather than as a psychological means toward achieving a fuller life. But the writings of Thomas Merton offered insight. He understood integration as a process of spiritual and psychological growth that is essential not only for mental patients but for everyone. While this was a standard enough view, Merton differed with modern psychoanalytic goals and argued that *"final integration* . . . is not just the 'cure' of neurosis by adaptation." Indeed, he found "adaptation to society" to be a totally inadequate goal because it merely "helps a man 'to live with his illness rather than cure it.'"[1]

I identified with Merton's views. I yearned to get beyond both the cure of, as well as the widely held bias that I must simply learn to live with, my illness. At the same time, I was being asked to advise others. And that advice—as demonstrated in a January letter to a man seeking help for his wife, an MPD patient—usually followed the traditional psychoanalytical view of "adaptation to society": "Tell [her] she is not alone. . . . If she can only come to know she is an important individual, without this long and painful search for self; if she can accept herself, then she will find that others will, also."[2]

Yet in writing such letters, I was aware that "self-acceptance" and "adaptation to society" had not enabled me to deal with all of my own anxieties. Here again, Merton was helpful. He determined that "there is an important distinction between mere *neurotic anxiety,* which comes from a commitment to defeat, and *existential anxiety,* which is the healthy pain caused by the blocking of vital energies that still remain available for radical change." More specifically, he described "healthy pain" as "a summons to growth and to painful development."[3]

I realized that in terms of development I had only been growing in normalcy since the summer of 1974—less than five years. Why, then, should I not expect pain and anxieties? Being successful at the chronological age of fifty-two did not erase the fact that, on some levels, my personality still had no more experience in *coping* with life than that of a child in elementary school.

By the mid-eighties, psychiatrists who specialize in MPD treatment would routinely caution unified patients to view integration as a slow process and to expect that a span of three to five years of uninterrupted unified personality development may be required before both the psychiatrist and the patient can be confident that the patient's integration is "holding." But, once again, neither Dr. Tsitos nor I had such guidelines available in the seventies. We only had his good counsel and my instincts. And my instincts led me not to resume therapy following the fugue state. Instead, I chose to face my family and friends just like anyone else who fails. . . .

Unwittingly, Elizabeth Taylor played a role in my decision. At the time, she was married to U.S. Senator John William Warner, a Virginia Republican, and they lived in Middleburg, not far from Herndon. My first opportunity to meet the famous actress came shortly after the senator took office. I was invited to a February reception in her honor at West Springfield High School.

Upon meeting her, what initially struck me was that she seemed even more beautiful than I remembered from her movies or television appearances. However, as she conversed with others, she also seemed painfully shy and somehow lacking in self-confidence. I couldn't believe the contrast to her image in the media.

During the previous year's campaign for her husband's senate seat, she had been controversial, often outspoken, and rarely lacking in confidence. Many political observers had attributed her husband's victory, narrow as it was, to Elizabeth Taylor's remarkable ability to draw crowds and to influence voters. But mixing informally, she was a charming opposite to her public persona. In fact, her "star quality" did not emerge during the reception until she was asked to come forward and speak. And when she did, her comments were concise, witty, and delivered with a flair. On cue, she had seemingly transformed herself into the woman who mesmerizes men and inspires women.

I left that day with no illusions that I could be an Elizabeth Taylor. But the contradictions that she openly demonstrated did encourage me. Since going public in 1975, I had not allowed myself that luxury. Instead, I had struggled to appear consistent. Perfect. Never moody. I had wanted no one to seize upon a wayward gesture or a sudden moodiness and thereby mistakenly infer that I was still mentally ill. But Elizabeth Taylor had shown that women in the public eye don't have to be a grown-up version of a Shirley Temple doll. It was the observation that the prominent British psychiatrist had offered about Eve Black's role among my most famous alters: To be normal is to be inconsistent.

Once again, then, I probed the only personality I had left and sought in it acceptable ways of coping as a public figure. Clearly, I had to become selective and more resourceful. I had to accept fewer public appearances and to space the ones I did accept so that I minimized the stress. Three months later, a reporter from *The News and Observer* would quote me as affirming, "I can draw on the good qualities from the personalities and incorporate them as I build my new life."[4]

By the time I said that, I had spent nearly four months of rest and reevaluation and preparation. Making infrequent public appearances, I had spent productive time in private. I had read all the literature on MPD that I could find. I had also written, polished, then rewritten a basic lecture on my case history and MPD in general. If I was going to succeed as a professional lecturer, then I had to be thoroughly prepared. And if I was going to minimize stress during such public exposure, I had to perfect my presentation. These efforts were essential. Otherwise, I might again be vulnerable to that one unusually stressful moment when I would cope not by relying on solid preparation but by further dissociation.

During my brief and unannounced sabbatical, however, major national developments set the stage for renewed public interest in patients' concerns. Since April 1978, when the special Commission on Mental Health had filed its report to the president, Rosalynn Carter and leaders of the National Mental Health Association had repeatedly testified before subcommittees in the U.S. Senate and House of Representatives. These efforts eroded the governmental malaise that had existed through several administrations and changed the direction toward improved health care for mental patients. Then, during the early months of 1979, the First Lady increased her efforts, addressing professional and lay organizations across the nation to seek support for new federal legislation on behalf of mental patients.

The immediate result was a small but influential movement to improve the plight of the mentally ill. Within a year, some advocates called for an investigation of patients allegedly being overmedicated in psychiatric institutions with the rationalization that "drug use has cut the population of mental institutions in the United States from 600,000 in the early 1950s to some 300,000 [in 1978]." Other advocates, while agreeing that overmedication was a major problem, called for an even broader approach to mental patients' concerns. These views were eloquently expressed by Wade Hudson, an ex-inmate activist then working in California:

> In the effort to demystify what is happening with people labeled "mentally ill," one critical factor to keep in mind is the importance of economic pressures. . . . The poor stand as a visible threat to those who are better off, demonstrating what could happen to [the latter] if they chose not to serve the system.
>
> The lack of adequate income is a serious problem for most mental patients. Not only are they poor before institutionalization, but the chances for improving their economic situation are greatly reduced by the discrimination (in employment, housing, etc.) they suffer once released. . . .
>
> And the theory that psychiatric drugs were responsible for the wholesale release of inmates from state hospitals starting in the 1950s, for example, is widely and falsely perpetrated. The "harmlessness" of these drugs is still another widely circulated myth that needs to be debunked. Debility and impaired intellectual functions in the short run and permanent physical injury in the long run are to be expected. In fact, the primary effect and purpose of these drugs is to diminish the ability [of the patient] to feel and think.[5]

In May, some of these issues were addressed when President and Mrs. Carter made a joint appearance at the White House to announce and submit to Congress the Mental Health Systems Act. It promised to be a milestone piece of legislation implementing many of the recommendations from the earlier presidential commission. That same month, the First Lady also addressed the Medical Society of the World Health Organization in Geneva and called for an end to "mental health care where in too many cases those who are without power or influence suffer severe discrimination in the delivery of services."[6]

As I watched from a distance while these events unfolded, I felt inspired by Rosalynn Carter's example. Granted, she was the president's wife, but she was also a woman and a southerner. And discovering that she and I had been born in the same year, I resolved that if the First Lady could make a great deal of difference as a national mental-health advocate, then I could make some difference wherever I was invited to speak.

So I resumed my work that May with a five-city, eleven-day tour on behalf of the Mental Health Association in North Carolina. My paintings were exhibited at Duke University in Durham, then moved to Kinston, Greenville, and Rutherfordton. In conjunction with these exhibits, I also lectured in each city, and the responses to both my art and new lecture presentation were very positive. So much so that Duke University scheduled a longer exhibition of my paintings in the fall; the state's MHA leaders asked if I would return for a longer, more comprehensive tour in 1980; and MHA leaders from Pennsylvania invited me to do the same but in the autumn of 1979.

As a result, I returned to Herndon with renewed confidence that I had succeeded. And I had worked harder for it. Harder than any previous effort in my life.

But instead of success immediately driving me back to more lecture appointments or tackling some new challenge, it made me desire another extended period of time with my family. Particularly the women. Over the years, a lot of women friends had gone out of my life. For a while, success and fame and the excitement of being one person had made up for these losses. But by the summer of 1979, I needed the companionship of my family in that close, special way that we had experienced the previous summer at the Sizemore homeplace. In the best sense, I was maturing.

In July, Taffy and I established Hotel 1776 in Williamsburg, Virginia, as our retreat. My daughter had convinced me that some of my stress could only be relieved by occasional "escapes" from home, the telephone, the mail, and any routine responsibilities. And during this first retreat, I was reminded that Taffy had a fine mind and was an avid reader; my independence in recent years had prevented us from enjoying the time necessary to communicate what we had individually learned and felt.

Williamsburg made this possible. We discussed my efforts to incorporate the alters' good qualities into my own, and Taffy demonstrated an uncanny ability to react to all these emerging aspects of my personality. She had known most of my alters and could gauge how my behavior related to theirs. It was an invigorating time. It was an intimate mother–daughter time. But it was also the period when she and I began relating to one another simply as two women who enjoyed one another's company. Later that month, I spoke to one of Bobby's classes at George Mason University, and once again, I received a sense that my new life was meshing with my son's.[7] My children, though too old to be mothered, were finally striving to ensure that there would always be a place in their lives for me.

But there was one relationship that, over the years, had not been allowed to heal, and that was with my sister Elise "Becky" Walton. The unresolved problem was not conflict but loss: Becky had been extremely close to the Turtle Lady; consequently, that alter's disappearance had deeply hurt my sister. And after the unification, that grief subsequently interfered with Becky's ability to accept me. Ours had remained a friendly, benign relationship, but the closeness was not what it had been between her and the Turtle Lady.

So in August, while Don and I vacationed with Becky and her husband, George, at Goat Island, South Carolina, the opportunity finally came to address this estrangement. After Don and George left for a day of fishing, I asked Becky what had happened to our closeness.

"You've been a totally new sister these past five years," she said, "and I still don't know how to deal with it." She paused, as if pondering what honesty might do to me. But being a bright, tough-minded woman in her own right, Becky soon pushed forward, saying, "I've known you as so many different people that, through the years, it seemed like we were *always* having to get to know one another from scratch. And that was hard. Maybe too hard at times. Because I've had my own problems to deal with, Chris, and you know that."

"But I love you," I said, "and we may now need one another more than ever."

"I love you, too, Chris," my sister responded, her expression clouded. "But the Turtle Lady just seemed like my true *soul* sister. That's why I miss her. And sometimes just being with you makes me miss her more."

"She hasn't gone anywhere, Becky. She's still here. She's with me," I said. "But it was necessary for her to go away in order for me to get well."

Becky smiled, fighting back tears. "I just never thought about it like that," she said. "But I do see her, every once in a while, in some of the things you do. So what you say must be true."

"Then help me bring more of the Turtle Lady out in myself," I said. "The good that was her, the specialness that made you two close—surely some of those qualities are mine, too. We just have to find them. Nurture them. And let them surface."

To my sister's credit, she worked with me that week. It was not a normal sister-to-sister exchange, but Becky showed a remarkable willingness to try. She wanted me as a sister, as much as I wanted her. And she was willing to work in order to achieve that.

During the monthlong exhibition of my paintings at Duke University in September, the major focus was on "The Attic Child" series.[8] Patrons purchased several installments, including "At the Gazebo," "Playing Hopscotch," and "Jumping Rope." These scenes of childhood play seemed to touch a nerve—even with those who knew nothing about the South Carolina setting at the Strother Place. One reason seemed to be the paintings' ties to the Great Depression. With the seventies drawing to a close and with stock prices, interest rates, and unemployment reaching high levels, some financial observers were comparing the 1979 economy to the explosive era preceding the Crash of '29. But my paintings were giving viewers and patrons a positive link with that otherwise negative period in American history. And this positive approach, exactly fifty years after the onset of the Great Depression, seemed to make "The Attic Child" paintings irresistible.

This return to Durham also enabled me to renew my relationship with Elen, the cousin and friend who had labored so lovingly as coauthor of *I'm Eve*. After the book's publication, we had gone in separate directions.

Elen also encouraged me to meet with Dr. Mattie U. Russell, who was then the manuscript curator at Duke's William R. Perkins Library. At that appointment, which turned out to be a delightful luncheon, Dr. Russell extended Duke's invitation to provide a permanent home for all my papers.[9]

Though I had expected the invitation, it also stunned me. I was being asked to donate the correspondence, diaries, and memorabilia that had belonged to all my alters, plus all the material that I had collected since the unification. These would be placed in archives alongside collections that contained correspondence from such respected writers as Walt Whitman, Fred Chappell, Reynolds Price, William Styron, Edmund Wilson, John Dos Passos, and Robert Penn Warren.

It was a great step for a woman who, just months before, had doubted her ability to recover from failure. Yet there was another implication: Donating one's papers to an archive was what public figures often did at the end of their careers. But I was only fifty-two years old. Did Duke's invitation imply that my career was over?

Audiences the next month in Pennsylvania and Virginia, however, did not reflect that. The crowds were generally large and enthusiastic as I toured Pittsburgh, Greensburgh, Beaver, and Butler on behalf of the Pennsylvania Mental Health Association, then returned to Virginia to address the Mothers of Twins Club at Sugarland and the Danville–Pittsylvania Mental Health Association.

But the most intriguing responses came in mid-October at the Loudoun campus of Northern Virginia Community College from a parapsychology group led by Jean Eek. Some years earlier, Dr. Thigpen had suggested by correspondence that I consider writing about reincarnation, spiritualism, and astrology as "kinds of explanations other than psychological for multiple personality" while Elen and I drafted *I'm Eve.*[10] We did not follow his suggestion, but I remained open to such alternative views of MPD. And Jean Eek's group provided them in abundance.

They cited parallels to ESP and energy transference in some of the experiences my alters had shared. They noted striking similarities between what my alters had "seen" and accounts in spiritualism of mystics seeing visions and apparitions. And they suggested relationships between my alters' separate, dissimilar existences and accounts of reincarnation.

As I left the group, I was not convinced that their parapsychological insights represented solid answers for MPD. But I had to admit that they came nearer to understanding what I had subjectively experienced in multiplicity than most psychologists did at the time. In fact, as I continued to explore the existing literature on MPD and to consider alternatives to psychological studies, one startling realization became clear: Even though I was no psychiatrist, *I understood more about MPD than most clinicians.*

Underscoring this was the American Psychiatric Association's reluctance to recognize MPD as a bona fide disorder. For example, in 1979, the available edition of the APA's *Diagnostic and Statistical Manual of Mental Disorders*—which had not been revised since the second edition's publication in 1963—classified MPD as a form of hysterical neurosis but provided no description for it.[11] Consequently, many clinicians dismissed both popular accounts, such as *Sybil* and *I'm Eve,* and about a dozen professional articles or books that were published on the subject each year during the seventies.[12] In addition, few psychiatrists attended my lectures, or at least they did not introduce themselves as such. And virtually no professional articles had cited *I'm Eve* since the book's publication.

As such dismissals continued, I became concerned. I understood that the scientific process is exacting and slow, but Drs. Thigpen and Cleckley had first presented findings concerning my case history to the APA in 1953.[13] Since then, nearly three decades had passed, during which I and many others had suffered from an illness that most psychiatrists refused to recognize as valid. In fact, I had been cured of, and had already begun lecturing about, the illness before the APA actually accepted its first substantive papers on MPD at their annual meetings in 1978 and 1979.[14]

In a sense, then, MPD patients in the late seventies were like Vietnam veterans who suffered from post-traumatic stress. Both groups had endured psychological horrors. Their lives had been irrevocably changed, and their symptoms were often painfully disruptive. But American psychiatry, while observing the unmistakable effects of such trauma, played close to the vest. One leading clinician involved in MPD studies during this period nearly lost his professional privileges to admit MPD patients to the hospital where he practiced. Though the peer-review committee ultimately voted in his favor, Ralph Allison, M.D., wrote of his peers' prevailing attitudes, particularly toward the parapsychological and religious aspects of MPD:

> Many of my fellow psychiatrists view these concepts as superstitious nonsense. They want to deny everything that can't be proven conclusively by scientific methods. They may be right, but they also may be closing themselves off from a reality greater than we can comprehend with our present knowledge. After all, most of the advances in medical science that we take for granted would seem miraculous to people living only 150 years ago, when barbers handled many of the medical procedures![15]

Barbers? I remembered what the Scottish reporter had told me: that the actual man upon whom Stevenson had based *The Strange Case of Dr. Jekyll and Mr. Hyde* had been a nineteenth-century barber in Edinburgh. So it was interesting to speculate how "advanced" that lone barber's understandings may have been in terms of establishing vital links between psychology and parapsychology.

Experts point to 1980 as a milestone year in the diagnosis of MPD patients, with the primary impetus being that the *Diagnostic and Statistical Manual of Mental Disorders* was fi-

nally revised. In this third edition, multiple personality was classified as a disorder and basically described,[16] giving MPD a
legitimacy in the eyes of psychiatrists that the disorder had always had among its sufferers. This difference was crucial. Under
the sanction of *DSM-III*, clinicians could diagnose and treat MPD
without the shadow of controversy that had surrounded the disorder throughout my adult life—and, in some ways, because of
my case history.

DSM-III also described MPD as "apparently extremely rare,"
which perpetuated with both clinicians and patients the *mythic
quality* of MPD that had surrounded both my early treatment
and the extraordinary publicity about my case history. For many
years, I had mistakenly thought I was the only living person with
MPD. Dr. Thigpen had instilled this belief in me, and his writings
with Dr. Cleckley had shored up that assertion within the psychiatric community. In fairness to my former therapists, researchers
have subsequently identified only eight MPD cases to have been
reported and published between 1945 and 1969[17]—roughly the
years when MPD disturbed my life the most.

However, when *DSM-III* supported the belief that MPD was
extremely rare while also sanctioning the disorder's diagnosis,
one primary result was an explosion of reported MPD cases.[18]
On a personal level, I no longer believed—at least intellectually—that I was the only living person who had suffered MPD.
Since 1977, a few had introduced themselves, though always dis-
creetly, following some of my lectures, and I had corresponded
or exchanged telephone calls with many MPD patients and their
alters. Through such controlled circumstances, then, I had
learned a great deal about what MPD patients have in common,
including the fact that the disorder was not as rare as most experts claimed.

But until 1980, I had never spent an extended amount of time
with another person who had suffered MPD. The reason? Even
though I had previously sought to meet Sybil, I had deep apprehensions about such an encounter. Apparently, Sybil shared
these apprehensions, and that's understandable: Being perceived
as *unique* is a powerful personal myth. Despite my apprehension,
however, I needed a face-to-face encounter that would emo-

tionally dispel this myth. And such an opportunity came in February. I will never forget it.

The meeting had been planned as a luncheon in a Virginia city, where I would meet a woman whom I will call Rita. A few months earlier, she had written a very insightful letter. Her sentiments reflected the uncertainty among MPD patients at the time: "Now that the integration has taken place, I am finding it very hard to deal with other people's nonacceptance that my situation ever existed, or their nonacceptance of me as a total person. . . ."[19] In a concise, honest manner, Rita had expressed the essence of what I had privately felt for nearly six years, so my anticipation about the luncheon was enormous. Somehow, I expected her to be exactly like me—looks, behavior, interests, and experiences with multiplicity—a psychic twin.

But at the restaurant, I could see none of myself in her, and Rita made it clear that she was there only for information, not for friendship. Her interests were exclusively her own, and her first question was, "What did it feel like to integrate?"

When I responded with a brief answer that alluded to *I'm Eve*, she said, "I don't want my people to die. It's an awful feeling, waking up and discovering that some of them have disappeared. I don't want to lose them during the night, and then to wake up and find that they are gone!"

I attempted to reassure her that "they do not die, they're still with us," but her reaction to *I'm Eve* had undergirded that of other MPD patients. As much as they had benefited from my book's honesty, they found it inadequate in terms of explaining unification or the problems they faced afterward.

But the basic difference between Rita and me was that she didn't seem to understand how multiplicity worked. I knew about myself, and I assumed that other MPD patients also knew about themselves. Yet this woman indicated that not all of them do. The other surprising aspect about this woman was that she spoke loudly. During my decades of experience with multiplicity, the "voices" in my head had spoken loudly, so I could have developed a loud-voiced alter. But I did not, though Rita had. She spoke during our luncheon as if accustomed to talking so that everyone could hear. Maybe she was as nervous as I? Maybe it was just as important to her to meet another MPD sufferer as it was to me? In any case, she appeared to try too hard, and I could not relate to her. Coming from my southern background, a loud woman was offensive because of my upbringing.

But as disappointing as the luncheon was for me, it yielded an important lesson. I had expected it to be like a reunion of sorts—that two women with a common experience, uncommon to the world at large, would have a meeting of the minds. Yet I came away with the understanding that MPD patients are as different as the alters that make up their multiplicity. That they are as restricted as the environment in which they live. And that each MPD patient needs to escape the personal myth that he or she is a lone sufferer of the disorder.

But I did find a new sisterhood that same month. I was installed as an honorary member in the Virginia Tau chapter of Alpha Delta Kappa, an international honorary sorority for women educators whose headquarters are in Kansas City, Missouri.[20] And this proved to be an important personal step.

Being accepted by these schoolteachers, professors, and school administrators gave me a sense of belonging with other women who were outside the realm of MPD studies and mental-health professionals. With them, I was not just a former mental patient, now working as an advocate and lecturer. They did not relate to me as if I were legendary or mythic. Instead, the ADK sisters treated me as just another career woman whose friendship and companionship mattered. And in so doing, they unwittingly provided a certain compensation, a substitute for what I had lost, years before, when my alters had disappeared behind the "screen" in my mind. In addition, my ADK sisters became a circle of friends who were interested in my life as it was progressing. Not in what it had been. We were a sisterhood of possibilities, blind to the past.

In retrospect, the spring of 1980 was when my life and career finally blossomed, beginning with George Mason University's three-week exhibition of fifty-four pieces from my collection. At that point, it was the largest single show that I had assembled. Included were the nineteen paintings that seven of my alters had done, four drawings done by Jane, and thirty-one paintings that I had completed since the unification.

In the middle of the exhibition and two days before my fifty-third birthday, *The Washington Star* ran a feature story that treated my work not as a novelty but with the respect afforded other artists whose exhibitions represented years of hard work and artistry. Though its headline alluded to my past—THE PAINT-INGS OF THE MANY EVES—the focus of the article was on my life in 1980, noting, "Sizemore sells many of her paintings to universities, museums and private collectors for sums up to $1,000. She is also working on another book, which will combine her poetry and art work."[21]

It meant a great deal that my paintings were actually commanding prices that, along with my lecture earnings, were finally enabling me to earn a respectable living. Wade Hudson had been right: Former mental patients' "chances for improving their economic situation are greatly reduced by the discrimination . . . they suffer. . . ." By persistence and talent and pluck, however, I had beaten the odds. And interestingly enough, the first purchase from this exhibition was made by Lilla Dunovant McCutcheon Richards, then a Virginia resident. She was a descendant of the Dunovants from my hometown of Edgefield, and that family had owned the Strother Place where many of "The Attic Child" paintings were set.[22]

But the event that was most personally satisfying came a week later, when all of my Virginia family consented to have a group interview and a family photo published in *The Reston Times.*[23] Though linked to the exhibition at GMU's Fenwick Library, this interview was the first in which Don, Bobby, Taffy, Tommy, and the grandchildren talked openly about both the joys and the difficulties they had encountered during my years of multiplicity. While the reporter asked them questions, it was obvious to me that the hesitancy of the *60 Minutes* interview in 1976 was a thing of the past. With the buffer of four years during which they had seen me grow stronger, my family responded with humor and candor.

And when the issue containing the story and photo arrived, I first rubbed my fingers across the picture. In it, each family member was smiling, obviously proud to be publicly identified with me, even in a newspaper that circulated throughout the area where all of us lived. And gone from their expressions were the traces of stigma that secrecy had forced upon us for so long. In this, the first published portrait of our family, there was at last evidence that *all* of us had recovered from the effects of my mental illness.

Buoyed by the supportive experiences that had occurred almost weekly during the first four months of 1980, I left Herndon in early May for a sixteen-day, nineteen-city tour of North Carolina—my second to benefit that state's mental health association. Surprisingly, even though I had visited some of these cities the previous year, media attention on this tour was greater than before. Television, radio, and newspaper correspondents were at every stop, and the clippings and tapes generated by this tour seemed to reflect the positive attitude I felt.

"I don't think I'll need therapy for multiple personality again," the High Point *Daily News* quoted me as saying. "But that's not saying I wouldn't need therapy for something else. If I need therapy, I'll just get it because I'm just like everybody else now." And many people in the audiences also seemed affected. As one local MHA leader wrote, following the tour, "We have had other recovered 'celebrities' speak to us in the past. . . . Through her unique insight, warmth and genuineness, however, Chris Sizemore had a greater impact . . . than any who came before. Hers is far from simply a story of recovery. Chris's message is one of hope and victory over the stigma of mental illness."[24]

Midway through the tour, however, two staff members with the state's MHA left me speechless. At least momentarily. Peggy Hill and Dot Ling had accompanied me from city to city and had witnessed the responses to my appearances from both audiences and the media. As a result, they asked if I would permit them to nominate me for the Clifford W. Beers Award, given annually by the National Mental Health Association.

I knew that Beers, a former mental patient, had founded the NMHA early in this century, but I knew nothing at the time about the award. When they explained its prestige, I felt that they were wrong about supporting me. Despite the responses during this tour, I didn't feel that my lectures since 1977 had produced a significant enough impact to merit a national award. But I was complimented, and grateful, so I consented. And during the remainder of the tour, Peggy and Dot collected newspaper clippings about my efforts and letters of recommendation from MHA leaders across the state to document the nomination.

The tour culminated in a two-day event hosted by The Friends of Duke University Library. Earlier, I had accepted Duke's invitation to donate my papers and had periodically deposited them in boxloads. Included were all my alters' diaries and correspondence from the fifties through 1980; the manuscript and documentation for *I'm Eve*; memorabilia; legal papers; newspaper clippings, television, and radio tapes; and over three hundred letters from Dr. Thigpen and other therapists. My only stipulation was that during my lifetime, persons wishing to examine the material must first obtain my written permission.

By May 24, Dr. Russell had sorted through a portion of this material and had prepared an archival display at the William R. Perkins Library. But this turned out to be only part of the celebration. The Duke Friends also feted the library's acquisition with tennis and golf classics, a reception, and a showing of *The Three Faces of Eve*.[25]

At the presentation ceremony, North Carolina's MHA president, Hernando Palmer, told the invited guests that my tour had been "the most successful speaking tour ever held in our state."[26] Dr. Russell described my papers as one of the most important and historically significant donations she had acquired for Duke. And my entire family shared in the experience, including my husband, children, sisters, aunts, and cousins. The two-day event was even more meaningful for me because it included recognition of my son Bobby's twenty-first birthday. In a sense, mother and son were coming of age together.

But the donation did evoke some controversy. In advance of the event at Duke, officials from the University of South Carolina contacted me and asked that I consider placing the papers in my native state's leading university. I thanked them but explained that the decision had already been made.

A few days later, U.S. Senator Strom Thurmond telephoned. The South Carolinian Republican, who had also been reared in Edgefield, encouraged me on the basis of our mutual loyalties to the same hometown to reconsider USC's request. "The boys back home sincerely want your papers, Chris," he said in a tone that implied the senator was rarely refused.

I didn't want to be one of Senator Thurmond's exceptions, but I had already committed to Duke. "I'm very sorry, Senator," I said, "but I've already deposited them."

"What?" he responded, incredulity apparent in his voice.

"Duke already has the papers."

"Well, that's no problem," he said. "Go get 'em."

I declined, said good-bye, and expected that refusing Senator Thurmond might result in Edgefield disowning me forever. Instead, the owner of one of Edgefield's weekly newspapers, Emily Bull, ran an editorial in praise of my career and my decision. The editorial's theme was "A prophet is not without honor, save in his own country."[27]

Despite the controversy, giving up the material from my decades of mental illness brought a deep sense of relief into my life. *The Reston Times* quoted my precise feelings at the time:

> It was like giving up a treasure—not because they are so valuable but because I lived inside of those papers for so long. . . .
>
> But now I've moved on to a new era. For a while those papers were telling me who I was. They gave me a sense of self-worth. Now, I don't need them anymore.[28]

It had taken almost exactly six years from the July 1974 unification until the Duke presentation, but I had finally survived the aftermaths of mental illness. As the summer of 1980 began, I could relax in the security of knowing that my family relationships were restored. My self-confidence and talents had been raised to levels where I could earn a living and attain respect for the work that I did. And MPD itself was no longer considered a pseudo-illness. In every important sense, then, I was entering a new era.

B y autumn 1980, a new era for my career *did* begin. *DSM-III's* recognition had played its part, but other events dovetailed with MPD's legitimacy. While the Ninety-sixth Congress was finalizing legislation to meet the needs of mental patients, several highly publicized acts of violence were committed by psychologically troubled individuals. These stories dominated American headlines, and the mental-health community, caught in the crossfire, sought credible, experienced spokespersons.

In a sense, I was the right person at the right moment because, during this same period, some medical journalists, psychiatrists, psychologists, and researchers suddenly viewed both my case history and the various accounts of it with renewed interest. And with greater professional respect. In September, for example, *Time* magazine determined that the predominant American image of a psychiatrist/patient relationship had been established twenty-three years earlier by Lee J. Cobb's performance as Dr. Luther (Dr. Thigpen) in *The Three Faces of Eve.*[1] The following month, two leading experts on MPD included *I'm Eve* in articles for the *Journal of Clinical Psychiatry* and *The Journal of Nervous and Mental Disease*—marking the first published professional references to my autobiography since its release.

One of them was Indiana researcher Philip M. Coons, M.D., who noted that, through 1980, "there [has been] relatively little written about multiple personality in the modern, professional, psychiatric and psychological literature," and that, previously, "the diagnosis of multiple personality has been controversial."[2]

Georgia clinician George B. Greaves, Ph.D., agreed. In addition, he credited *I'm Eve* with vivid descriptions of how MPD affects an individual's life, and he affirmed my autobiography's contentions that my first therapists had failed in their treatment. As he stated it: "In turning to [Morton] Prince's work in their attempts to treat Eve, Thigpen and Cleckley adopted a compromise strategy of using hypnotherapy . . . but rejected Prince's integrative strategy. As history was to show, this was the backward choice."[3] Dr. Greaves's conclusions marked the first time that any clinician had gone on record in my defense.

But beyond this professional recognition, new public attention focused on my nomination for the 1980 Clifford W. Beers Award. Though I did not win it at the November presentation ceremonies, I still benefited from the exposure. That same month, the *Today* show filmed a feature during "A Day with Chris Sizemore"—an event at northern Virginia's West Springfield High School in which students performed a dance to music that had been set to my poem "Black Tambourine." And the nomination itself added legitimacy to my efforts as a lecturer and an advocate. The Mental Health Association in North Carolina had compiled nineteen press clippings and thirteen letters of recommendation into a nomination book, and that book's introduction stated:

> Since Mrs. Sizemore's recovery in 1974 . . . she has revealed her story in a positive way to let hundreds of thousands of people know that there is hope for [patients with] mental illness—even the most rare form. . . .
>
> In her message, Mrs. Sizemore does not emphasize her own, rare form of mental illness as much as she does the fact that mental illness is a terrifying and dehabilitating disease, but a disease for which there is help.[4]

In response, MHAs from across the country sent invitations for me to visit their state chapters and to lecture. From this convergence of events, then, I became a full-time lecturer, making over a hundred annual appearances during the next six years.

However, the foremost reason for enthusiasm and optimism throughout America's mental-health community that autumn was the fact that in October President Carter signed into law the Mental Health Systems Act. The bill had been passed by a solid bipartisan majority of both houses. And earlier, it had been developed by the First Lady and the president's special commission, which had carefully considered two decades of experience with the federal Community Mental Health Centers in order to make the legislation work effectively. The resulting MHSA was a humane approach to treatment for mental patients. It promised to change the primary focus of mental-health care from large institutions to predominately outpatient, community settings. And it promised to reduce the stigma of mental illness under which thousands of institutionalized patients had suffered for generations.[5] The era demanded such changes.

Directed by Rachel Roth, over eighty-five adult volunteers from George Mason University and six northern Virginia mental-health organizations monitored network television during February 1981. Their plan was to rate prime-time shows in the District of Columbia's metropolitan area by judging whether each program contained references to mental illness, then to record the mental-health messages communicated through, as well as the descriptive characteristics of mentally ill persons portrayed in, these television programs.

In the broad view, the results of this monitoring did not appear troublesome. About 40 percent of prime-time movies communicated something about mental illness, and 18 percent portrayed a mentally ill person. Close behind movies were the TV police/detective series, in which about 36 percent involved references to mental illness, and 16 percent had a mentally ill character. However, I was concerned that other types of informational shows—such as the news programs and talk shows where I had appeared—rarely contained mental-health messages or featured guests who talked about mental illness.[6]

But on closer examination, the television portrayals were what really disturbed me. Usually, the mentally ill character was portrayed as the villain. Most implied that mentally ill persons "look and act differently from others; that they are not like 'us.'"

Many implied that mentally ill persons "are both physically and sexually threatening," and most characterized the mentally ill as "active, confused, aggressive, dangerous and unpredictable." The study concluded that "mentally ill persons on TV are disenfranchised, and not a part of the usual fabric of home and work. Such portrayals can only add to the public's tendency to view them as special, distinct and probably inferior."[7]

Published alongside these findings was a survey that had been made during the late seventies by Dr. Otto Wahl, assistant professor of psychology at George Mason University. He had collected samplings of TV program listings from *TV Guide* and *Soap Opera Digest.* The following excerpts illustrate how such casual references were reinforcing the stigma of mental illness:

"Charlie's Angels"—The Angels are lured to a tropical island where they find themselves at the mercy of a diabolical madman.

"Hawaii Five-O"—McGarrett's efforts to use reason instead of force on a deranged psycho fail miserably when the man shoots a cop and kidnaps a teenager.

"The Jeffersons"—A comedy of errors lands George in a mental hospital, where he almost goes crazy trying to convince the staff that he is sane.

"Happy Days"—Richie is driven to see a psychiatrist after reading a book on abnormal psychology.[8]

The February 1981 study also noted that such listings appear in spite of the following guideline in effect at the time through the television code of the National Association of Broadcasters: "Special precautions must be taken to avoid demeaning or ridiculing members of the audience who suffer from physical or mental afflictions or deformities."[9]

Armed with these facts, MHAs across the nation took notice. Whenever I or other advocates made public appearances on their behalf, media work became as much a part of our efforts as the traditional lectures and seminars. As a result, what I had begun simply as a lecture career quickly became a media career, too. Local talk shows on TV and radio. Call-in shows. Public-service announcements. Advance promos for seminars and fund-raisers.

Thus, without much preparation or training, I had to learn quickly how to make the camera and the microphone my message's best friend.

Awareness levels were also increasing among law-enforcement officials, as I discovered in March while conducting my first workshop for the Federal Bureau of Investigation. I was hesitant on this first visit to the FBI Academy in Quantico, Virginia, because I was not sure what the FBI expected of me. But the agents-in-training were very responsive. During the question-and-answer session, one woman asked if I thought law-enforcement agents in general were given sufficient psychological training so that, at the time of making arrests, they were qualified to make determinations about whether a defendant should be put in jail or sent to a mental hospital.

"How many hours of training in psychology are most officers required to have?" I asked.

"In most programs, about four hours," she responded.

I was appalled and said that wasn't enough training to qualify an officer to make such a decision. She agreed, and apparently the FBI did, too. For the next five years following that first lecture, the academy consistently invited me back as a guest lecturer. Along with other mental-health professionals, I served as part of the expanded psychological training that would be introduced into an increasing number of law-enforcement programs during the eighties.

That same month, however, Reaganomics not only entered American life but posed a surprise threat to mental health. Newly inaugurated president Ronald Reagan immediately proposed repealing the bulk of the MHSA. Specifically, he sought to place 75 percent of the 1981 mental-health funding into a block grant to states—a plan that promised to divert monies needed for psychiatric care into ongoing programs, such as drug abuse and alcoholism, which at the time actually needed the funding less than the psychiatric services. In practical terms, this meant a serious reduction in community mental-health services, and most certainly the loss of access to these services for many Medicaid-eligible poor people, especially children and the elderly.[10]

Beyond the fiscal reasons for the Reagan administration's drastic cuts in federal spending, however, there appeared to be political motivations for these actions. Former First Lady Rosalynn Carter had made the MHSA one of her primary concerns. But when President Carter lost his bid for reelection one month after having signed the MHSA, it bore the earmarks of eleventh-hour legislation and the stigma of a lame duck's legacy. In a sense, it was destined to be attacked by the new administration.

Nonetheless, this threat spurred many of us into action. One NMHA executive committee member, Jeff Van Sickle, testified March 17 before the Senate Subcommittee on Labor, Health and Human Services, Education and Related Services, and he eloquently opposed the Reagan administration's proposals. Others of us lobbied directly with congressmen and even state legislators. But both figuratively and literally, we were marching uphill. Reagan had wielded a mandate from his landslide victory over Carter. And the new president viewed this mandate as a license to cut federal spending, no matter what the costs to human services.

Reaganomics, then, was the harsh reality to which mental patients awakened, and many of us began to appreciate more fully the debt we owed to the Carter administration. Though our lobbying efforts could not halt the hemorrhaging of federal funds from mental-health programs, we were determined to show the Carters that their work on the MHSA had not been in vain. Three months later, several of us would get the chance. Intervening, however, was one of the strangest experiences of my life.

On March 27, during a Friday luncheon with one of my ADK sisters, Ann Flack, the conversation turned to the topic of psychic phenomena. I told her that recently some psychic-type experiences had been disturbing me. Several times I had heard sounds coming from the radio, only to discover that it wasn't turned on. Similarly, I had seen scenes on the television set, only to discover that the set was turned off. Beyond the bizarreness of such occurrences, what concerned me most was that mental patients suffering from schizophrenia often reported such experiences. Yet I knew I wasn't ill. Ann, a high school librarian, agreed that I seemed fine and certainly not mentally disturbed. But neither of us had a clue as to what such experiences meant.

The next day, I was scheduled to participate in my second parapsychological conference with Jean Eek as the conference coordinator. Since I had enjoyed such a stimulating time with her group the previous year, I was excited about the event. So much so that I invited Ann and my daughter, Taffy, to go with me.

When I asked Ann at the restaurant, however, she suggested that my recent psychic disturbances might be related to the fact that I had allowed myself to be more receptive to such experiences in preparation for my lecture. Momentarily, we accepted that explanation and, minutes later, left the restaurant. Then, while I was driving the car from Annandale to Herndon with Ann as a passenger, suddenly my vision of the road became interrupted by what I can only describe as *a visual flash*. It was a distinct black-and-white picture interspersed with the full-color vision I had of the highway. And in this visual flash, I saw a scene. But just as quickly, it disappeared. Then I saw it again, and again it disappeared. When I saw it for the third time and it disappeared, I became frightened. I knew what was happening, and it was not dissociation.

Any time before, when I had experienced such visual flashes in groups of threes, they were always precognitive. That in itself did not alarm me, because I had experienced premonitions before and they usually proved to be helpful. But what did frighten me was what I had seen: In each of the three visual flashes, I saw President Reagan, who looked as though he were dead after having been shot. Finally, I said to my friend, "Ann, the president is going to be shot."

My friend replied, laughing, "You ate too much hot food back there." But when she saw that I was serious, she stopped laughing and added, "Tell me what you saw."

"I saw him on the street. He got shot. And, oh my God, he's dead."

For several seconds, neither of us spoke. Then Ann said, "If you ever have one of those flashes about me, I'm not sure I want to know the details, but warn me anyway."

With that, neither of us continued to talk about what I had seen. It was too tragic, too awful, to consider. Whatever political differences I had with the new president, I could never wish him the victim of the horror I had just envisioned. Still, I worried about this premonition because it was unique among all that I had previously experienced: It was the only one that had involved someone I didn't know; and it was certainly the only one I had ever had that involved the president of the United States.

Earlier in the year, my chiropractor had fitted me with arm braces because I was suffering from carpal tunnel syndrome. The years of lifting heavy luggage on lecture tours had taken their toll, so my hands were fixed in position by braces made of metal bands that had been wrapped in leather. These braces held my hands in place and prevented strain on the ligature. But the braces had been fitted with a slight curvature in the metal to allow some movement and use of the hands. And I was wearing these braces, the day after my premonition about President Reagan, when I participated in the sixth annual Consciousness Frontiers Day at the Loudoun campus of Northern Virginia Community College.

In addition to my workshop, other conference leaders that day included Charles Rose, an attorney and congressman from North Carolina who conducted a workshop on miracles and intervention by angels; the Reverend John Nicola, a teacher and author who discussed his experiences as a technical consultant during the filming of *The Exorcist*; and Robert Monroe, author of *Journeys Out of the Body,* who conducted a workshop on altered states of consciousness.

After conducting my workshop, Taffy and I attended a seminar described as exploring "the transference of energy being channeled in unknown manners." And that's where I experienced another psychic disturbance. Midway through the workshop, its directors dumped dozens of bent spoons in the middle of the floor but gave each of us a spoon that had not been bent. Then they instructed us to concentrate on the spoons we held. Soon, nearly everyone's spoon appeared to be bending. But mine remained motionless. When I broke my concentration and looked at the other participants, they seemed as puzzled as I that my spoon was the exception.

Later, as Taffy and I headed to my car, she said, "I wonder why my spoon bent and yours didn't? Could it be you were just too tired after conducting your workshop?"

"That can't be it," I said. "Almost everyone else had conducted, or assisted in, an earlier workshop; but it still worked for them. All of their spoons bent." I also knew, but did not say, that the premonition about the president was still worrying me deeply. So I decided that my secret concern had hindered my concentration.

Yet when we reached the car and I tried to grasp the steering wheel, I realized that the braces on my arms were abnormally curved. The metal wrapped inside the leather had bent far more than the slight curvature created by my chiropractor's fitting. In fact, the braces were so twisted that I couldn't move my hands, making it a struggle to drive home.

But I did, and then immediately telephoned the workshop's directors to tell them what had happened. The woman said, "Well, of course. The metal closest to the body would be the one to bend—instead of your spoon—because the braces were absorbing all the energy being transferred from you."

By itself, this incident would have seemed hardly more than a novelty. But in combination with the other psychic disturbances, it made me wonder: *Am I the focus of unexplainable psychic disturbances for some reason?* Unfortunately, I would have an answer in two days.

I awakened late. It was March 30, a rainy Monday in the Washington area. The kind of morning when I didn't want to find out what was going on in the world. So I didn't read the newspaper, listen to the radio, or watch television. Instead, I began wearily cleaning our Herndon home. The morning passed. I ate leftovers for lunch, and my first telephone call of the day came about three o'clock.

When I answered it, I recognized Ann Flack's voice. But she seemed extremely upset as she said, "Chris, have you got your television on?"

"No."

"Do you know what has just happened?"

"No. What?"

"President Reagan has been shot."

I could not believe what I was hearing. "Are you sure?"

"It's on the news."

"My God." It had been frightening enough to have a premonition about the president, but it was horrifying to hear about that tragedy's *reality*. Then I realized the implications. "Ann. Have you told anybody what I said?"

"I didn't dare."

"Then let's don't tell *anybody.*"

After I hung up the phone, I rushed to the television and watched for any details about the assassination attempt. Gradually, news reports revealed that the president had been shot in the chest at about 2:30 P.M. as he left the Washington Hilton Hotel, where he had addressed a labor meeting. His press secretary, James Brady, had suffered a serious wound in the head, and both a Secret Service agent and a District of Columbia policeman had been injured. Apprehended at the scene was a twenty-five-year-old man, John Warnock Hinckley, Jr.

But for me, the most terrifying aspect of these reports was that the scenes being flashed as news footage looked strikingly similar to those I had seen three days earlier in precognitive flashes. The only difference was that the body on the street had not been the president's. And I kept asking myself: *Why had I not telephoned the FBI as soon as I got home on Friday?* Less than a month before that premonition, I had worked for the agency. Surely they would have accepted my warning as something serious.

The fact is, I did not call them. Had the premonition been about any member of my family or any of my friends, I would have acted on it. But a premonition about the president? The remarkableness of it had been so surreal on Friday that I had not dared to tell anyone—much less federal agents who had only recently met me. As a former mental patient, I knew that many people still did not truly believe I was well and that such an admission would have confirmed more doubts about my sanity than it would have afforded protections for the president.

But faced on Monday evening with the reality of what that tragedy had done to the president, his press secretary, and two law-enforcement agents, I harbored profound regrets. Could I have made a difference? Had I been given the premonition for a reason?

Because I did not trust my psychic abilities enough, I'll never know the answer to such questions. And it would be several years before research would hint at reasons why dissociation-prone individuals appear to have greater psychic abilities than most people.

The following month, the Mental Health Association in Georgia and the Mental Health Association in metropolitan Atlanta began planning a tribute to Rosalynn Carter, in recognition of her enormous efforts on behalf of the mentally ill. I received a call from Dot Ling, who had worked so diligently through North Carolina's MHA on my nomination for the 1980 Clifford W. Beers Award. She asked if I would accept an NMHA request to do two paintings—one of which would be chosen to be part of the tribute to the former First Lady.

I accepted and immediately called Taffy, but I didn't tell her the news. It was too special to relate over the telephone. Instead, I asked her to spend the weekend with me. Two days later, we settled into our same corner room with a fireplace at Hotel 1776 in Williamsburg. It was before lunch, and I telephoned room service for a bottle of champagne, cheese, and crackers.

"Mother," my daughter protested. "Isn't it a little early to be drinking?"

"Not for what I want to talk to you about," I said.

When the bellboy arrived with our order, I asked if he would also start the fire in our hearth. The young man looked at me quizzically, because it was a warm spring day and the room did not appear to need a fire for warmth. But he said, "Yes, ma'am," and made a fire.

Then I asked him to draw the blinds, move the table in front of the fireplace, place a candle on the table, and serve the champagne by candlelight. The young man did exactly as he was told, though I suspect that he was wondering what these two women were going to do in such a setting.

When I told her about the request, Taffy got up from her seat, walked over, and hugged me. "That's wonderful. Absolutely wonderful."

"But I'm not sure that I'm good enough—"

Interrupting, Taffy said what any mother would want to hear under such circumstances: "You're good enough to do a painting for the queen of England."

"—and I'm not sure what kind of painting to do," I continued, not knowing how to respond to her encouragement.

"We'll talk about all of that," Taffy interjected again. "But first, a toast." Then she took her glass and held it in salute to me. "To the artist of the year. My mother."

As we sipped our drinks and discussed this special opportunity, Taffy added, "This will prove to the world that mental patients *do* have something of worth to offer. And you're the right person to do that."

Thereafter, we discussed a variety of options for the paintings I could do. By midafternoon we decided to eat in our favorite Chinese restaurant and then go shopping. As we walked along the handsome brick sidewalks of Williamsburg, we held hands. Like two sisters. Coincidentally, we had even dressed in the same colors that day: black, red, and white.

In an elite dress shop we looked for something I might wear to the painting's presentation ceremony. Among the displays of beautiful clothing, we were discussing the lengths and styles and colors of the dress I might wear when I put my arms around her and asked, "Taffy. Will you go with me?" Then I stopped myself. I knew it was a difficult question. Except for *The Reston Times* interview the previous year, Taffy had made few public appearances with me. She had remained my confidante and supportive daughter, but she wanted none of the public life. So I added, "But of course you'll have to ask Tommy."

"This time, I don't have to ask anyone, Mother," Taffy said. "This time, I *will* go with you."

It was the moment I had waited for. Though I had always had my daughter's love and support in private, her hesitancy to appear with me in public had created an emptiness in my life. No glorious moment in life is truly fulfilling if it cannot be shared with those you love. So my daughter's willingness for all that to change meant a great deal.

The next week I began to work on the paintings, and it took about three weeks to complete them. The first, entitled "Early Beginnings," was a peaceful Americana scene of an unpainted house positioned beside a lake and a large tree. The other was of the lighthouse and western shoreline on Saint Simons Island, where the first family had spent a lot of time during President

Carter's administration. I called this second painting "The Shores of Home."

In fact, working on this tribute to Rosalynn Carter was so invigorating that only one other task could have diverted me: the opportunity to present my views on MPD to the American Psychiatric Association. And in May, that opportunity came when thirteen of us were invited as faculty to the APA's 134th annual meeting, held that year in New Orleans, Louisiana.

Our three-day course for psychiatrists' continuing medical education was the first national gathering to deal with the full range of multiple-personality studies since the APA had recognized it as a disorder the previous year. As a former therapy patient, I felt very privileged to be a participant at this conference. It provided my first face-to-face contact with all of the disorder's leading authorities, and my role in the convention was one of the earliest occasions for any former mental patient without a medical degree to serve on an APA faculty.

On another level, this annual meeting was personally rewarding because it was the first time that my artwork had been exhibited at any nationwide gathering of psychiatrists and mental-health professionals. While thousands of clinicians filed past the display at the Rivergate Convention Center to register for the convention, I felt as though my art itself was functioning as a solid advocate for MPD's validity.

But the historic significance of this event proved to be the scope and depth of information about MPD that was provided to psychiatrists. Philip M. Coons, M.D., and Bennett G. Braun, M.D., presented papers that detailed the history of MPD and its clinical manifestations. Roberta Sachs, Ph.D, Renate E. Braun, Ralph B. Allison, M.D., and Richard P. Kluft, M.D., discussed the origins of the disorder in family life and in the patients' personality formations. Then Cornelia Wilbur, M.D., and Drs. Coons and Allison detailed various ways to diagnose MPD. In the final sessions, all of these authorities—plus Tony A. Tsitos, M.D., David Caul, M.D., Joel O. Brende, M.D., and Bernauer Newton, Ph.D.—discussed various treatment methods to use with MPD patients. As a former patient, I responded to most of these discussions by focusing on the MPD sufferer's perspectives of the disorder's manifestations, diagnosis, and treatment.

Though I was warmly received by most conventioneers, a panel discussion exclusive of our MPD course offended me. A prominent psychiatrist was arguing the case that mental patients created for therapists many unique "hassles" that other types of physicians did not have to endure. He cited several examples and concluded by asking the APA to study guidelines that would improve conditions under which psychiatrists worked.

But in relating his examples of how mental patients cause professional stress for therapists, the psychiatrist became excessive. He gestured wildly from the lectern, at one point slinging his leg across it as if it were an ottoman. And he used condescending terms such as "crazies" and "nuts we have to deal with" to describe mental patients. This offensive manner persisted throughout the remainder of his speech until I could take no more. But I first leaned over and whispered my concern to the psychiatrist seated beside me.

This kind gentleman said, "Then tell him how you feel."

I looked around the enormous conference room. I appeared to be the only nonpsychiatrist present, and none of them seemed to be disturbed by the speaker's use of language about mental patients. So my first thought was to keep silent. I had never publicly challenged a clinician. I had never criticized a psychiatrist. But when the speaker concluded, I was on my feet before I could stop myself.

I asked the panel's chairman for permission to respond. When he consented, I said, "I am opposed to this doctor, or any professional, using such derogatory terms in reference to mental patients. All of us—including most patients—know the proper terminology. So this speaker has insulted the very people from whom he earns his living. Mental patients deserve more respect than that. And I believe they deserve an apology from the speaker."

"Your objections are duly noted," responded the chairman, obviously seizing my pause as an opportunity to halt the criticism. And immediately, I felt a definite shift of mood in the room.

But I remained obstinate. I intended to speak for mental patients, even if none of these psychiatrists agreed with me. So I added, "I also believe the speaker owes this body an apology."

The psychiatrist under fire leaned into the microphone and

said, "I will apologize to the lady from the South." But his tone made it clear that he thought, You might need an apology, lady; but there's no need to apologize to my peers because they understand.

I suddenly felt exposed, as if the majority of therapists in the room *did* believe that I was wrong and that the speaker had behaved appropriately. And when the event concluded, my suspicions were confirmed. Gone was the warmth with which I had been received throughout earlier APA sessions. No one greeted me as I departed. It was apparent that many of these professionals drew a sharp line between the physician and the patient. An immovable line. And I had offended many of them by daring both to step across that line and to criticize one of their peers.

Afterward, Connie Wilbur invited me to lunch. Though we had exchanged telephone calls and letters, we had not met until this convention. But I found her to be a charming woman. This day she was particularly lovely, her carrot-red hair and sparkling blue eyes contrasting tastefully with her emerald-green dress.

Initially, we discussed our unique link: that Joanne Woodward had portrayed each of us in the *The Three Faces of Eve* and *Sybil.* Connie praised the actress's enormous abilities, having seen them firsthand while serving as a consultant during the filming of *Sybil.* Then she asked if I had met the actress.

"No, I've never had the opportunity," I said, "but I did meet her husband once." Then I recounted the incident that would subsequently be reported in *The Washingtonian.*

Several of us went to an auto race in West Virginia, and on our arrival, we learned that Paul Newman was an entrant. So, during a break in the competitions, we walked around the grounds and looked for him. Finally, we spotted him beside a trailer. He wore sunglasses, a racing shirt, and blue jeans, but he still looked like a Greek god as he stood casually in the sun, a drink in his hand.

"Chris, you must introduce yourself," my friends encouraged. But I hesitated. They insisted. I hesitated. And so it went until I summoned the courage.

Then, walking toward him, I repeated in my mind how I intended to introduce myself by explaining my relationship to his wife's career. However, when I stood in front of the man and he pushed his sunglasses down the bridge of his nose, I froze. His remarkable blue eyes penetrated mine, and I was mesmerized. So, instead of repeating my rehearsed lines, I simply said, "Hi, I'm Eve."

Paul Newman grinned, pushed his glasses back in place, and responded, "Well, honey. I'm Adam."[11]

Connie seemed to enjoy the story, laughing with me about my mishap. And at that moment, I knew I could trust her. So I recounted the conflicts I had encountered that morning at the panel, and she offered some advice.

"Now, I'm going to tell you a story," she said. "When I became a psychiatrist, I was the only woman participating in most of these conferences. The male doctors ignored my papers and wouldn't refer patients to me." Then she detailed several incidents that had been troubling, early in her career. Finally, she said, "So I know, Chris. If you're going to work in this man's world, you're going to need a lot of grit. But if you don't have the stamina and if you don't want to be hurt, then now is the time to decide whether or not to continue.

"But whatever you decide, don't let it hurt you," she added. "It's their weakness. Psychiatrists have problems, too, you know. So it's their problem to deal with."

On June 23, about seven hundred dignitaries, including members of the former Carter administration, joined a host of NMHA members at Atlanta's Omni International Hotel in tribute to Rosalynn Carter. It was a southern gala. Bert Lance, a former budget director during the Carters' White House era, served as emcee for the tribute, which included comments by Jack Watson, a former White House chief of staff under President Carter, Andrew Young, former United Nations ambassador, Archie Givens, Jr., the NMHA president in 1981, and Coretta Scott King.

In addition, Mrs. Carter was named Mental Health Volunteer of the Decade by the NMHA leadership. This recognition covered her volunteer work from the time her husband became governor of Georgia in 1970 through the end of his term as president of the United States in 1980. During the governorship, Mrs. Carter had served as a member of the Governor's Commission to Improve Services for the Mentally and Emotionally Handicapped and as a member of the Mental Health Association of Georgia. Then, less than a month after her husband was sworn into national office, President Carter had established the President's Commission on Mental Health. And we all knew what she accomplished after that.

Midway through the tribute, it was a great honor for me to unveil "The Shores of Home" and to present it to Mrs. Carter. The former First Lady wore a white, starched eyelet dress and looked elegant. With sincerity, she thanked me and the NMHA, then she addressed the audience.

Her speech's primary concerns were the Reagan administration's threats to the programs she had worked so diligently to put in place. "We took a great step forward, and although we may have to take a step backward, we will not be defeated," she said. "But if you do not act with us, four years of hard work could be wiped away without any public discussion."[12]

While she spoke, I left the stage and started back to our table. Taffy met me halfway along the aisle, grabbed me around the neck, and hugged me, saying, "Mother, I could not be more proud of you." When I looked around, a cameraman from *PM Magazine* had captured that moment on film. Later, it would appear in a *PM Magazine* segment about my life, and that footage became very special to me: It confirmed how dramatically my daughter's attitudes toward my public life had changed.

Later, one of the NMHA leaders told me that Mrs. Carter took my painting to her room, placed it on the floor so that the frame leaned against the wall, then sat across from it. She looked at the scene from Saint Simons for a long time before saying, "It's remarkable. And it's even more special because a former mental patient created it."

I have subsequently been told that my painting still hangs in the Carters' home in Plains, Georgia, and I savor all these memories. It meant a great deal to share the limelight with such extraordinary southern women as Mrs. Carter and Mrs. King. Their lives have been role models for millions of us women in Dixie because, somehow, they have managed to have it all: to be loving and supportive wives and mothers but also to be women of stature, exclusive of their husbands' careers. And after the recognition that the APA exhibitions and "The Shores of Home" brought to my career as an artist, I felt that I, too, was finally becoming an extraordinary woman of the South.

In fact, it was that summer when I discovered something extraordinary about my perceptions as an artist. During the previous twelve months, I had taken painting lessons at the Lands' School of Art in Falls Church, Virginia. Originally, I had enrolled with Emmy Land, one of the school's instructors, because I wanted to learn to draw. But my inability to draw proved to be a symptom rather than the problem.

During that first session in June 1980, I had shown Emmy some of my paintings and then had asked if she could teach me to draw.

She looked puzzled, glanced back at my paintings, then asked, "Who drew these on the canvases for you?"

"Nobody."

"Well, you can't paint if you can't draw," she responded. At that, both of us looked back at my paintings, to which Emmy's rule didn't seem to apply, and we both laughed. But she added, "At least I don't know how you painted *those* without having drawn them first."

I explained that it had not occurred to me how drawing and painting might be related. I had always considered them different skills, since I could paint but couldn't draw. Only my alter Jane had been able to draw.

"Then how *do* you paint without drawing?" Emmy asked.

"I have a total picture, in color, in my mind before I ever start," I said. "Then I just paint toward that image on the canvas."

Emmy admitted that she had known other painters who didn't draw, though she said none of them had been good painters. At least not academically good. "The problem is usually form," she said. "For example, if there are no lines on the canvas from which to work, how do you judge perspective?"

"I don't have problems with perspective," I said, "but some viewers of my paintings do." The most consistent criticism of my work had been that perspective and the lines seemed too awkward for realism but not daring enough for other styles. I had always listened politely to such comments but had never really understood. My paintings looked real enough to me.

During subsequent sessions, then, Emmy struggled to teach me how to draw. First she observed me working in class. Then she taught fundamental drawing techniques. But form was virtually impossible for me to draw, simply using lines. And squares *were* impossible.

After several months, Emmy relented. "Academically, I can lay paint on a canvas better than you," she said. "But I can't do what you do. I cannot imagine a painting *before* it's there."

"Really?" I said, incredulous that others didn't perceive their paintings as I had been doing for years. "My vision of what I paint is constant," I explained. "Even if I leave a painting unfinished— as I'm having to do more often these days—I can come back to it, weeks or months later. And as soon as I stand in front of the canvas, the vision returns. Intact and exactly as before. That's why I never needed to draw on the canvas. The whole thing was already laid out in my mind."

Emmy just shook her head, and thereafter gave up teaching me how to draw. If I began a painting in her class, I would describe the image and point out its dimensions on the blank canvas. Emmy would draw. Then I painted, roughly following her lines. As a result, by the summer of 1981 I had improved my sense of form and perspective in painting, but I still couldn't draw.

Then, one day, another student and I were talking. I mentioned my inability to draw and, on a whim, wondered if this inability were somehow related to the puzzling psychic disturbances I had experienced that spring.

"I don't know about the psychic stuff," he said. "But what do you mean, you have a 'total picture' in your mind? Can you perceive more than you can put on canvas?"

"Of course," I said, thinking his a silly question coming from another artist.

"Then describe a painting you've done—say, one based upon a scene you have not actually visited. One you've only imagined."

"Well, I did four seasonal installments in 'The Attic Child' series. And the constant elements in each are a pond in the foreground, the girl on the pond, then the bank and trees in the background. I never saw that exact place, except in my own mind."

"Okay," he said, "but you've seen ponds and trees somewhere, so those paintings could have been modeled after any that
you had seen. Right?"

"Sure," I responded, "except that I couldn't put everything on
the canvas that I saw in my mind."

"Is it that canvases are flat, but the world isn't?"

"That, too," I said. "But the real problem is that I can't paint
all of the beauty that my mind sees. Take a tree, for example. You
can paint the front of a tree, and you use certain techniques to
make it *appear* rounded. But you really can't paint all of the
tree—the front, the back, the top, and the sides—in the same
place on the same canvas at the same time. Yet that is my mind's
image of a tree, so it's frustrating. I can paint only *part* of what I
envision."

"That's what painting is," he said. "All of us can only paint in
two dimensions. Height and width. And we can only approximate
depth."

"But I want to paint the roundness."

"You want to paint more than one perspective but at the
same time," he said. "Well, Chris. That's called *sculpture*. Painters
can only convey an object to canvas from one perspective at a
time. A canvas is flat, and people can only envision an object
from one perspective at a time."

"What do you mean?" I asked, understanding what he said
about sculpture and flat canvases but not what he said about envisioning. "I can see *all* of an object in my mind."

Now, he appeared puzzled. "Are you saying that, when you
envision a painting, you don't see it in your mind from any single
perspective?"

"No," I responded, "though I know what you're talking about.
I painted my first installment in 'The Attic Child' series because I
had such a dream. And that dream was the first time I was ever
inside the overall picture. It was bizarre. I momentarily became
the girl in my dream. But looking through her eyes, I could not
see all around every object. Everything suddenly seemed flat and
the lines stark. But just as quickly, I was no longer the girl. No
longer looking through her eyes. And it was such a relief to be
dreaming normally again. Seeing everything. All sides of every-

thing at once. The total picture. That other way was too much like being awake."

"I don't dream like that," he said.

"Like the girl in my dream, or like me?"

"Like you."

"Oh, that's too bad," I said. "It's so beautiful to see everything at once. That's why I paint. The real world doesn't look like the world in my mind, so I keep struggling to bring that world into this one."

Sometime later, I thought of this conversation again when reading about the work of two Harvard Medical School researchers, David H. Hubel and Torsten N. Wiesel. Their findings imply that the world we see is actually limited by how our eyes function. They studied the thicknesses of ganglion cells in both the eye's retina and that portion of the brain's cortex that receives information from the retina. And what they discovered was that more "constraints" had been placed upon the retina than on the cortex.[13] In short, we can see less than we can comprehend.

Their work noted other complexities in the eye/brain connection, including the "column systems," and the researchers concluded, "Why evolution has gone to the trouble of designing such an elaborate architecture is a question that continues to fascinate us. Perhaps the most plausible notion is that the column systems are a solution to the problem of portraying more than two dimensions on a two-dimensional surface?"[14] The retina, like a canvas for painting, is basically a flat surface on which a round world must be conveyed. Thus, my problem as a painter seemed to be the problem of working under the "constraints" of a single pair of human eyes.

But my imagination. *My mind's eye.* Somehow that seemed to be a different story. If a normal brain that had never experienced multiplicity could, nonetheless, comprehend more than the eye's retina could convey, then what could my mind comprehend? Over the years, it had perceived the world through many "eyes." And if I received their individual memories, did I not also receive their individual imaginations?

I have no answers to such questions. I only know that my dream world is richer in form and in colors than the world I see when I'm awake. And what I envision for a painting is total—

rounder and more beautiful than I can paint. It's as though I have a *collective control* of my alters' former, and singular, perceptions. And this collectiveness may also explain why, as in the spring of 1981, I experienced so many psychic disturbances. It's as though my alters—who remain behind the "screen" in my mind but are no longer in control of my life—use imagination and psychic experiences to communicate their perceptions to me. As though, after the "screen" separated us in my 1977 dream, these extraordinary means are the only ways they have left to communicate. Otherwise, they position themselves around that circular room, which is my mind's eye, and provide me with their collective perspectives, which is my visual imagination.

Two years later, interestingly enough, I would be interviewed by a woman, Iona Deering, who was working on a dissertation in art therapy. She observed my paintings and subsequently wrote, "Mrs. Sizemore uses an almost naive, childlike style of painting in 'The Attic Child' series, which is more representative of her child theme. We know she possesses the skills to create the illusion of three-dimensionality because it is revealed in the faces of 'Sisters' and in the hand of 'Journey into Darkness'; yet her 'attic children' are more two-dimensional, leaving me to assume that this style of painting is a deliberate choice by her unconscious. . . ."[15]

9

As remarkable as change had been in my lifetime, Don's life had seemed unalterable for nearly thirty years. In late autumn of 1981, for example, he was fifty-eight years old, yet his weight had barely varied from its constant of 175 pounds. He looked almost exactly like the muscular, trim, erect man in Jane's wedding snapshots from 1953. And he acted like that man, too, as though underneath his calm, easygoing demeanor throbbed a driving, impatient energy. Without ever needing coffee to awaken, he still got up at five-thirty every morning. He rarely missed a day on the job as an electrician at the Greater Southeast Community Hospital in Washington, D.C. And each evening, he returned home like clockwork to do more tasks until dark around the house, yard, and garden. Particularly his two-thousand-square-foot garden in our backyard.

When we had moved to the Armada Street property four years earlier, Don's garden was a no-man's-land—its thin, gray soil the apparent result of a gas-pipeline project that linked Houston, Texas, to the East Coast. Only weeds and seedlings seemed capable of flourishing along the pipeline's route, making it look as though a dead riverbed cut through the suburbs. But Don spotted potential.

"You don't need a lot of space for growing vegetables," he said that first autumn. "You just have to convince the land that it can do the job." And convince it he did. He bought a Rototiller, fertilizer, and seeds, then wedded himself to the task. Within a few weeks, a patch of turnip greens began sprouting from the weak but finely worked soil. Other plant covers gradually emerged. And by the first snowfall, Don's garden was bedded in for winter.

The following spring, he plowed under his cover crops and resumed the Rototiller's assault. Using zodiac principles that he had learned as a boy, he planted seeds according to their most favorable signs. Everything in the ground by Good Friday. And the first sprouts soon came, as if they were also part of some divine plan. Onions, peas, cabbage, radishes. And in the following weeks, cucumbers, butter beans, Silver Queen corn, okra, bell peppers, green beans of the variety known as Kentucky Wonders, and Big Boy tomatoes. Finally, beets, squash, and Tommy Toe tomatoes came up. Even gourd vines began climbing up the fence.

But Don's husbandry didn't stop once the plants broke through the soil. Indeed, it intensified. He staked the green beans and overhung them with twine. Then he interspersed the bean plants with tomatoes so that both grew, benefiting from the support of stakes and twine. He also put mulch underneath the tomato vines to keep the fruit from rotting in contact with the bare soil. And his prize tomato plants he encircled with construction wire, allowing the vines to be protected from wind and animals. By midsummer 1978, Don's garden was the talk of the neighborhood. As much for where it was as for what it produced. He had made life spring up where none had seemed possible.

And so it had gone, autumn to winter, spring to summer—Don's garden growing more impressive during each of our first four summers in Herndon. The previous summer, for example, his garden had been so bountiful that, from it, I had been able to can forty quarts of Kentucky Wonders and the same amount of Big Boys. I also dried scores of onions by tying each bulb in a knot along a nylon stocking.

These were skills that my mother had taught my alters. But the summer of 1981 had been the first chance that I had to use them. And as I got into the tasks, I enjoyed remembering Mother in Edgefield. There, canning and drying produce from the garden were the only ways we had of ensuring self-sufficiency during the Great Depression. But practicing these timeless skills in Herndon also affirmed that Don and I were finally living the southern life we had been raised to appreciate.

Yet little in our marriage had been consistent, and our comfortable home life would be no different. During the early months of 1982, I first noticed changes in Don's appearance. His shoulders started to bend slightly. The line that separated his high forehead from his wavy black hair also began to recede. And his soft brown eyes suddenly showed more exhaustion. About the same time, our family physician discovered a white ring around the pupils in Don's eyes. The doctor explained that this was a sign of high cholesterol and prescribed an increase in Don's dosage of Inderal, which he had been taking along with a diuretic since 1971 for high blood pressure.

After the doctor's diagnosis, Don dismissed my concern about his health and went straight back to work. But I continued to worry. Something more was wrong. I was convinced of it. As surely as if I'd had a premonition.

Even with my concern over these uncharacteristic changes in Don, I also had work to do. More work, in fact, than ever. MPD's legitimacy had been secured just long enough for new controversies to arise. And foremost among these was the much-debated but legal defense of "not guilty by reason of insanity." I had my first insight into the problems that MPD posed for the so-called insanity defense in February while I was at the FBI Academy in Quantico for another presentation to new agents. Bob Ressler and Dick Aul, two special agents with the FBI, had asked that I come early to review some film in the academy's library. Ressler described the film as evidence which had previously been obtained in the case of a felon whose attorneys used their client's diagnosis of mental illness to seek the insanity defense.

Without commenting on the phone, I had reacted to a strange feeling. John W. Hinckley, Jr., was seeking this defense based on his treatment for schizophrenia prior to his assassination attempt on President Reagan's life. What if this FBI film was of Hinckley? His trial was scheduled for June, and press reports indicated that the insanity defense would be challenged. If this was the case, did I dare admit my premonition of the assassination attempt to these agents? Moreover, was I qualified to participate in legal proceedings that involved the president of the United States?

As I watched the videotapes, however, I recognized the man in the film as Kenneth Bianchi, the Hillside Strangler. In 1979, Bianchi had already received one life sentence after having pleaded guilty to the murder of two coeds in Washington State when the former security guard was arraigned in California on new charges. As the Hillside Strangler, Bianchi was alleged to have raped and brutally murdered thirteen other young women in the Los Angeles area.[1]

Bianchi, then twenty-eight years old, maintained his innocence in the Hillside Strangler charges and was remanded for pretrial psychiatric evaluation. During a subsequent videotaped interview, however, a hypnotized Bianchi manifested behavior that some psychiatrists diagnosed as MPD. I remembered the case vividly, because the Hillside Strangler evoked sensational headline stories across the nation shortly after the release of the paperback edition of *I'm Eve.*[2]

So during the February 1982 session with the FBI, I intently observed Bianchi in the films. In particular, I concentrated on the slim man's eyes and facial features, because the agents had asked for my opinion on whether or not Bianchi evidenced traditional symptoms of an MPD patient, as a number of prominent defense psychiatrists had contended.[3]

But what I saw during more than an hour of videotapes, which we watched twice, was that Bianchi's eyes remained the same when he was presumably changing personalities in response to requests by interrogators for him to do so. The same thing appeared to be true for Bianchi's voice: It never really changed from personality to personality. His voice did get higher or lower, but the timbre of his "voices" remained the same. And the changing facial expressions did not alter the basic form of his face.

I concluded that Bianchi had been very clever during the filmed interrogations, but that he did not seem to be an MPD sufferer. Subsequently, I would learn that prosecution psychiatrists and many police officers familiar with the 1979 proceedings had reached similar conclusions. One of them, Philadelphia psychiatrist Martin Orne, M.D., had "convincingly testified that Bianchi 'confabulated' his personalities."[4]

"Do you think he is a multiple?" Ressler asked.

"I don't think so," I responded, citing as reasons the fact that

Bianchi did not exhibit the traditional characteristics of an MPD patient when "switching" from one personality to the next.

"But if he were a multiple," the other agent asked, "could he have committed these crimes and not remembered his actions?"

"He could have," I said, explaining the aspect of amnesia found in all MPD cases.

Then Ressler asked, "If he were a multiple, do you feel that he could have determined right from wrong at the time of the murders? And should he be held responsible for those acts?"

This was the hardest question. It hit directly at the heart of legal issues in the insanity defense. And I could only base opinions on my personal experiences of having lived within the disorder. After some consideration, I said, "Unlike schizophrenics, MPD patients do not lose touch with reality, and most of their alters can tell right from wrong. So, yes, I believe he should have been held responsible for his acts."

I illustrated this by personal observations about the only times that one of my former alters could *not* have assumed full responsibility for acts done by another alter. Foremost in my mind is the 1952 incident, dramatized in *The Three Faces of Eve*, when Eve Black attempted to choke Taffy. While I cannot *personally* remember that incident, I know it happened because I saw it during an abreaction in 1974. But other such confusing periods occurred in the fifties when Dr. Thigpen was manipulating my alters by extensive hypnosis and again in the mid-seventies when the Strawberry Girl was regressing toward childhood under Dr. Tsitos's psychotherapy. During these highly regressive states of mind, my alters may not have known right from wrong because they were undergoing such intense therapies that their conscious awarenesses were vacillating from maturity to childhood.

"But as a well person," I added, "I have no choice but to accept responsibility for *everything* that all twenty-two of my alters did. It was my life and my body that they were using. I cannot escape that, and neither can other persons who have been cured of MPD."

Bianchi had also accepted his responsibility. In late 1979, he signed a plea-bargaining agreement, pleaded guilty to five of the murders and implicated his cousin, Angelo Buono, then forty-four years old, in the remaining Los Angeles murders. Buono was arrested, charged in ten of the Hillside Strangler slayings, and the California court gave Bianchi another life sentence.[5]

But studying the Bianchi films two years after those proceedings, I was concerned that he had been incorrectly diagnosed as suffering MPD and that using such a diagnosis to seek the insanity defense had been a disservice to other mentally ill criminals who might warrant it. This diagnosis had also been a disservice to MPD sufferers, because it could mislead the public to believe, mistakenly, that all MPD patients are criminals. I told the FBI agents this, and they seemed to appreciate my candor.

When I subsequently expressed these same opinions publicly and among mental-health professionals,[6] however, I drew sharp and immediate criticism. I became an object of disdain by a growing number of clinicians across this country. Most of them said essentially that, given my case history, I should be more protective of other mental patients and should not distinguish MPD sufferers from other mentally ill defendants.

My response was, and has remained, that I can only speak about MPD patients; that unless they are under intense therapy or unusual stress, their alters do know right from wrong; and that under our legal system, when a defendant can discern right from wrong, he should bear the responsibility of his actions. If convicted, he should be punished. And if he is also mentally ill, he should immediately receive proper psychiatric care, because all mental patients deserve quality treatment for their illnesses, no matter what their legal status may be.

But if a defendant truly suffers from MPD, how can you punish one alter and forgive the other? Both resided in the same body and mind at the time of the crime. The answer lies in how multiplicity works. Despite authorities' claims to the contrary, my former alters were not fragments of my birth personality. They were entities, whole in their own rights, who coexisted with my birth personality before I was born. They were not me, but they remain intrinsically related to what it means to be me.

This distinction is explained by levels of awareness. When my birth personality retreated at the age of two, it did not abandon my life. It simply left center stage in my consciousness. And in so doing, it abdicated control of my life and, more particularly, moved beyond the awareness of my alters.

This created a void in which the alters were free to function in my lifetime according to their individual awareness levels. Eve White, for example, was an alter of limited awareness, so she functioned poorly in my life. In contrast, Eve Black functioned with a flair as long as her awareness was dominant in my lifetime. But as the birth personality, I was always alive and, in effect, always waiting in the wings of my life. I was simply not a part of my life's conscious memory or awareness. I existed only in my life's unconscious state. In a sense, for forty-four years I was the dream instead of the dreamer.[7]

Julian Jaynes described how this is possible in his book about the *bicameral mind:* "Consciousness is a much smaller part of our mental life than we are conscious of, because we cannot be conscious of what we are not concious of. How simple that is to say, how difficult to appreciate! It is like asking a flashlight in a dark room to search around for something that does not have any light shining upon it. The flashlight, since there is light in whatever direction it turns, would have to conclude that there is light everywhere. And so consciousness can seem to pervade all mentality when actually it does not. . . ."[8]

Ultimately, however, the responsibility for all my alters' actions lies with me. As the birth personality, I had unconsciously chosen to be beyond awareness or, in Jaynes's terms, beyond the reach of the flashlight's beam within my mind. So I believe that, even though MPD patients are certainly mentally ill, they should not use the insanity defense because their disorder is, in a sense, *a willed negligence of responsibility* for their own lives. Under our legal system, when negligence results in harm to others and when those inflicting the harm know right from wrong, then the negligent person should be held responsible for criminal actions.

Nonetheless, the insanity defense continued to stir heated discussions. At the APA convention in May, Michigan psychiatrist Emanuel Taney, M.D., attempted to put the controversy into perspective. He noted that "less than two percent of criminal defendants who go to court opt for an insanity plea."[9] And beginning that same year, various states implemented a new option for mentally ill defendants. This "guilty but mentally ill" law provides that after a jury decides that a person was legally insane at the time he committed an act, then the person must be treated for his illness until a psychiatrist and the court can certify that the illness has abated. Subsequently, the person must serve the rest of his established sentence in a correctional facility.[10]

This new option conforms with the stance I have taken. It allows a more humane treatment of mentally ill defendants while still assuring sufficient protection from harm for society at large.

One day that spring, I returned from a lecture tour to find Don lying on the living room floor of our Herndon house. It was so uncharacteristic of him to be idle that I believed he had fallen. But when I reached him, I saw that he had a pillow under his head and was resting.

"Are you all right?" I asked, kneeling beside him.

"It just seems like I'm always so tired," he responded in a muffled voice, and soon went back to sleep. I left him to rest, but I was puzzled. This was a workday, and it was unlike Don to come home from work and immediately lie down. When he awakened and came to sit with me in the kitchen, he said, "I stay tired all the time. I don't understand it. I'm doing the same job, and I'm not working any harder. So why don't I feel the way I used to?"

When I finally convinced Don to see our family physician again, the doctor asked him to come every two weeks for blood-pressure checks. Soon a pattern developed where each biweekly test indicated an increase in Don's blood pressure, and each time the doctor increased Don's dosage of Inderal. All the while, Don grew weaker and weaker. It was as though either some unidentified illness or the medication itself were draining every ounce of energy and passion for life that Don had enjoyed, uninterrupted, for decades.

Yet seeing him in such a condition made me realize how much I had depended on his constancy, all through the years. When I was mentally ill, his constancy had ensured my survival. During the integration process, even when his stubbornness had infuriated me, it served as an anchor for my ultimate acceptance of responsibility for my life. And since 1977, the knowledge that he would always be there had enabled me to travel and explore and grow. Simply because he *was* seemingly changeless, I was free to change.

But what now? I was so involved in my work, so committed, that 1982 hardly seemed the time to cut back. During May, I was scheduled to participate for the second time as a faculty member at the American Psychiatric Association's annual convention, to be held in Toronto, Canada. Then I was to spend the remainder of that month on tour in Alabama and Florida on behalf of those states' MHAs. How, with these commitments, could I also remain close to home—particularly when Don refused to accept that something more serious than blood-pressure levels might be his problem? And how was I, at the age of fifty-five, going to pull away from what had become my passion for living? *My work.* I just couldn't.

During the tour for the Mental Health Associations of Florida, I spent a few days on the Gulf Coast with Pam Davis, who, at the time, was that state's director of MHA chapter services. During this break in the tour, she told me that she was spearheading my nomination for the 1982 Clifford W. Beers Award.

Even though I had known little about the award in 1980 when my nomination had not succeeded, I subsequently learned to appreciate both the award and the man for whom it is named. In particular, I felt a spiritual kinship with Beers, who had been the founder of our National Mental Health Association (originally called the National Commission for Mental Hygiene and established in 1909).

The organization was a personal cause for the Connecticut native, his passion. In 1900, three years after his graduation from Yale University, he suffered a mental breakdown. Then he spent three years in psychiatric hospitals, where the methods of treatment that he observed so aroused his concern that he resolved to change them. Following his recovery, he studied his own case, and in 1908 published an autobiography, *The Mind That Found Itself,* which received international attention.[11] Years later, the NMHA established the award in Beers's honor and designated that it be given annually to a former consumer of mental-health services who best fits the image of Clifford Whittingham Beers in efforts to improve conditions for, and attitudes toward, the men-

tally ill.[12] So when Pam explained why she was supporting me for
this prestigious award, I was deeply affected.

"The thing I admire most about the work you're doing, Chris,
is that it's all positive," Pam said. "You do express hope for mental patients. You have asked for better housing for them. You've
asked for their rights to be respected. You've gone to legislatures
and have fought for mental health associations' agendas. Those
are all very positive things, and you didn't have to do them. You
didn't have to go public. You had a husband who could have
supported you. You could have quietly stayed in the background,
remained anonymous as Sybil has, and nobody would have benefited from your experiences."

"I appreciate that, because a lot of people are working on
behalf of mental patients," I said, fighting back tears. "But I had to
do something about them. They've become a part of my reason
for living."

Pam also showed some of the supporting evidence for my
nomination that she had already garnered. Letters of endorsement and newspaper clippings were in stacks, and she said that
all of them expressed accolades for my work. Somehow, I didn't
have the nerve to read them. But just seeing them, I realized that ·
whether I won the award or not, the fact that this many people
believed in me made all the difference in the world.

He was stocky. He wore a brightly colored sports jacket,
slacks, and an open-collared shirt. His head was dominated by a
heavy thatch of reddish-brown hair. And when he first interrupted during a speech I was giving in May for the Montgomery
Mental Health Association, I thought he was drunk. In retrospect,
however, I believe that I reacted to his public criticism because,
in fact, it had never happened to me. Nòt in nearly six years of
working in the public eye.

"Lady," the man said with a slur, during one of the first sessions of my Alabama tour, "I don't believe a damn word you've
said." Then, for about five minutes, our conversation in front of
the audience of about eight hundred persons bounced back and
forth like a Ping-Pong ball. His, hurling jabs and insults. Mine,
attempting to defend my positions.

Finally, he said, "You haven't convinced me a bit. Whatchu gonna do to prove it to me?"

"Nothing," I said. "I didn't come here to prove anything. I am here simply to share my experiences, to give information to others, and, hopefully, to help somebody else."

"Well, I think you're just a *feminist.*"

I considered that for a moment, realized that the man was sober, determined, and—to my surprise—accurate in his last observation. So I said, "If believing that becoming everything you're capable of being—whether you're a man or a woman—makes me a feminist, then, yes, I guess I am."

"And is multiple personality something that only women get?" he asked.

At the time, statistics indicated that about 80 percent of patients who had been diagnosed as suffering from MPD were women, so I told him that fact and noted that most of these women were from the Deep South.

"And how do you account for that?" he asked.

"In part, it's because of the double standards in this region," I responded. "For example, some women in the South still have to get permission from their husbands in order to go out for lunch. Even when her husband knows who she's with. By comparison, how many husbands call home for permission to go to lunch?"

The man's response was even louder than his earlier comments: "Well, there ain't a thing wrong with that. A woman ought to ask her husband if she wants to do something."

I looked at the audience and said, "I rest my case." But the man had unwittingly succeeded in making me acknowledge publicly, for the first time, the debt I owed to the feminist movement. Ironically, the federal Equal Rights Amendment would die two months later.

June 30, 1982, had been the deadline for obtaining a sufficient number of ERA ratifications from state legislatures. But the deadline passed without the amendment having obtained full ratification. Though I had not actively supported the cause, I regretted its demise because I had benefited from the overall efforts of the women's movement. My public career could not have been possible before activists such as the National Organization for Women began asserting the rights of women to be full participants in our society.

*   *   *

In late June, after his fifty-ninth birthday, Don finally agreed to undergo a series of tests at Duke Medical Center. There, Caulie Gunnells, M.D., determined from these tests that Don had been overmedicated for years, which was partially responsible for his hypertension, high cholesterol levels, leg cramps, and an irregular heartbeat. In particular, Dr. Gunnells said that the Inderal had been robbing Don's system of potassium, which had been the primary cause of his exhaustion. So the physician took Don off of Inderal and predicted that, in about six months, my husband's energy level should improve.

But privately, Dr. Gunnells confirmed that Don's having taken Inderal for so many years, often in high dosages, had caused irreversible changes in my husband's body. The doctor said that nothing could restore the losses and that, most likely, my sex life with Don would never be the same.

For weeks I refused to believe that Don and I were aging, that irreparable limitations were becoming a factor in our relationship and in our lives. It all seemed so unfair because, in all of what was then nearly twenty-nine years of our marriage, we had only enjoyed comfort and peacefulness during the last five. Had we not *earned* the right to more?

And this feeling of injustice colored almost everything that happened. For example, that summer a British nonfiction book by Ian Wilson described *I'm Eve* in terms of MPD as being "the best introduction to the condition's myriad of astonishing features." It also summarized my case history and drew upon it favorably when making comparisons to other phenomena of the mind.[13]

But I could take little joy from this, even though it was the first international recognition of my autobiography's contributions. The only personal joy that either Don or I seemed to find that summer came in August, when our son, Bobby, completed his work for a bachelor of arts degree from George Mason University.

Bobby was the first grandchild in our family to get a college degree, but his accomplishment was particularly important to me for another reason. I had missed his birth and those early childhood years when his personality had developed; those had belonged to the Bell Lady. And I had missed most of the earlier milestones of his education; those events had been attended by the Turtle Lady or the Purple Lady. So it was important to me that I was in control of my life when Bobby earned this degree.

"You know that I didn't like *I'm Eve*," Bobby said one night. "But I now see that the book's success made it possible for me to go to college. So I appreciate what you've done, Mom. It hasn't been easy on you. It certainly hasn't been easy on us. But our lives *are* better."

As Bobby left to spend the evening with friends, it was as though a young Don Sizemore had just walked out of the room. Bobby possessed that same inner force, the same quiet manner, and the same independence. Time was bringing forth new strength to replace the former. A son like the father.

During early October, I returned to Augusta, Georgia, for my first public appearance there since leaving in the fifties. And I dreaded it. This was where my life as Eve had been most painful. But Richard E. "Dick" Hitt had insisted on this stop in the tour that he, as the executive director of the Georgia Mental Health Association, had planned to benefit various MHA chapters across the state.

Though I was warmly received by large audiences throughout Georgia, I felt uneasy on the morning of my lecture in Augusta. I changed clothes three or four times. I just wasn't sure how this city was going to accept me. This was Dr. Thigpen's territory. He was still practicing in the city; we had not spoken in years; and he reportedly maintained an authoritative role in the area's mental-health and psychiatric communities. My greatest fear was that the lecture would be boycotted. After all, Augustans had solidly rejected me in the fifties, and I had no reason to believe that anything had changed during the intervening years.

"So, Chris, how do you feel about coming home?" Dick Hitt asked when he picked me up at the hotel.

"Nervous as a cat," I said, "which is the way *you'll* feel when nobody shows up."

"They'll be there," he said. And when we arrived at the Augusta motel, he was right. A crowd was gathered on the lawn, and huge speakers had been erected for them to hear because, inside, the banquet room was already full after having been opened to double capacity. There were so many people that a third, separate area had to be set aside for the extraordinary number of media representatives who were there.

The scene was more like the set of *This Is Your Life* than a typical lecture. My twin sisters, Becky and Tiny, had been invited, and greeted me with hugs at the entrance. And there were other people who had been in Augusta during those early years of my psychiatric care—including a woman whom I will call Mrs. Anderson. She had been the ward nurse who had taken walks with Eve White and had played cards with Eve Black.

"I was privileged to be part of psychiatric history that was made here in Augusta," Mrs. Anderson said when introducing me to the audience. "I knew Chris when she did not know herself very well. I loved her then, and it is an honor to be welcoming her back."

I began my address with an opening statement: "I left twenty years ago a sick woman. But I return today as a well person." As soon as I said these words, the entire audience interrupted with solid, resounding applause. And the shock of it, the sudden reassurance of it, seemed to lift away decades of anguish that I had associated with Augusta. It also helped to ease the disappointment that, even though they had been invited, Drs. Thigpen and Cleckley were noticeably absent.

Afterward, I visited the Partridge Inn and the Bon-Air Hotel, both located on Walton Way. Eve White had been a telephone operator in the hotel, and in the evenings Eve Black used to frequent that inn and listen to an organist who played classical music in the lounge. As I walked through these buildings, I could picture my former alters enjoying their youthful days here, and the experience made me understand their feelings more than ever. But time had stolen the charm from these buildings. They were in worn condition, and the Bon-Air had been converted into a home for senior citizens.

When we reached University Hospital, where I had been hospitalized in the fifties, the white-columned, brick building had been boarded up and was overshadowed by the new Talmadge Hospital complex nearby. But seeing the old facility was like visiting a homeplace that had fallen into disrepair. That hospital had been "home" to my first healing processes; yet time had been better to me than to it.

Then we rode along Broad Street where J. B. White's and Davidson's were still in business. Eve White had been a clerk at both department stores until Eve Black's escapades cost them those jobs. And the marquee of the Miller Theatre still jutted out above the sidewalk, just as it had when its placards announced the world premiere of Joanne Woodward's movie.

At the end of the tour, I felt satisfied. Overall, downtown Augusta did not appear to have changed that much. It was as though the city remained nearly as locked in time as my inherited memories of my alters' lives there. For me, then, revisiting was like encountering ghosts of another era, people from a time outside of my own, yet people who were also very familiar to me and places for which I held intimate feelings. This had been Don and Jane's town. But in some ironic and yet comforting way, going back had made it mine as well.

Heading out of town, we also passed Dr. Thigpen's office. It was a substantial brick building. His name was on a sign in the front. But it had not been the building where my alters first went in the fifties. Time had been better to him, too, and my Eves had played no small part in that.

That same month, *Psychology Today* published startling news about MPD. Neuroscientific evidence seemed to prove that alters are not merely "metaphors" in the minds of the disorder's sufferers. Indeed, as I had believed all along, alters are distinct, unto themselves. Entities, in a sense. Or as the researcher, Frank W. Putnam, M.D., explained:

> The notion of multiple personalities was always more readily accepted in popular books and movies—*The Three Faces of Eve* and *Sybil,* for example—than it was by psychiatrists and other doctors. Now, however, there is a strong indication that two or more separate personalities can exist within one brain and one body, alternating in response to environmental clues and stresses.
>
> At the National Institute of Mental Health, we have discovered brain-wave patterns for each of the personalities of

people who display [MPD]. We use a technique that combines electroencephalograms and computers to measure averaged evoked potentials (EPs)—brain-wave activity produced in response to specific stimuli such as flashes of light. . . . We studied ten people, each of whom had at least three distinct identities, [and we examined] each identity on five separate days to determine the stability of its EP over a period of time.

As a further test, every individual with MPD was matched to a control person of the same age and sex. These controls deliberately created and rehearsed imaginary alternate personalities, who were then tested in exactly the same fashion as . . . the MPD subjects. We wanted to see whether the control subjects could change their EPs simply by pretending to be someone else.

They couldn't. Whomever they pretended to be, their EPs were virtually identical. In contrast, the alternate personalities of the people suffering from MPD showed significant differences in their averaged EPs. This indicates that alternate personalities are not merely an elaborate act but are actual shifts in personality accompanied by significant changes in brain activity. These changes further suggest that the various personalities may process sensory information in different ways.[14]

Though Putnam's findings were initially received with minimal fanfare and subsequently questioned by other authorities, they were vital. To me, this discovery would ultimately do more, in terms of public opinion, to confirm the validity of MPD than had *DSM-III's* earlier recognition of MPD as a disorder. Data from EEGs and computers meshed with the mentality of the eighties in ways that a clinician's manual never could.

But there was an irony in this landmark news from NIMH. Earlier in the year, the Reagan administration's budget director at the time, David Stockman, had spearheaded cuts that reduced by about 18 percent the federal government's funding for the Alcohol, Drug Abuse and Mental Health Administration. Since NIMH was a subsidiary agency of the ADA/MHA, these federal cuts threatened to hinder MPD research at the very moment it was experiencing breakthroughs.

I was furious. And the Associated Press would quote me as saying that cutting research monies for studies in mental illness while sustaining funding for research into physical illnesses such as cancer represented a perpetuation by President Reagan of the stigma against mental illness and an unrealistic perspective on life in America. "I don't care how physically healthy you are," one reprint of the AP article would quote me as saying, "if you're not mentally healthy you cannot have a good quality of life."[15]

When my tour reached Atlanta, where I was to speak at the Colony Square Hotel, I met with George B. Greaves, Ph.D., who was to become one of the foremost MPD authorities in the South. We discussed the impact of the federal cuts on NIMH researchers and the more general problem that there was no central means for supporting the study of MPD.

Dr. Greaves said he was working on a plan to establish a society to support such work and asked if I would help. I agreed, and during the remainder of 1982 and throughout the following year, I spent a lot of time compiling names and addresses of doctors, therapists, and other mental-health professionals who could benefit such a society. At my various public appearances, I also promoted the concept of a society devoted exclusively to MPD, and encouraged professionals to support Dr. Greaves's plan.

Five months later, this group would be formally organized in March 1983 as the International Society for the Study of Multiple Personality and Dissociation. Dr. Greaves would be recognized as founder of the ISSMP&D, and I would serve as one of eleven members on the society's first steering committee.[16] It would be an important step. Until then, no psychiatric group had committed itself to a serious program of research, publication, and public information about the disorder. Its time was long overdue.

"Chris Sizemore is the only artist in the world who can give a seven-woman art show all by herself." This enigmatic but evocative line was the lead to a feature in *The Washingtonian,* which prefigured a monthlong exhibit of my art at the National Mental Health Association's headquarters, then located in Arlington, Virginia.[17]. But as prestigious as the event was, it was still a prelude. Later in November, at the NMHA national convention, I was to receive the 1982 Clifford W. Beers Award.

Actually, Dick Hitt had defied decorum in October and, in the puckish manner that makes him likable, had leaked this news to the press when I was in Augusta. So when the NMHA subsequently told me that I had won, it was not a surprise. However, the *experience* of the art exhibit at NMHA headquarters was. At the gala reception in November while NMHA leaders from across the country were congratulating me and admiring my paintings, thoughts raced through my mind. And they were thoughts of solid conviction and resolve that I had never before allowed myself to say aloud: *At last I am no longer stigmatized by mental illness. Not because the stigma no longer exists. But because I refuse to let people ascribe that stigma to my life. I simply won't allow it. And the time has come for mental patients across this nation to declare the same to the world and to their families. The message is simple. In spite of their illnesses, the mentally ill are okay. They need no pity. And they don't want sympathy. All that most mentally ill persons want is the opportunity to receive quality psychiatric care and to be considered a human being with a problem.*

Five years earlier, I had thought I was strong enough to take this stand. I had wanted my autobiography to be entitled *I'm Chris,* emphasizing that I was no longer the Eves who had been associated with mental illness for so long. But I wasn't that strong in the seventies. And through the promotion of that book and the early years of my career, I was totally dependent on having been the famous Eves. Why else, I wondered, would anyone come to hear me speak? Why else would they buy my paintings? In effect, then, I had carried society's stigma of mental illness as my calling card. While fighting that stigma, I had been unwittingly perpetuating it by the very means through which I was working.

But at the NMHA reception, people seemed more interested in *my* paintings than in any that my alters had created. And people were congratulating me on the award I was to receive. Not because I had been the famous MPD patient. Nor because I had recovered from the disorder and had written a book about the ordeal. But simply because of the work that I had done since 1977. Work that none of my former alters could have accomplished. Work that only *I* could have done.

At one point during the reception, I slipped away from the crowd and walked to the historic mental-health bell. This NMHA emblem—which remains on display in the national headquarters and is moved only once each year to be rung at the national convention—had been forged from shackles, chains, and other restraints once used in mental institutions. I read its inscription: "Cast from shackles which bound them, this bell shall ring out hope for the mentally ill and victory over mental illness." Then I stood in silence. I was one for whom the tolling of the bell had real meaning. My shackles had now been forged into hope, too.

Though I invited all of my family to the award's presentation ceremony in Dearborn, Michigan, no one agreed to go. My sisters, who had seemed to enjoy the events in Augusta, said they couldn't make another trip so soon. Elen, my cousin and coauthor of *I'm Eve*, had also declined. Don had not fully recovered from the aftereffects of overmedication. Bobby was in his first semester of graduate school and had exams. And Taffy's children were in school, so she said she probably couldn't go.

So I went alone to receive the most important recognition of my life, and that depressed me. Why, I wondered, did my family not want to be part of the good times, when they had not abandoned me during mental illness and all the miserable times? But when I arrived at the hotel in Dearborn on November 11, there was an excitement—other people's excitement for me—that seemed to permeate the entire convention. Everybody I met seemed to share it. Their comments were more than polite. It was as if they were as thrilled as I was that I would be receiving their award.

"You're probably the only person who has ever received this honor whom three-fourths of the people at the convention already know," said Dick Hitt. "And we already know how much you've done to earn it. Most of the other recipients—though they certainly deserved the award—were not individuals known by MHA members across the country. But everybody knows you, Chris, and everybody here knows what you've accomplished by working in our towns and lecturing to benefit our chapters." Then Dick smiled and gave me one of his winks. "You're *our* winner," he said, "and that's what all the excitement is about."

That night, I struggled to get to sleep in my hotel room. Dick's words kept running through my mind. As did faces from the convention corridors. And their words of congratulations. Then, about 2:00 A.M., not long after I had finally fallen asleep, the telephone rang in that jolting manner that late-night calls do. I sat straight up in the bed and grabbed the receiver. Had something happened to Don? A heart attack? When I answered it, and Taffy said, "Hello, Mom," the sound of her voice convinced me even more that there was trouble.

"What's wrong?"

"Nothing's wrong," she said. "We just arrived at the hotel, and I'm calling from the lobby."

Immediately, my eyes gave way to a flood of tears and my voice faltered. This was the same daughter who, only a few years earlier, had accepted my well personality with some misgivings. But in driving half the night from Virginia to Michigan, she was saying, "All that's behind us, Mom." She was expressing love for *me*, woman to woman, daughter to mother.

The next afternoon, Taffy helped me dress prior to the awards banquet. It was another moment of reversed roles in our lives, her mothering me as if I were the daughter and a bride getting ready for a wedding. She helped me select a navy dress with a pleated shawl, and she loaned me a pair of rhinestone earrings for good luck. I practiced my acceptance speech on her so many times that she could have done it herself.

Then, just before I left, Taffy put her arms around me, hugged me, and said, "You'll never know how proud I am of you." Bolstered by her love and primping, I felt very attractive as I walked along the corridor toward the elevator.

Downstairs, there must have been six hundred people in the banquet hall. Minutes later on the dais, I looked out over the audience and recognized face after face of persons with whom I had worked over the years. *This is the main difference between multiplicity and normalcy,* I suddenly reflected. *When I was an MPD patient, other people found places only in my mind. But now that I'm a well person, other people have found places in my heart.*

Having practiced my speech well, I probably said most of it from the podium. But I cannot be certain about what I did say, because I cried throughout the speech. And scores of people in the audience were crying, too. However, I do remember telling my fellow workers in the field of mental health, "You are sharing the most momentous event of my whole life. You are sharing the greatest honor that I shall ever know. I did not win this award. You allowed me to receive it."

At that point, I looked at the four members of my family who were there: Taffy, Tommy, Jimmy, and Christi. Their eyes were shining, their faces glowing with love and pride. *They don't belong down there,* I suddenly thought. *They belong up here.* So I asked them to join me onstage. I wanted everyone to see the loving family. The children who never gave up on their mentally ill mother.

When they had gathered around me—Taffy placing her arm about my shoulders the way she had done the day when I first emerged in Dr. Tsitos's office—I told the audience, "Many times these dear ones helped me up when I could not stand alone. So this is their honor, too." Then I turned and handed the award to my son-in-law.

When I faced the audience once again, I said, "This award means that I will never stand alone again, telling the world that mental illness is nothing to be ashamed of. This award means that you stand beside me, too. That you support my view that mental illness is to be expected. That it is treatable. That it is curable. And that the most important thing we can ever do for another is to reach out and touch their lives when they are hurting. But God help us all if the time comes that we no longer care."

At that point, the audience interrupted me with a fervent, uplifting applause. It was ethereal. Like the Good Little Girl being baptized as a child. Or the Freckle Girl feeding Taffy for the first time. Or Jane having a minister say, "I now pronounce you man and wife." Or the Bell Lady hearing Bobby say his first word. The feeling at that instant in Dearborn was like all of those glorious moments wrapped into one. Except: This one was mine.

But in spite of my honor, the stigma had not really diminished. Just a month before I received the award, the results of a California poll had indicated that 60 percent of those interviewed would not vote for someone who had undergone psychotherapy. Had we learned nothing from the shameful treatment of U.S. Senator Thomas Eagleton, ten years earlier, during the fiasco that resulted in his name being withdrawn as the Democratic nominee for the vice-presidency?

"Sizemore said she was astonished," a California reporter would quote me as reacting to the poll's results. "'That shows a lack of understanding about what mental illness really is,' she said. 'One in seven people will undergo therapy this year. That is your average, everyday American.'"[18]

PART III

Everyone May Have Multiple Selves

T hough the Clifford W. Beers Award recognized my work as a spokesperson on behalf of mental patients, it was becoming increasingly clear that I didn't speak for *all* mentally ill persons. Not even all MPD patients. And this was particularly the case for patients who refused to integrate. Before July 1974, many of my alters had resisted unification, or the first stage of integration. Most notable among these was Eve Black. Yet they resisted because they mistakenly viewed becoming one person as death. I now understand their fears and resistance. But only with hindsight. And going into 1983, hindsight was a perspective rare to MPD studies and treatment in America.

The clinical focus at the time was almost exclusively on the disorder itself—countered by an emerging controversy over unification and, ultimately, integration. The reasons were obvious. Most clinicians were either diagnosing MPD or guiding MPD patients toward unification for the first time in their psychiatric careers. The vast majority, then, were in the fascinating stage of MPD treatment when the disorder seems almost as hypnotic for the therapist as it is for the patient.

Following the patient's unification, however, many clinicians and patients were asking what Dr. Tsitos and I had pondered nearly a decade earlier: *Where do we go from here?* The road map leading toward integration, or the means for successfully enabling an MPD patient to remain one person, had still not been published. In addition, clinicians and patients were discovering, as I already had, that the subsequent journey to wholeness is anything but fascinating.

"Maybe we're being sold a bill of goods by therapists," one MPD patient said in December 1982. "There's always a drop in creativity and energy when you fuse. But I'm too productive to stop doing what I'm doing. I'd rather keep two or three personalities."[1]

This woman, whom the Gannett News Service called Judy, claimed twenty-seven alters. But unlike my case history of MPD, Judy described her multiplicity as a *consistently* productive state. Among other accomplishments, she had earned a six-year Harvard degree in half the normal time.[2] Seemingly, then, she had harnessed the collective abilities and energies of her alters into a highly functional existence.

Nor was Judy an isolated example. Prior to 1983, Los Angeles psychologist Susan Kuhner had opened the Kuhner Institute for Multiple Personality with the expressed purpose of helping "multiples who don't want to fuse." She reportedly set out "to convince the outside world to accept multiplicity rather than mold it to the one-personality standard."[3] Within a year, however, the institute closed when it could not support its theories. Nonetheless, even stronger arguments for this view would come four years later in a highly controversial book, *When Rabbit Howls.*

My first encounter with that book's author, Truddi Chase, came following a lecture I gave at the University of Maryland in March 1983. At the time, I did not know the attractive red-haired woman. She seemed to be just like the other audience members who stood to ask questions. But when her turn came, she said in a whimsical, almost defiant tone, "Two, four, six, eight. I don't wanna integrate,"[4] and then waited for my response.

Though I intended to show respect for her right to differ with my opinions, I bristled. I felt a personal attack in her words because my speech had summarized over two decades of personal struggles in therapy to achieve integration. Yet her chant seemed to mock all that I had achieved and, for the previous six years, had been publicly advocating.

"Without that goal, the patient does not have a commitment to get well," I responded, more harshly than is my habit. "Such patients are really not thinking about anyone but themselves. Because if you care about your family and the people who love you, then you will *not* want to remain mentally ill."

Afterward, I realized that Truddi Chase had been the first person in my experience to assert, face to face, that *not* integrating might be a viable option for MPD patients. But more than that, I would learn from her book that the causes and traumas she had endured during childhood were radically different from mine. Like Sybil, Truddi had been sexually, physically, and emotionally abused by her parents. In contrast, I had suffered no such abuse. But as a result of the horrible conditions in Truddi's life, she was left with over ninety alters—so many, in fact, that the byline of her book would be not a single name but "The Troops for Truddi Chase."

Alongside the controversy over some MPD patients' refusal to accept unification, then, it was also becoming clear that my childhood experiences leading to multiplicity had not been typical. In fact, very few MPD patients develop the disorder as the result of psychological traumas such as my encounters with death and injury. Instead, according to surveys conducted in the early eighties by Dr. Putnam, over 80 percent of MPD patients are victims between the ages of two and five of repeated and severe sexual and physical abuse. And such childhood abuse usually extends over long periods of time beyond childhood.[5]

Consequently, this encounter with Truddi Chase and the growing evidence about childhood abuse in MPD cases led me to do a lot of reevaluating. Yes, integration had been right for me and my family. And, yes, without both unification and integration, an MPD patient could never truly say, "I am well." But were unification and integration what *every* MPD patient needed? Or had the healing process developed a myth of its own, implying that one size fits all, when MPD actually seemed to affect each patient differently?

As *When Rabbit Howls* would argue, "Your clues, the only two you need, are the amnesia and the headaches which resemble migraines. Forget the manner in which the persons emerge or the overall operating pattern. [MPD patients] as a rule have got their own individual patterns, and survival is uppermost in their minds. . . . These people are the survivors. If the world blew up tomorrow, guess who'd walk out of the rubble? Unless, of course, they commit suicide first, and nobody has those statistics."[6]

Related to childhood abuse, another long-held assumption about MPD came under scrutiny in 1983. For decades, dating back to Morton Prince's publication of findings in 1905,[7] through the fifties when Drs. Thigpen and Cleckley treated my alters, and into the 1980 publication of *DSM-III*, all authorities seemed to believe that cases of MPD were extremely rare. While that assumption obviously contributed to both public and professional interest in my case, it also affected my self-image. Even as a healthy person, I felt as though I and other well-known MPD victims were somehow set apart, peculiar, one-of-a-kind persons.

Then, in April, I boarded an airplane en route to a speaking engagement. Once the flight was under way, I reached into the seat compartment and pulled out the airline's complimentary magazine. Flipping through its pages, I was surprised by an article's subtitle that stated, "Cases of multiple personality, such as the one portrayed in the movie 'The Three Faces of Eve,' have been thought to be quite rare. [But] some California researchers are challenging this assumption."[8]

The article quoted Donald Schafer, M.D., a psychiatrist at the University of California, Irvine, Medical Center, as saying, "From where I sit, multiples are coming out of the woodwork. Our group of ten to fifteen mental-health professionals is treating fifty multiples, and the rate at which they are being identified implies there are another fifty diagnosable multiples in Orange County, which has a population of two million. On the basis of that, we conservatively estimate there are fifty cases of multiple personality per million of population nationwide."[9]

I quickly calculated that Dr. Schafer was projecting significantly more than ten thousand MPD victims in America. How could that be possible? At the most recent MPD conferences where I had been a participant, the highest projections by the best authorities had established no more than 160 MPD patients, nationwide, since the illness was first reported.[10] Yet I also had to admit that an increasing number of MPD patients seemed to be coming to my attention. More therapists were showing interest in the disorder and indicating that, to their surprise, they were also diagnosing more MPD patients.

Even though Dr. Schafer's projections would be discredited by most professionals, including Drs. Thigpen and Cleckley,[11] his work served a useful purpose. Like the controversies over integration and the linkage of MPD to childhood abuse, Dr. Schafer's projections were a harbinger: MPD was becoming a disorder that society could no longer ignore. And motivated by these controversies, I ventured into a new aspect of mental-health work during that spring. Clinicians began asking me to serve as a consultant during their treatment of MPD patients. And I accepted.

In April, a Virginia therapist asked me to visit one of his patients in the hospital. He said he had diagnosed her as suffering MPD but noted that she was also suicidal. My consultancy, he believed, might help the patient understand reasons for her to live and to get well, because he knew that several of my former alters had also attempted suicide.

But I accepted this case because I also understood why suicide was an inevitable choice in many MPD patients' lives. Most of their alters are fragile entities. Inexplicably given existence in a life that does not belong to them, alters initially delight in being "out," being in control. But, gradually, most are faced with the reality that, as alters rather than as the birth personality, they are locked in time. For example, only one of my alters ever aged, ever matured in any significant way, and that was Jane. But she was an alter created, in part, by Dr. Thigpen's manipulative use of hypnosis. In contrast, my other alters remained locked in their time frames whether their existence in my body lasted six months or six years. So, once my alters realized that they had no real future or that, individually, they possessed no past of any consequence, for some, suicide attempts became inevitable.

Armed with this personal understanding, then, I visited with the MPD patient whom I will call Kate. Not long into that first dialogue, I was convinced that the therapist's diagnosis was correct. She seemed mercurial and suicidal. But there was more: A couple of her alters were the most violent personality types that I had encountered in any MPD patient.

"When I was a child, I killed animals and skinned them," one of her alters said during that first session in the hospital ward. Then she proceeded to detail with a certain relish how she had repeatedly inflicted violence, pain, and death on small animals. At the end, she added, "And it wasn't sport. It was my childhood pleasure." Then the woman's eyes flashed a sudden disdain for me, and she said, "I'll bet the very idea of that makes you sick."

I did not respond. I could see that she enjoyed telling this. And she, or another alter, would subsequently tell this same story every time we met. Though we would talk at length during each session, her resentment toward me gradually increased. One day she blurted out, "You must really think you're somebody. You got well. But the rest of us haven't. I'm certainly not well, and that's not fair."

Thereafter, Kate's alters vacillated between direct, unyielding resistance to my efforts and a clinging dependency on me. Some of them sent small gifts and notes confirming how good our visits were for her. Others would lambaste me, be derisive and verbally abusive. Though I understood that such a mixture of reactions was typical at various stages of MPD, I was personally unprepared to cope with Kate's violent moods. Previously, I had only talked by telephone with a few MPD patients or met with them in the protected environments of lecture halls or other public places. None of them had been violent in my presence, and my involvement with them had been buffered by the circumstances.

But working with Kate, I was on a psych ward. I was not shielded by the blindness of telephones. I was face to face with a patient whose symptoms were of a type that I had only read about. And though I empathized with her suffering, I could see little resemblance to the types of personalities my alters had been. Gradually, however, I realized a crucial aspect of MPD treatment from working with her and seven other patients that year. Role models, which became so important to me *after* unification, are not always helpful to patients in the midst of multiplicity. They already have in their minds all the "people" they need. So my function as a consultant was not to develop a relationship of role model to patient. Instead, my function was to empathize and, within the bond of that empathy, to offer hope.

About two years later, Kate did experience unification, and her psychiatrist was ultimately successful through follow-up therapy in diminishing Kate's violent behavior. Her suicidal tendencies never went beyond the stage of threats. In fact, despite the violent, criminal aspects of MPD described in *The Minds of Billy Milligan,*[12] only a small percentage of MPD patients bring harm to anyone other than themselves. But, as I would discover later in the year, self-inflicted harm can be horrible.

When you become involved in an MPD patient's life, you also begin communication with that patient's alters. So it is not uncommon to have all the alters telephone you, one after another. Or for many alters to write separate letters and seek individual appointments, even though all of them basically discuss the same problems. In some ways, I soon realized, it had been easier being the patient, because I found myself interacting that spring with not only eight patients but also nearly ten times that many "voices" and "personalities" among their alters. Just keeping all the names straight was a herculean task.

What's more, even with my best efforts and counsel, I couldn't fix everybody's lives. A few of these MPD patients seemed unalterably locked within their disorder. Their childhood abuses had been too severe and had lasted too long, some into the teenage years. And the sheer numbers of their alters complicated their existences. Even though I had never coexisted with more than four alters at a time, some of these patients, like Sybil, coexisted with many, many more. So I had to face the prospect that, with some, nothing I could do would help them reach unification, much less integration.

As a result, consultancy added more strain on my time than I had anticipated. Admittedly, I knew that time is a meaningless concept to MPD alters. But I had not experienced the impact of that timelessness on normalcy until I began consulting. Suddenly, it was not uncommon to receive telephone calls in the middle of the night or on holidays. Alters who might not have been "out" for weeks or months would surface in the patients with whom I was working; these alters would quickly discover that *I* was involved in their treatment; and their first impulse was to get in touch. So my consulting became a twenty-four-hour-a-day, seven-day-a-week endeavor.

And my prior commitments made no allowances. In May I was scheduled to speak in Canada, then to launch a monthlong exhibition of my art at La Galleria in San Mateo, California. Thereafter, I was to speak on behalf of mental-health associations in Tulsa, Oklahoma City, and St. Louis, then to return to Georgia for a second statewide tour. Consequently, nowhere that spring was there time *just . . . for . . . Chris.*

And I needed to devote some time exclusively to being myself. On lecture tours since 1977, I had been center stage so much that it was once again becoming diff-cult for me to relax. And never was there a time on tour when I could simply say that my feet were hurting or that I would rather be wearing blue jeans or that my teeth felt dirty and I needed to go brush them. I had to be whatever it was that I was being paid to be. I couldn't just be myself.

It was as though I had to prove something. Particularly since receiving the Clifford W. Beers Award. And the reason was ironic. The prestige of that award had actually left me feeling unworthy. Instead of believing that the award had crowned my labors, its ultimate impact was a compulsion to justify what I had already accomplished. Yet I had no idea how to prove myself deserving. And consultancy was proving more difficult than I had imagined. From the start, I felt like a failure. It just didn't seem possible, having been such a vital part of my own healing, that I could not help others heal faster and more easily than I had been healed.

So I began to wonder: Had the magic gone out of my life?

Addressing the Art Therapists Psychological Institute of Washington, D.C., in June, I discovered from them the beneficial ways in which art was beginning to be used as an adjunctive treatment for mental patients. During my years of psychoanalysis, art therapy had not been part of my clinical treatment. In fact, Dr. Tsitos did not see my paintings until after the unification. Nonetheless, my mind had intuited the healing powers of its talents and had used both painting and writing as aids to help me get well. But I learned from the ATPI that art therapy was particularly helpful with MPD patients because creativity and multiplicity go hand in hand. And painting seemed to be a talent particularly linked to MPD patients' abilities to remember in pictorial form, as had already been demonstrated by paintings done by Sybil, Billy Milligan, and me.

Coincidentally, an art therapist interviewed me and carefully analyzed my collection of paintings that same month. The woman, Iona Deering, subsequently wrote her observations: "As a small child there was a physical space . . . where she could be immune from negativity. [It was] a sacred space where she felt loved. She now resides in that space, and she has expanded that space to include the whole world. This is not to say that she has regressed . . . to that child in the attic; this is to say that she always had that space within herself. Her positive myth now governs her, and she presents this to us visually in her Attic Child [series]."[13]

I was intrigued. Not only by what this observer, using Jungian concepts, had discovered about the therapeutic nature of my work. But also by what she found to be unique in the "Attic Child" paintings I had been doing since early 1983. As her dissertation explained, "The most recent painting, 'Riding the Unicorn,' shows the child galloping off on a unicorn. . . . The unicorn is a mythic animal with head and forelegs of a horse, the tail of a lion, and one horn on its head. *[But] she has created her own special unicorn,* making it a white horse with a horn. Animals, especially horses, are symbolic of aggressive feelings, and white horses are magical; so she is presenting a magical symbol of her emotive and motive powers."[14]

And she was right. I identified with this legendary creature, even though I could find no evidence to confirm whether or not the unicorn had actually existed. Yet that only served to increase my empathy for the lonesome, one-horned being. Somehow, creating my own style of unicorns and painting them in action with the attic child seemed to fill the gap within me. In a sense, I was creating on canvas a magic that I felt ebbing from my life, and a uniqueness to replace what had made me legendary in the first place.

Interestingly enough, my family and friends seemed to recognize what was happening in me, and they responded by giving unicorn objects to me. Bobby gave a daybook with unicorn art displayed throughout each month's pages. Taffy gave a bell ornamented with a unicorn. And friends began sending unicorn knickknacks. It was as if the persons closest to me had sensed the subtle changes that were only being expressed in my art.

Art, then, was still functioning therapeutically in my life. And this realization motivated me to explore art therapy on a deeper level. So, the following month, I met at Duke University with Irving Alexander, Ph.D. He was a psychologist who taught and held the chair in that department, but he was also a registered and certified art therapist. When I had telephoned to arrange for this meeting, he asked that I bring a collection of paintings that included one done by each of my former alters.

In his office that day, Dr. Alexander was very methodical in his approach. He asked that I turn the paintings so that they faced the wall, then he suggested that my friend and I go to lunch to allow him time and privacy in which to consider the works.

When we returned a few hours later, Dr. Alexander seemed perplexed. "I had been prepared to see different scenes, different paintings," he explained, "but I was not prepared to see the work of seven different people." He went on to observe that the techniques and the brush strokes were very different, comparing one painting to another. Then he offered some specific comments about the works. The following is a sample of what he observed:

About the Bell Lady's painting "Splitting": "It indicates she believed that she was born with this disorder and would die with it, because the two strong lines at the top and bottom of the painting indicate an unalterable pattern." The Bell Lady was right-handed.

About the Card Girl's painting "Eve's Inferno": "She was very much aware of her alters because of the three trees that are starkly centered in the painting. And I see a lot of pain and fear expressed by the reds in her work." The Card Girl was left-handed.

About the Retrace Lady's painting "Journey into Darkness": "The use of disembodied eyes indicates psychosis." But all multiples use eyes symbolically in their paintings, I have learned.

Leaving Duke University that afternoon, I felt as though a new avenue of work and creative challenges had been opened up for me. I could use art-therapy techniques to study the *Eve* collection and glean from it insights to benefit both myself as a painter and the MPD patients with whom I was consulting. My source of private joy could become a solid tool in my public career.

*   *   *

And my private life needed joy. Earlier in 1983, I had begun having dreams about Mamie Lee Sain, my mother's sister and the aunt I considered my second mother. At the time, she was seventy-three years old, and in early February she had been hospitalized for surgery to replace a valve in her heart. One of her daughters, Elen, had coauthored *I'm Eve* with me. So Aunt Mamie Lee was special in my life. Along with my other aunt, Elise Weaghington, the two were the oldest surviving women of their generation in our family.

In these recurring dreams, I could see Aunt Mamie Lee going down through a green meadow surrounded by hills and stands of trees. She wore a white voile dress, with points along the hem. Her hair was gathered in a ball on her head but slanted along the side in a style fashionable in the early twenties.

She seemed to float through the tall grass toward a narrow creek that ran through the middle of the pasture. On the opposite bank stood my father and mother, Acie and Zueline Costner, and Aunt Mamie Lee's husband, Uncle Ellis. Like her, they appeared to be young again and dressed in Gay Twenties styles. My father's hair was black, thick, and parted in the middle. My mother wore a long-waisted dress with an embroidered hem. and her hair was pulled back over her ears. All four looked the way they had in family pictures taken before I was born.

And in each dream, as my aunt approached the creek, the three on the other side were laughing and smiling. Theirs were innocent, youthful, inviting expressions, and each time my aunt responded by floating across the creek to join them. But at the moment my aunt touched down on the opposite bank beside my mother, I would always awaken. After the third or fourth of these vivid, full-color dreams, I became convinced that these were premonitions of death. Our three other relatives in the dreams were already dead.

Aunt Mamie Lee did survive her surgery in February, but she did not get better. Another surgery was required a week later, and for the next two months her condition grew progressively worse. She suffered more surgeries and more pain until nothing the doctors could do seemed to make a difference. She died on May 13. A month later, Aunt Elise died.

Their passings were deep personal losses, like losing my own mother a second time. But unlike my mother, who died long before I emerged from the unification, Aunt Mamie Lee and Aunt Elise had known me as a whole person, an integrated personality. So we had shared something as women that I had not been allowed with my mother. My aunts knew *me*, but my mother never did.

On Christmas Eve, my family had just arrived at our home in Herndon and were unloading their gifts when the telephone rang. Immediately, I recognized the caller's voice as that of a woman whom I will call Tara Sue. She was an MPD patient from North Carolina, and I had been consulting in her case for several months.

"I'm committing suicide," she said calmly, "slashing my wrists."

This was not the first time that Tara Sue had called to say she was putting an end to her life. Wealthy and aristocratic, she was a strong-willed woman whose alters consistently resisted help from the clinician. But Tara Sue's threats had become so repetitive that I had, much earlier in my consultancy, confirmed with her therapist and with Dr. Tsitos exactly how I should respond to such threats. So I took Tara Sue's statements in this telephone conversation to be sincere. She was contemplating the act.

Initially, I attempted to keep Tara Sue talking by asking her to describe what she was going to do to herself.

"Don't you know what 'slash' means?" she responded as if agitated.

I knew what she meant. I had seen the results of self-mutilation on her wrists and on the bodies of other MPD patients, but her therapist had advised that generally such self-inflicted wounds were not life-threatening. Most authorities agree, and indicate that when MPD patients mutilate their bodies by cutting, it usually mirrors some form of abuse by cutting that someone else had inflicted upon the patient as a child. The general pattern is that a parent first uses a knife to punish a child. Then, when the child has become an adult, he or she associates guilt with punishment by cutting and somehow translates that memory into self-mutilation.

But when I told Tara Sue that I understood, she said, "Oh, no. This is different. This will get the job done."

I sensed no urgency in her voice, so I attempted to change the subject. I asked about the gifts she would be giving her son and husband on Christmas Day. About the decorations she had put up that year. And about the meal she planned for that evening. Tara Sue readily discussed the holiday activities as if she were not locked away in her bedroom and contemplating suicide. There was still no trace of anxiety in her voice.

"Well, I'm sure you'll want to see the pleasure on your son's face when he opens his gifts," I said.

"No," Tara Sue said, the conversation's original darkness returning to her voice. "Nobody can get in here, and I'm never going back out alive."

"Don't you think it will hurt your son, if something were to happen to you?"

There was a silence on the line. Then she said, "It's already too late. I'm bleeding all over the floor."

I suddenly realized that she had not called in anticipation of committing suicide. The act had been done. Instead of self-mutilation, this woman had probably severed a major artery or vein.

"Is your husband there?" I asked, struggling to remain calm.

"Yes."

"Then may I speak with him?"

"No."

"Well, why don't you hang up and just let me call him? That way you won't have to tell him what's happened. I can do that for you."

"You can hang up, but I won't," Tara Sue said. "This one's for real."

I immediately hung up my phone and switched to another line. When I dialed Tara Sue's number, I heard a busy signal. Next I telephoned her therapist. He handled the crisis from there, calling the police and then meeting them at Tara Sue's home. The authorities had to break down her bedroom door and rush her to the hospital. So Tara Sue did not die that Christmas Eve. And after physicians had her stabilized in the hospital, her husband telephoned me. His voice sounded exhausted, hollow, but still compassionate as he thanked me for helping to save his wife's life.

When I hung up the phone, I glanced into our living room. Don, the children, and the grandchildren were laughing, telling stories, and arranging the gifts to be opened. I remembered that just days before, Don and I had celebrated our thirtieth wedding anniversary. But none of this would be happening had he and Taffy not intervened for my alters years before. Like Tara Sue's bewildered alters, mine could not have saved themselves without a family's relentless, ever-forgiving love.

I had learned during 1983 how to open my mind to new areas of growth and my heart to God. The seriousness of my consultancies with MPD patients had compelled me. Caused me to pray but not to have great expectations. To hope for peace of mind and good health but also to reach a new level of *acceptance about limitations.* Mine. Those of the MPD patients with whom I was working. And those of the clinicians. The Tara Sues of this world are trying to warn us. No matter how positive multiplicity can be for some patients, no matter how solid the arguments against integration may be, MPD has definite limitations. And some of them are deadly.

How present I become,
As though there were no more yesterdays.
Sudden silences separate the moments
While I walk the crooked line
That only faith can make straight.
Starshine encircles me with grace,
Butterfly wings sing a lullaby,
And reveal pink fragrant rose beams. . . .
While my trembling soul
Reaches for the hand of God,
Beyond the realm of angels,
And
A soft "amen" gently brushes the edge of my face.[1]

I had written this poem, entitled "Wholeness," in the spring of 1983, during another period of *sleepwriting* similar to what I had experienced periodically since the seventies. The poem was part of *The Attic Child* manuscript, which I continued to complete even though the book still had no publisher. But this poem stood out because it provided a personal glimpse, nearly a decade after the unification, of how integration was persistently working within my psyche. Working to provide a deeper appreciation of time. The "present," in particular. And working toward a deeper understanding that "wholeness" is not something one achieves but a process that one "becomes." Yet the poem also affirmed that this process is not easy. Indeed, it is the journey of a "trembling soul" along a "crooked line." And though "grace" and beauty make the journey easier, and "faith" helps to make that line "straight," there are only occasional "amens" to assure the wayfarer that the process is heading in the right direction.

This brief sleepwriting period also occurred about the time I began consulting with MPD patients and their therapists. Was there, I wondered, a connection between my inner perceptions of "wholeness" and my reactions to these deeper involvements with MPD patients? As these consultancies continued throughout 1983, I was often reminded how desperately I had wanted, before the unification, to distinguish myself from the persons my alters had been and, more specifically, to distance myself from the suffering of MPD. But after working with people suffering from multiplicity, I no longer had such negative feelings about dissociation. Only about the disorder itself.

In fact, I felt a real kinship with the MPD patients. I understood what they were experiencing. And I had genuine empathy for how each one felt during a "switch" of personalities. Yet I was determined to avoid the pitfall of fascination with the disorder, which has proven so detrimental to the relationships of many MPD patients and clinicians. So I never asked a patient "to switch" in my presence. Or when one did, I called no more attention to the change than the patient seemed to want.

As a result, I grew to accept what many people cannot. Having overcome earlier fears of my unconscious and of some *positive* forms of dissociation, I became more open to extraordinary aspects of consciousness. This broadening awareness would manifest itself in my life during a peculiar event in late 1983. And after I had sorted out that experience in relation to my clients' multiplicity, the Associated Press would quote me as saying in late 1984, "It's strange. It awakens something in me."[2]

Nothing seemed to herald that the day would be anything other than ordinary. I had been alone at our Herndon home and had worked vigorously, cleaning the house. By late afternoon, I decided to take a shower before Don got home from work. So I went to the upstairs bath, undressed, and adjusted the faucet controls to produce a steady hot flow of water.

But as I stepped into the shower stall, my foot rested on some soap residue and I slipped. I could feel my feet sliding out from under me. Fearing the fall, I panicked. Just as suddenly, however, I was startled when I felt my body being jerked back into a standing position by what seemed to be a pair of strong hands that lifted me along both sides of my rib cage.

Despite an immediate sense of relief at having been spared possible injury, I was terrified. Who had done this? None of my family was at home and the house was locked tight. Had some stranger entered the bathroom? I slowly turned to see. But no one was there.

The next morning as I slipped from my gown to get dressed, I discovered blue bruises, like handprints, on both sides of my rib cage. Again I was frightened, and at first I was determined to tell no one. Former mental patients acquire an acute sense of discretion.

Then I remembered how sympathetic Stanley Krippner, Ph.D., had been toward discussing psychic and paranormal experiences when I had lectured at San Francisco's Saybrook Institute two months earlier. He was professor of psychology, former dean of that institute's graduate school and research center, and a close personal friend. He was also doing research into the relationship of personal mythology to unconscious states.[3] So I wrote to him for advice.

His February 1984 response indicated, "Of course I found your experience in the shower interesting, [though it] is not all that unusual. . . . I feel that some people reach *such a high degree* of personal and transpersonal [development] that they are able to pull upon inner/outer resources in times of great emergency. Whether these resources are 'spirits' or elements of our own unconscious is debatable. To me, the important fact is that these resources are available, and that we can be more open to them than we are."[4]

Stan's assurances reinforced my own belief that such psychic experiences must be a *positive* aspect to the innate vulnerability—or the proneness for dissociation—that had made me susceptible to MPD in the first place. During childhood, when my alters had genuinely believed that they saw ghosts on the Strother Place or spirits in that house's attic; or when one of my preteen alters told the family that she had seen Jesus in a dream and He had warned her that my sister Becky had diphtheria; or, more recently, when I had the premonition about President Reagan's assassination attempt—surely some of these experiences possessed a meaning exclusive of MPD. In fact, given how little we scientifically understand about consciousness, who can say with certainty that at least some of what MPD patients perceive is not a valid mirror for testing what normalcy really is? Or that once an MPD patient is cured, his or her "high degree of personal and transpersonal [development]" does not allow meaningful, though sometimes paranormal, encounters to continue into periods of mental health? Indeed, is it possible that we are all *multiple* to some degree? A grand literary tradition affirms that we could be.

"Dostoyevski, Goethe, Guy de Maupassant and, in our time, Jorge Luis Borges have all been fascinated with the *doppelgänger,* a duplicate self or imagined twin," wrote Richard Restak, M.D., in *Science Digest.* "Could this image of the double express an inner feeling of multiplicity? Then the ancient Greek dictum, 'Know thyself,' might more usefully read, 'Know thy multiple selves.'"[5]

That spring, a Lander College student posed the question differently. Following my annual lecture in Greenwood, South Carolina, he asked, "If you could live your life over, would you want to have been normal?"

Without a pause, I told the student audience that I would not have chosen a normal life if normalcy meant fear of my unconscious and a lifetime of ignoring the positive awarenesses that dissociation can bring. Instead, I would elect to work through mental illness again. But I hastened to explain that such a choice was not a glorification of mental illness.

"Anguish and pain and confusion are not experiences to recommend," I said. "But few of these so-called *negatives* in life can be avoided if any person is to possess true joy, the freedom from fear, and the comfort of inner peace. Had I been normal, I don't know who I would have become. It took *all* the struggles to make me the woman I am."

* * *

The positive implications of multiplicity seemed an appealing topic to both the media and my lecture audiences that spring. CNN aired an interview with me on *Healthweek* during that network's series about MPD early in 1984. The USA Cable Network interviewed me for *Alive and Well.* Then I lectured in various parts of the northern Virginia area, including my annual appearance at the FBI Academy. And at virtually every appearance, the questions usually turned to the role that dissociation plays in everyone's lives.

This was particularly the case during May, when I was the keynote speaker for a series of annual meetings: in Birmingham for the Alabama Council of Community Mental Health; at Andrews Air Force Base for the Mental Health Association of Prince George's County; as well as in Baltimore and at Ohio State University in Columbus for both metropolitan areas' MHAs. Clearly, some of the public's long-standing fascination with MPD seemed to be rooted in the fact that most people recognize in the drama of multiplicity the roles that dissociation plays, to a lesser degree, in everyday thinking.

As Dr. Restak would subsequently explain in *The Brain,* released that autumn in conjunction with a PBS series, "From studies of multiple personality, neuroscientists are beginning to change some of their traditional ideas about altered states of consciousness. . . . Multiples may represent extreme examples of things we all do every day. . . . This doesn't imply that we all are 'multiples.' But it does suggest that our everyday personalities aren't nearly as coherent and integrated as we like to believe."[6]

Then, alluding to Dr. Putnam's NIMH research, Dr. Restak added, "Changes in our brain-wave patterns often accompany these changes in our mental state. Drowsiness and reverie, for instance, are marked by a slowing in the [brain's] background rhythm. Full alertness, in contrast, is marked by a well-organized, sharply defined background rhythm. . . . From studies of the evoked potentials of multiples, then, we may soon learn more about the neurobehavioral mechanisms underlying normal personality."[7]

Apparently, other professionals agreed, because during this same period four respected psychiatric journals would be dedicated to the topic of MPD.[8] And some of these studies reflected the view that a better understanding of multiplicity and dissociation might help explain more fully what normalcy is.

No matter how positive the implications of dissociation, however, MPD patients were still suffering. Particularly those who had been sexually abused as children. And I learned from one such MPD patient, a black woman whom I will call Olivia, that some clinicians were as prejudiced against diagnosing, and dealing with, the results of child abuse as they were about diagnosing MPD.[9]

At the time, she was a government employee with a demanding job. According to her supervisor, she consistently worked with a high degree of professionalism and productivity, so Olivia's switching from one alter to another did not prevent her from being a high-functioning multiple at work. Even though her first therapist had identified as many as six coexisting alters in her life, she complained of no interference on the job. Her most severe problems, she said, came after quitting time.

"One of them wanders through life as if it were a sleazy movie," Olivia told me, describing nights when her alter frequented exclusive singles' bars in a fashionable area of an East Coast city.

"I would never go to places like that. But she does. And she gets all of us into trouble," Olivia said. Though she did not switch personalities in my presence, I could see them reflected in the changes that came to her eyes. It was as though several of her alters were listening, hovering near us while Olivia continued to talk.

"She has no taste in men. She will sleep with salesmen or married men, conventioneers or any lonely man with money. And all the while, I am there. Not out and capable of stopping them. But *there.* I am a prisoner inside my own body while she is using it in ways that break my heart."

This promiscuity, Olivia was to understand, had its roots in the sexual abuse that had been inflicted upon her. Alternately, her father and her uncle had forced four-year-old Olivia to have sex with them. And this abuse had been repetitive, spanning a number of years.

But Olivia came to me because of another abuse: what her first therapist had done. "It took such a long time in therapy to discover what the men I had loved had done to me as a child," she explained. "I had forgotten all of it. And when my therapy sessions approached those hurts, I refused at first to go further. It took all of the courage I had simply to let go and let it all come out."

However, the day this revelation came during Olivia's therapy, the white clinician responded to his now highly vulnerable patient, "But isn't it *common* for blacks to have incest?"

"It's not!" Olivia said she had retorted, deeply hurt by the betrayal and the prejudice implicit in his words. Then she said she had whispered, "It's common for white men to rape black women." Thereupon, she left the session.

Some days later, Olivia came seeking from me a recommendation for a new therapist. One who was black. One who could understand her African-American culture and heritage. Fortunately, I was able to locate such a clinician practicing near her residence. But the incident reinforced in my mind the obvious conflicts within the clinical community. When, I wondered, would MPD patients be assured, not only of proper treatment for their disorder, but also of unbiased consideration for the abusive traumas that trigger the illness?

In May, MPD authorities tried again. During the annual meeting of the American Psychiatric Association, convened that year in Los Angeles, child abuse was the primary focus of MPD studies. Dr. Kluft had reported on a case of severe abuse that resulted in a child suffering from MPD. It was the first reported diagnosis of childhood MPD since 1840. And Dr. Wilbur—generally credited with having discovered such abuse as MPD's primary causal factor—called for "a massive approach across the country toward the prevention of child abuse." Concurrently, the American Medical Association was studying the child-abuse crisis and preparing guidelines for both diagnosis and treatment. According to their estimates, more than a million American children were suffering from abuse and neglect, creating a situation that the AMA described as "serious" and often "life-threatening."[10] And potentially, a situation that promised more MPD sufferers in years to come.

But both the APA and the AMA seemed more concerned about physical and sexual abuse to children than about the more elusive emotional traumas that, at least in some MPD cases, can be equally damaging. So when I spoke for the Children's Conservation Convention, held in Columbus that same month, I focused on children who experience trauma simply by witnessing violence directed at others—including the watching of violence on television and in movies.

"Of course, all of us abhor the subjection of children to direct physical or sexual abuse at the hands of adults," my prepared text for the Columbus audience stated. "But what about indirect abuse or violence to others which a child witnesses before he or she is old enough to deal with such trauma? When a child merely witnesses extreme violence, and that child is five years old or younger, then significant psychological damage may be inflicted. Damage which may not manifest itself in that individual's life until years later."

Illustrating from my case history, I explained how the casual events that apparently triggered MPD had occurred when I was two years old. And all three traumas were incidents that I witnessed within a span of three months. I saw a man who appeared to have drowned and was being pulled from an irrigation ditch, and I heard my father say the word *dead.* Next I saw a man who had fallen onto a saw and was cut in half at the lumber mill where my father was the superintendent. Then I saw a jar explode and cut my mother badly. While none of these moments of violence was direct, or intentional, abuse on my childhood consciousness, all of them had a traumatic effect on my fragile, developing personality.

"Admittedly, researchers have determined that less than ten percent of all MPD patients have the disorder as the result of indirect trauma outside themselves," I told the Columbus audience. "But if merely witnessing violence could trigger MPD in my life, what are the many popular, but bizarrely violent, movies and television shows doing to the preschoolers of this nation today? Unfortunately, we may not know the definitive answers until they become young adults around the year Two Thousand."

Though I only discussed my case history with the Columbus audience, I was consulting at the time with a patient whose MPD had also been triggered by witnessing violence. The woman, whom I will call Angie, had been referred to me by her therapist after they had discovered a puzzling aspect during her therapy. Angie was a middle-aged MPD patient who had originally been diagnosed as having a sleep disorder. Her initial symptom was that in the middle of the night she stopped breathing, and this awakened her. But her therapist soon discovered that when Angie stopped breathing in her sleep, she also experienced a switch of personalities.

He began treating her for MPD, but he remained unable to affect the breathing problem. Actually, it worsened. Angie could be sitting, talking with a friend, then she would suddenly begin choking. But whether asleep or awake, whenever this choking sensation occurred, Angie said she only gained relief by switching personalities. Yet she said that she had no control over the switching process.

Finally, during one session with her therapist, we discovered a probable cause. At the age of four, Angie had seen her brother commit suicide by hanging himself. But she had not been able to remember having witnessed this violent act since she was seven years old—the age when she first experienced the choking. Her therapist ultimately concluded that by repressing that psychological material as a child, Angie was acting out her brother's hanging each time she experienced a switch of personalities. Her MPD, lasting from childhood into middle age, had not then been triggered by sexual abuse but by the trauma of witnessing a violent act—the death of her brother.

How, then, can we save our children from such pain and its lasting effects? I told the audience in Columbus that protecting a child from being psychologically damaged includes reporting to the authorities all direct physical or sexual abuse of children and obtaining for the child victims immediate psychiatric care from a clinician trained to work with children. But protections must also include a more realistic approach to parenting, particularly in terms of how we prepare even our youngest children to understand death and violence.

"If a child has been prepared from his or her earliest years to accept that everybody can be hurt badly and that everybody will die," I concluded, "and if a child has been taught to feel *comfortable* in the presence of death, not to fear the threat of death, then that child stands a greater chance of not being traumatized by whatever violence he or she may witness—whether in life or on TV or in the scenes of a movie."

In June, prior obligations prevented me from participating in a tour of China that I had organized for educators and mental-health professionals. So others went without me on an eighteen-day excursion to such exotic places as Shanghai, Suzhou, Nanjing, Beijing, Xi'an, Chongqing, and Guilin. By August, I was still thinking wistfully of the Yangtze River cruise I had missed when, in effect, a neighbor of the Orient came to me.

The young man wore a well-tailored and obviously expensive three-piece business suit. Observed downward from his starched collar and his silk four-in-hand tie, the man's appearance could have been that of any successful entrepreneur. And since a mutual friend had arranged for this visit, I knew in advance that my visitor lived in a mid-Atlantic state, was very intelligent, and was experiencing psychological problems that he believed to be similar to MPD. What I didn't know seemed to be sculpted on the visitor's face when I greeted him at the door of our Herndon home: He was a native of India. I will call him Vijna.

The gaze from Vijna's deep black eyes was direct, sparkling, and animated. His face was bearded, handsomely toned and contoured. And his head was meticulously wrapped in a black turban, secured by what appeared to be a large, gleaming emerald set in a gold pin.

After we sat down in the living room, Vijna said, "My problem, Mrs. Sizemore, is that I am experiencing more than one spirit."

"Did you intend to say 'spirit,'" I asked, "or do you mean 'more than one 'personality'?"

"Oh, most definitely do I mean *'spirit.'* We are all reincarnated," Vijna said. "But normally, we possess no memories of the lives which have come before this one. Our spirits have spiraled upward, and each higher being has no need of memories from a lower life. Yet that, you see, is my problem: I *do* have memories and thoughts from more than one spirit." He paused, folding his hands serenely, then added, "This is peculiar. This is not as it should be."

When I asked Vijna to describe his spirits, he said that four were coexisting in his life and that one of them was "very old . . . from a past life . . . from an era long ago." But the other three, he said, "seem to be in the present state. It's as though my lifetime is theirs as well." Then he smiled curiously and asked if it were possible that my case history had been *misinterpreted* as MPD when, in fact, it might have been a problematic reincarnation such as he believed himself to be experiencing?

"Well, it does sound like the same type of experience," I said. "But could you not be experiencing multiple personality?"

"Whatever we call this, Mrs. Sizemore—*because of it,* I am a man who is paying a very large karma at this time for something from a past life."

For nearly an hour, we discussed the differences and similarities between MPD and reincarnation. Finally, this still-energetic young man asked me what I would recommend so that he could get help.

"If you really want to get rid of these other spirits, then I believe you need psychiatric treatment," I said.

"Do you not believe that a guru could help me?"

"I don't know," I responded, and asked if he had already gone back to India, sought such help, and found any relief from his problems.

"Yes," Vijna said, "but I am still here and so are my spirits."

Then the young man looked at me with what, at the moment, I assumed to be a more profound gaze, and he said, "I don't know what I might have done to have to pay this kind of karma. It is so confusing, so frustrating. I just can't seem to get on with *my* life."

At that point, his eyes began to flutter. He shifted body positions in the chair. And his shoulders slumped as if his body were suddenly becoming ten years older. Though he remained humble and gracious, his voice deepened. He spoke slower, more deliberately. What he said seemed wiser. Then, what I perceived to be an older man described the spirits within Vijna as being frequently confused: "Madam, his body is crowded with them.

When more than one is present, none can find peace. They do not know how to deal with this."

"And have *you* gone back to India and sought help from a guru?" I asked again.

"I am *certain* some guru could help," the deeper voice said with none of the hesitancy that Vijna had evidenced earlier.

"And is your *guru* the same as our *psychiatrist?*"

"No, madam," he said. "They do not do the same things."

Because of our ideological and cultural differences, I seemed unable to offer this older man any advice he would accept. Our conversation dwindled, and soon he informed me that he was tired and must leave. He rose cautiously from the chair. His manner of walking was not smooth and confident, as Vijna's had been upon entering. And bidding me good-bye, the man's eyes seemed clouded. When I closed the door behind him, I was convinced that the man who had come to my house was not the same man who left.

During the visit, however, neither my guest nor I had commented on the apparent changes within him. It was as though both Vijna and the older man considered this "switch" to be normal. Prior to this day, I had observed such changes only in MPD patients or, earlier, in my own struggles with that disorder. But what I had just witnessed in Vijna seemed distinctly similar to MPD switching. Did this mean that MPD and reincarnation might somehow be related?

Two years earlier, British author Ian Wilson had explored this question by examining over two decades of research by Ian Stevenson, Ph.D., professor of psychiatry and neurology at the University of Virginia. Though Wilson concluded that "Stevenson has let in rather more fraudulent reincarnation claims than he would care to concede," the British author did find in Stevenson's research several common characteristics between MPD patients and adults claiming "hypnotic memories of past lives—the usual variety of modern past-life claims."[11]

All that I had previously read about the emergence of past lives in the conscious awareness of an individual had reportedly occurred while the subject was under hypnosis, as in the highly controversial Bridey Murphy case. Yet when Vijna was with me, he did not seem under a hypnotic or trancelike state. His initial demeanor was intense but not typical of a hypnotized person. And the older man's demeanor was slower and deliberate but still not trancelike. In fact, this *absence* of a trancelike state was one reason I had become convinced that Vijna's past-life "spirit" had, in my presence, apparently emerged in the form of the older man.

But the most striking relationship to MPD that Wilson had found in Stevenson's reincarnation accounts was that "the typical Stevenson subject is a child between the age of two and six who has professed *conscious* memories of having lived before. Such a child may talk and behave as if he has different parents and belongs to a different location to that in which he finds himself. He may recognize and name objects, places, and people he claims to have known in a previous life. He may 'relive' the circumstances of a violent past-life death. Above all, he may produce so much detail about the deceased person he seems to have been that it becomes possible to identify that person and check information with surviving members of the past-life family."[12]

By comparison, more than 75 percent of MPD sufferers report having personalities who are under twelve years of age, and virtually all MPD patients are found to have experienced at least a fugue state before the age of five. But few, if any, MPD patients report memories from past lives that seem credible. Nonetheless, the similarities do appear to indicate that MPD and reincarnation are related phenomena.

While I am not yet convinced that this relationship is solid, I remain open to the possibility that the connection—if there is one—will be discovered through research with children. For we were all born during a state dominated by dreaming. Wilson's book cites research by a British obstetrician and the published writings of Carl Sagan[13] as confirming the possibility that "a mother's mental imagery [is] somehow being transmitted to her unborn child."

Similarly, Stevenson's research with children in India revealed what the Charlottesville professor called "announcing dreams," or significant dreams in the mother's life while she was carrying the child who subsequently professed past-life memories. To Wilson, these "announcing dreams" are the most "authentic" aspect of Stevenson's work.[14] For if a fetus "may be dreaming all the time," as Sagan contends, and if a fetus can retain into adulthood the memories secured within the womb, as British gynecological research contends, then some unconscious—and dissociative?—influence may be possible upon an unborn child.

But whatever researchers may discover, I was convinced in 1984 that Vijna's problems had their source in some realm of the psyche that is vulnerable both to characteristics of MPD and to influences upon him in India—quite possibly before his birth. Unfortunately, Vijna was also a person whom I could not help. But my experience with him deepened my convictions that even though such phenomena are perceived by other cultures as reincarnation, it is very likely that MPD may either be the actual cause of, or at least be related to, what these people are experiencing.

Professionally, my husband has always been a skilled and handy man. He had never begged for a job. And since 1974, he had worked at Washington's Greater Southeast Community Hospital, where he and his foreman, Paul Conrad, were the team that installed and maintained all of the hospital's electrical systems. When new technology arrived for X rays, computers, and tele-. phones, no up-to-date health care could be provided until the two men secured the systems.

"But an electrician can't do anything without his hands and his tools," Don explained, "and that's how I first discovered my problem. It all started in the spring of eighty-four as frustrations. Little things at work. I'd have difficulty getting a nut on a bolt, or even when I was working on dead lines, I would have trouble keeping the positive and negative wires apart. All I knew was that I just couldn't control my hands like I once did."

Initially, Don dismissed these tremors as nervousness, the result of fighting the northern Virginia traffic or simply another by-product of aging. He was sixty-one years old. But by midsummer, the problems became so severe that he could no longer hide them. And when I took him to a physician in August, the diagnosis by Alan Joshua, M.D., was that Don had "Parkinson's-like tremors."

Though the actual problem seemed elusive to Don's doctors, it was clear that decisions had to be made in our lives. The possibility of Parkinson's disease, a neurological disorder most commonly striking persons over sixty, had grave implications.

If he did have Parkinson's—which is characterized by rigidity of the neck and limbs, poor balance, difficulty in initiating movement and body tremors—then he could not continue working for very long. Yet without two incomes, we could not afford to stay in northern Virginia. The cost of living there had skyrocketed. So that fall, we began discussing the possibility that Don might take early retirement the following year, when he would be sixty-two, and that we might sell the Herndon house.

Privately, however, I resisted the prospect of retiring. Though I was fifty-seven, I did not feel old. Certainly not old enough to retire. And as had been the case two years earlier when Don first became ill, I was not ready to give up my lecturing, consulting with patients, or my work in MPD studies. The timing was all wrong. In fact, my fall schedule promised to be one of the most productive of my career, in part, because MPD had once again become a focal topic.

In particular, the International Society for the Study of Multiple Personality and Dissociation was holding its first international conference the following month in Chicago. And the subject of dissociation in general was evoking wider interest. Reflecting this, the Phil Donahue show invited me to join Drs. Bennett G. Braun and Richard P. Kluft on a special segment devoted to new MPD information that had been generated by the milestone event. As one of the conference's sponsors would subsequently describe it: "In some senses, we experienced a 'first wave' resurgence . . . in the seventies when the studies of split-brain patients hit both the science journals and eventually the popular press with all the force of a new myth in the culture. . . . We may now be about to experience a 'second wave' of data on the subject with the recent resurgence of interest and research into the phenomena of multiple personality."[15]

Faced with the possibility, then, that I might have to retire in a year, or at least cut back significantly on my traveling to care for Don, I launched into my work with gusto. If this was to be my last season of full-time work, I intended to make the most of it.

My art was given several exhibitions, including major ones in Tulsa and Oklahoma City, Oklahoma, and a black-tie gala opening in Detroit, Michigan. Subsequently, *The Detroit News* published a front-page interview with me and reproduced eight slides of my paintings in a full-color layout.[16] And patrons at each exhibit bought a number of my original oils or commissioned new paintings. The most notable request was from the National Mental Health Association for a painting to be part of its seventy-fifth anniversary celebration, scheduled for November in Nashville, Tennessee.

So whenever I wasn't traveling, I often worked long hours at my easel in Herndon. By bedtime my mind would still be churning with ideas. Images to paint frequently came faster than I could put them on canvas. As a result, I would fall asleep most nights in a state of satisfying exhaustion. But I would also get up during the night and be in the same state of creative dissociation that I had periodically experienced for years. Particularly during times of stress.

However, I didn't realize how long it had been since Don had seen this. Previously, he had been a sound sleeper who rarely noticed my getting up in the middle of the night. But since his tremors had started, he, too, began awakening several times each night. And discovering that I wasn't in bed, he would search the house, only to find me up and writing at the desk or painting at the easel.

At first he thought I was suffering from insomnia. He said my eyes would be open, and whatever I was writing or painting would appear typical of the work I did during the day. He also described me as responsive, coherent, intensely involved in my work, and in every other way the same as I was at other times:

"Couldn't sleep, again?" he would ask.

"No, dear. Just have so much to do."

"Are you *sure* you're okay?"

"I'm perfectly fine," I would say, sometimes reminding him, "I've been doing this off and on for years. Oh, maybe more lately—I'll grant you that. But it's nothing to be concerned about. It's just another way of dreaming. Any time something bothers me, I get up, write it all down, get out all that's inside of me, and then I can look at it. That way I possess it. It belongs to me. It's no longer elusive. It's just a way of capturing my dreams."

But as this period of *sleep work* persisted, night after night,

Don did become concerned. Gradually, however, I realized that I hadn't changed. He had. For the first time in our marriage, Don was becoming dependent on me. In contrast to the years when he had seemed content for me to pursue my interests and him to pursue his, Don was increasingly expressing his needs for me. His being ill was eroding his independence. And, I realized, threatening mine.

Despite his concerns, I knew that my dissociative state of creativity was not a problem. Research at the time was asserting that dissociation plays a vital role in spontaneous fantasy, imagery, hallucinations, and dreams. According to Peter McKellar, M.D., dissociation may be "a switch into a different gear rather than a splitting."[17] Another researcher, John Kihlstrom, M.D., was linking dissociation to an individual's sense of control. He wrote, "All of us appear to have the capacity to dissociate, as in the case of dreams and other aspects of sleep. This level of dissociative skill appears innate, much like certain perceptual-cognitive and linguistic capabilities. At the same time, however, some of us are more prone to dissociate than others, perhaps rendering us vulnerable to hysteria, fugue, multiple personality, obsessions and compulsions at times of stress. And some of us have voluntary control over dissociative processes, an attribute that may differentiate hypnotic virtuosos from the rest of the population. The ultimate problem of dissociation concerns the nature of these cognitive skills, how they interact with declarative knowledge, how we acquire them, and how some of us gain access to, and voluntary control, over them."[18]

My control, then, was the crucial difference. I had survived the unknowns of my unconscious during mental illness, so I had already faced the worst that my unconscious mind could offer. But in using dissociation for creative efforts, I was once again making my unconsciousness work for me.

When I finished the oil painting to commemorate the NMHA's seventy-fifth anniversary, I called it "The Bell of Hope." It depicts a young girl dressed in a flowing white gown. She has plain features and is reaching toward rays of sunlight. She seems buoyed as she sits on the NMHA bell, that symbol forged from the shackles that once restrained mental patients in institutions all across America.

Later, at the Friday night session of NMHA's annual meeting, I presented the original painting to our organization, and "The Bell of Hope" now hangs in our new national headquarters in Alexandria, Virginia. I am deeply grateful to have been allowed this contribution, because for decades mental-health associations all across this nation had served me as an advocate while I was a mental patient and unaware of the work that NMHA did. Once I was healed and began lecturing, hundreds of mental-health associations welcomed me as a speaker, as a consultant, and as a mental-health professional who had something unique to offer their chapters. Then, in 1982, the NMHA had given me its highest honor. "The Bell of Hope," therefore, was my way of saying *thank you* to people and an organization that had given me more than any expression of gratitude could repay.

*T*he more complex the issues in MPD studies, the more apparent it became that I needed the resources of the ISSMP&D and the advice of experienced professionals. Fortunately, I found such a person in David Caul, M.D., a highly respected clinician who practiced in Ohio and served as my mentor from our first meeting in 1981 until his death in March 1988. Though best known for his work as Billy Milligan's therapist, Dave was a tireless and evocative participant at MPD workshops and on various professional committees. Among clinicians, he was admired for his insights and professionalism, exemplified by the fact that he was serving as president of the ISSMP&D during the year of his death. But among patients, Dave was valued for his compassion and, more particularly, for his open-mindedness. He always admitted that there was more to MPD than traditional psychoanalysis could explain.

Dave and I also became dear friends. But because both of us were busy people and I was often traveling, we rarely saw one another. Yet we shared an enthusiasm for new ideas and discoveries in our field, so we arranged to telephone one another on Sunday evenings, when possible, in order to exchange news about the work.

These conversations were invaluable. Because discoveries were coming rapidly in MPD studies, I needed Dave's advice in order to cope with audiences' questions following my lectures and to provide up-to-date consultancies for the therapists who involved me in their treatment of MPD patients. But I particularly trusted Dave's objectivity. He was a practical man of science who understood that sometimes my prior experiences with multiplicity affected my judgments: I tended to trust patients' perceptions above those of the clinicians.

During one memorable phone conversation, I asked him if the voices that MPD patients and their alters hear, and the visualizations they have of one another, were real. Or were they hallucinations?

As I expected, Dave's reply initially followed the standard clinician's tact: "Chris, anything you see or hear that is not real is a hallucination."

"Yet to the MPD patient," I countered, "these perceptions are real."

"Then let me tell you about one of my MPD patients," he said. "She had young children who liked to play outside. But then the woman became housebound, and that created a dilemma. If she persisted in refusing to leave the house, she would deprive her children of the playtime they enjoyed. However, MPD patients are most creative in solving dilemmas, so the mother began sending an alter outside with the children, while the mother, remaining in the house, stood at the window and watched."

"I understand how alters can be in different places at the same time," I said. "But how can a *body* be in two places at once?"

"Technically, a body can't," Dave said.

"Then was the mother hallucinating?"

"I don't know," he responded, "but I don't think so. At that point in her life, the mother could *not* have left that house."

"Did you talk with the children about the experience of playing outside with the alter while their mother stood at the window and watched?" I asked, wondering if the children saw both the alter with them and the mother at the window.

"No."

"Then did *you* ever speak with the alter who played outside with the children?"

Suddenly, the tone of his voice grew more excited, and he replied, "Oh, yes, many times," as if sensing where my thoughts were headed.

"Well, then, Dave, were *you* hallucinating?"

He laughed and said, "That's what I mean, Chris. This is a new field, and we are all learning. There are no absolutes. Be prepared to change your views about theories or research in progress. And even about your own perceptions."

"And what about *your* perceptions?" I asked. "For example, how did you react the first time you encountered an alter in an MPD patient?"

Dave, whose head was bald on top, replied, "A chill went up my spine, and the hair on my crown stood on end." At that, we both laughed. Then he added in a serious tone, "I *knew* that day that I was in the presence of a person *other* than the patient who had entered my office."

Then are perceptions a crucial indicator? After experiencing and subsequently studying MPD, I am convinced that the perceptions of both patient and therapist are radically affected by the *presence* of multiplicity. As a result, an open-minded approach is just as important to the clinician with MPD patients as the standard objective approach is with other patients. Indeed, both the patient's and the therapist's concepts of *self* are at stake in such circumstances. Every time.

When I discovered such open-mindedness linked with objectivity in Adam Crabtree's *Multiple Man: Explorations in Possession and Multiple Personality,* I readily endorsed the book.[1]

In this work, the Canadian author and therapist described intriguing relationships (and important differences) between MPD and possession. In particular, by defining *possession* as "the invasion of a person by *an entity* from the outside,"[2] his book recognized what scholars of the occult and some religions have been contending for centuries: that, previously, multiplicity was explained by possession just as readily as, in the modern era, it is being explained by MPD.

But I had no personal experience with possession. Nor had any MPD patient with whom I had consulted—with the exception of Vijna, who was not diagnosed as suffering from MPD and who viewed his multiplicity as more accurately reincarnation.[3] After reading *Multiple Man,* then, I remained convinced that my years of multiplicity had *not* been caused by possession in any of its forms. My alters did not perceive one another as invaders (despite the unfortunate title of *Strangers in My Body* for some editions of one of my books). Their voices were not perceived as alien to one another. Just different. And there was no hint of "demonic" qualities within any of my alters.

Yet they did perceive one another as *entities,* and this perception may be the strongest link between MPD and possession. In fact, every MPD patient with whom I have spoken in depth maintains the same belief. Each affirms—though not always in the presence of clinicians—that his or her alters are real entities, separate from one another, yet not alien to one another.

This, then, is the importance of *Multiple Man* for MPD patients. It was the first book by a clinician to maintain an open-minded approach to this concept of multiple entities within a single person—as seen most clearly in the book's conclusion, which reflects upon discussions about the occultists' views of *possession,* the psychiatric concept of a *hidden observer,* and clinical theories about MPD:

> Basically these terms describe *experiences.* How one *explains* these experiences is another matter. The challenge to anyone dealing with this field is to refrain from too facile interpretations. The Caribbean spiritist believes he *knows* what these things are. So does the American psychoanalyst. Each uses his interpretation to treat those plagued by forms of disturbing multiplicity, and each has his successes. But I believe at this stage . . . *all* speculation about what is behind these experiences must be considered provisional. Otherwise, the explanation becomes a screen that sifts out facts of experience which do not fit in, a censoring device that deprives us of the information needed to gain a deeper understanding of the nature of multiple man.[4]

The problem was, while occultists and many MPD patients appeared to have little trouble with Crabtree discussing both possession and MPD in terms of entities, many psychoanalysts were keenly resistant. One review of *Multiple Man* by a respected clinician objected to attempts at "driving out" or exorcising so-called entities that—according to standard psychoanalytical approaches—may be integral *parts* of the personality. In this sense, the reviewer argued, exorcism would be the precise opposite of integration.[5]

But the text of *Multiple Man* anticipated such controversy. The author, a historian of mesmerism, noted that while both occultists and scientists seek to understand the "human experience of multiplicity," they are "often portrayed in the modern world as warring against each other." The reason? Because the *occult* tradition, according to Crabtree, "tends to view the scientific as unacceptably analytical, reducing all of life's mysteries to mere mechanics," while the *scientific* tradition "tends to see the occult as both naive and dogmatic in its approach to explaining human experience. . . ."[6]

Beyond professional and philosophical controversies, however, I was more concerned about the impact of such ideas on mental patients themselves. By endorsing the book, I was not endorsing occultism, or occult practices. Instead, I was endorsing a fresh look at the relationship of scientific and occult traditions, because using the scientific method alone was creating problems. With clinicians viewing the alters of MPD patients as *parts* or *fragments* or *illusions* but the patients viewing their alters as *entities* or other *people,* basic communication was breaking down. And ironically, many clinicians seemed unaware of the breakdown. From their perspectives in the mid-eighties, MPD patients in therapy were experiencing unification and subsequently achieving integration in great numbers. So how could there be a problem?

The problem, often left to the integrated MPD patient to solve alone, is how to find meaning after therapy ends. Standard clinical terms like *splitting* and *parts* leave many integrated MPD patients feeling like shattered china that has been glued back together. Even terms like *unification* or *integration* seem to reinforce an unnatural view of self. Because even if the integrated MPD patient accepts these clinical terms on an intellectual basis, the patient still possesses what is best described as an unconscious conviction: *Once I was many. Now I am one. But I am* not *the puzzle put together from their parts.*

Another irony, then, is that the terms that function as workable tools during an MPD patient's therapy—and their work-

ability encourages clinicians to continue using such terminology—somehow lose their meanings when the patient
subsequently faces everyday life—a life where few *normal* persons accept Dr. Restak's speculation that all human beings have
"multiple selves." Instead, MPD patients who are healed face a
life where the norm is that healthy people are believed to be
single, isolated selves. A life where meaning is determined by becoming a successful *individual* who makes his or her mark in the
world Yet, in life after therapy, the integrated MPD patient remembers, *Even during multiplicity, I was an* individual self. *An
entity. Distinct from my alters.* How, then, can *self* have the
same meaning in sickness and in health?

To Adam Crabtree, however, the meanings of multiplicity
have not been solidly established—as if meaning were somehow
lodged between, or to be discovered through, an *interdependency* of science and the occult. "These traditions have had a
tremendous influence upon everyday thinking about human multiplicity in the modern world," he wrote. "The average man is, in
the conduct of his everyday affairs, both occultist and scientist.
Both traditions have formed his thinking, and each holds a powerful attraction for him as he searches to understand himself. Neither can be ignored if we wish to better comprehend the nature
of multiple man."[7]

But even if such a melding of scientific and occult were to
lead toward an ultimate understanding of what multiplicity
means, is such a melding really workable in treating patients? In
1987, my friend Stan Krippner reported that, at least in Brazil, it
is acceptable for patients suffering from either MPD or possession
to be treated not only by psychoanalysis but also by a variety of
occult techniques. And after interviewing some Brazilians who
practice this combination of *spiritism* and psychotherapy, Stan
concluded that the Brazilians "both agree with, and differ from,
the concepts of MPD held by most academic and medical psy-
chotherapists [mainly in America]. However, these differences
should serve as a reminder that the notion of the individual self
should not be taken for granted. Most native people live in a
matrix of social and kinship relationships that leave little room
for a concept of a singular, isolated self."[8]

Outside industrialized societies such as ours, then, *inter-*

dependency is more often the norm. The individual self is perceived as of less importance than the family or the tribe. And
among such people, the belief that everyone has "multiple
selves" is far more acceptable. Is it possible, then, that these people understand what we in Western industrial societies have forgotten? By elevating self above the family, have we in recent
generations somehow *internalized the family* and, thereby,
made our natural multiplicity into something abnormal? Have we
unwittingly turned a source of richness and health for the human
personality—our "multiple selves"—into a sickness?[9]

By 1985, Don and I had also gained a greater understanding
of interdependency as we prepared for his retirement. We established a financial plan for how we would live, which included
putting the Herndon house on the market and his accepting a
lower pension because of taking early retirement. I agreed to
limit my traveling. And we looked for a new home in North Carolina, close to the Sizemore homeplace. We were southerners
going home. And neither of us was demanding the independence
that had characterized the previous years of our marriage. Don's
illness ended all of that.

By May, we had bought a home in Ramseur, North Carolina. It
was a handsome residence, nestled in a peaceful wooded area of
a quiet town. And the house itself, constructed by a dedicated
brick mason, featured solid white brick walls, inside and out, plus
a gabled sun porch. Don and I liked it the first time we approached it along Williams Street. So, a month later, when we
saw the moving van off at the Herndon house, Don and I anticipated a comfortable retirement. A return to southern ways. An
end to the stress that, we believed, had contributed to Don's
tremors.

And one positive aspect of this interdependency was that, for
the first time since 1978, Don began accompanying me on my
travels. In late October, we went to New Orleans for the annual
convention of the American Art Therapy Association, Inc. There,
my paintings were on exhibit at the Hyatt Regency,[10] and the
artwork garnered an unusual array of comments. But those that
affected me most came from Don. During the previous decade,

he had attended only two exhibitions of my paintings. This time, however, he seemed genuinely moved by my work.

Listening to the professionals' comments, Don took advantage of a moment when he and I stood by ourselves. Looking at some of my alters' works, he said, "I didn't know you could hang this many paintings on a wall that would interest people so. You've really done something." I squeezed his hand and kissed him on the cheek. He smiled and added, "Looks like you can do anything you put your mind to." I had waited years for him to say those exact words, and hearing them at last, the waiting somehow seemed to have been worth it.

That night a hurricane struck the Gulf Coast. Don, exhausted from the day, slept solidly. But I wandered from window to window in our twenty-second-floor suite. The panes swayed in and out from the wind's force, and from this vantage, I imagined that I could see the entire city and all of the storm engulfing it. Outside, torrents of rain fell and rose in an eerie defiance of gravity. Down below, cars that had been parked along the street rocked like cradles while debris tossed about like tumbleweed.

Then I realized that observers during the art exhibition had assumed—as most everyone else does when viewing the *Eve* collection—that my alters had put on canvas their perceptions of multiplicity within the mind. How could I explain? As bizarre and boldly colored as many of the *Eve* paintings appear, I now understand that none of them were inner images translated to oils. Instead, like the storm scene I was watching while secure behind glass and high above the ground level of disaster, my alters had painted *the real world* as each one perceived it.

A year later, Tom Minehart wrote an Associated Press article about my life,[11] and that piece—reprinted in hundreds of publications in the following months—spurred a host of calls for interviews from reporters across the nation. By January 1987, Minehart's story helped open a new avenue for my work. That's when I was appointed to the human rights committee of the Dorothea Dix Hospital.

Located in Raleigh, it is North Carolina's largest facility for mental patients, and it is named after the nineteenth century's valiant advocate of mental patients' rights, Dorothea Lynde Dix of

Massachusetts. During her long lifetime, she was credited with achieving better institutional conditions in America, Canada, England, Scotland, continental Europe, and Japan.

But for me, this appointment was the first time that I would be in a position to have direct influence on the quality of health care being given mental patients. I felt confident. I had a uniqueness to offer that policy-making body: As a former consumer, I was bringing an expertise that the doctors and lawyers, the social workers and the ministers, did not possess. I had been the observed patient under the scrutiny of professional observers. But now, as a committeewoman, I could influence others as to the care and rights of mental patients. And I would be one person about whom the other committe members could say, "She was once one of them. She *knows.*"

This committee had been created several years earlier to facilitate the rights established by North Carolina laws on behalf of patients. But prior to my appointment, press reports had leveled serious accusations at Dorothea Dix Hospital, including stories alleging that the facility's patients were not receiving proper one-on-one care and that hospital security had been lax, allowing, on one occasion, a patient to run away. These charges concerned me deeply.

After attending several committee meetings, however, I came to understand some of the harsh realities about operating a state facility. For example, during the period when press scrutiny was so critical of the hospital administration, state funding was not adequate. As a result, Dorothea Dix was understaffed. And a lot of what was reported in the press had happened because the facility simply could not, at that time, afford to have on duty the number of technicians necessary to take care of the problems.

Our committee immediately set out to rectify the situation. We helped to write, and lobbied for, legislation that would increase state funding for more technicians. In subsequent months, we would work long and hard to improve other conditions for mental patients in North Carolina. And six months after my appointment, the committee would recognize my efforts by electing me as its chairwoman.

In spite of my repeated calls for open-mindedness in MPD studies, I harbored a personal prejudice against the use of hypnosis. Since 1957, when I was last treated with hypnosis by Dr. Thigpen, I had sworn never to submit to clinical hypnosis again. I was afraid. I knew that hypnosis in the fifties had aggravated my multiplicity, so for nearly thirty years I avoided hypnosis as if it were lethal. In addition, my fears had been confirmed by recent studies that indicated that "manifestations of multiple personality seem to occur most frequently when hypnotic procedures are employed in therapy."[12] This information paralleled earlier research that found that "patients who displayed the most elaborate and long-lasting evidence of multiple identities were those who were exposed to protracted hypnotherapy."[13] So I had many reasons to resist hypnosis and to nurture my prejudice against its usage with MPD patients.

But this prejudice was solidly challenged at the April 1987 conference on MPD in Akron, Ohio, where I met Moshe S. Torem, M.D. Following a gourmet meal with the Akron staff on the first night of the conference, Moshe asked if he could speak privately with me. That conversation lasted for hours, and it made us become immediate friends.

During this exchange, Moshe did not ask me questions about my previous alters, as everyone always does. Instead, he asked about the person I had become since the unification. And only when he sensed that some aspect of my previous alters' lives still affected my current life did he ask how I felt about them. He is one of the few people I have ever known who consistently declined to project his feelings onto mine. He won my confidence. I felt comfortable with him. And thereafter, we discussed a lot of mutual concerns about MPD therapy. In particular, he talked about the practice of reparenting, which is often used while MPD patients regress into childhood during a type of therapy designed to uncover early trauma.

"Some therapists cuddle and hug these adults whose minds are back in early childhood," he said. "But that's unprofessional. The therapist must draw the line. If the adult regresses to childhood, you don't treat him or her as a child. You treat the patient as an adult who has simply regressed."[14]

Later in the discussion, I admitted to Moshe my personal feelings of inadequacy: that I was ill-equipped to work because my formal education had ended in the tenth grade. He seemed surprised. But he assured me that I did not need more education in order to function competently in the roles that had evolved in my career.

"It isn't education that's important, Chris," he said. "Knowledge is what matters, and you have the knowledge we need. You have been *within* the confines of an extraordinary mental disorder. The rest of us can only study it."

The next morning when I addressed the conference, I gave the best speech I have ever delivered. I could feel the energy within the room as I spoke. And I knew this renewed self-confidence had come from the assurance that talking with Moshe had provided. But I also sensed that he had done something more, because I felt as though the burden of my inadequacy had been lifted.

That afternoon Moshe and I discussed the fact that, in recent years, I had gained considerable weight. I had tried numerous diets, but nothing seemed to help. So Moshe described his weight-control program and said he usually accomplished it through hypnotic suggestion. Then he asked, "Have you considered trying that?"

"No," I responded, attempting to veil my fears. "How is it done?"

"I use a light suggestion. It's not a deep hypnotic trance. You simply carry the thought with you." Then he told me the words he would use if I were under hypnosis: "Our body is a sacred trust. We must eat like a gourmet. We do not eat like a pig."

I laughed, then he laughed, and he asked if I wanted to try it. But I simply could not trust hypnosis, so I responded, "I don't know."

"That's fine," he said. "But if you want me to do it before you leave, just tell me and I will."

The next day, I did ask him to hypnotize me, and he again assured, "Now, Chris, if you're not certain you want me to do this, it's okay. I'll understand. But if you are sure, then I'll do so."

I insisted that I was, and he hypnotized me. The session lasted about five minutes. Afterward, Moshe told me that I had been extremely hypnotizable. "And I suggest that when you are in a trance or when you relax, you are thinking of the beach," he added.

"How do you know?"

"While you were under hypnosis, you moved your hands in a wavelike motion," he said. And with that, I realized what an astute observer Moshe is. In my most relaxed moments, my mind *is* a beachcomber.

But he saved the most significant observation until the end. That's when Moshe told me that throughout the hypnotic procedure I seemed "disgustingly normal." After the many lives I have lived and the anguish I have experienced, those words were a wonderful gift to bring home from Akron.

Some months later, I received a quarterly published by the Akron General Development Foundation. On its full-color cover was a reproduction of one of my "Attic Child" oil paintings, which depicts her suspended from a tree limb by an automobile tire on a rope. Barefooted, her left leg pointing skyward, her right leg stabilizing the makeshift swing, she is drawing in the sand with a stick. In such a state, she is both earthy and ephemeral—a creative victim of mental illness but also a typical child. When I painted it, it had been intended as a symbol of hope; but on this cover, it represented renewed hope in my contemporary life.

In that issue's interview with me, writer Ludel Sauvageot affirmed, "Today, she is a whole person—a charming and attractive sixty-year-old woman whose life is dedicated to bringing hope to the mentally ill and their families by simply being herself and telling her story. She is living proof of what she teaches. . . . Chris Sizemore is real."[15]

Notes

Chapter One

1. Corbett H. Thigpen, M.D., and Hervey M. Cleckley, M.D., *The Three Faces of Eve* (New York: McGraw-Hill, 1957), p. 218.
2. Corbett H. Thigpen, M.D., to Mrs. Christine Sizemore, May 23, 1974, in Chris Costner Sizemore Papers, Manuscript Department, Duke University Library, Durham, North Carolina (cited hereafter as "CCSP at Duke").
3. Ibid.
4. Diary, June 4, 1974, in CCSP at Duke.
5. Diary, June 6 and 7, 1974, in CCSP at Duke.
6. Diary, June 10 and 19, 1974, in CCSP at Duke.
7. Diary, June 19 and 23, 1974, in CCSP at Duke.
8. Diary, June 24, 1974, in CCSP at Duke.
9. Ibid.
10. Diary, June 26, 1974, in CCSP at Duke.
11. Diary, July 2, 1974, in CCSP at Duke.
12. Diary, June 25, 1974, in CCSP at Duke.
13. Diary, June 26, 1974, in CCSP at Duke.
14. Diary, July 2, 1974, in CCSP at Duke.
15. Diary, July 7, 1974, in CCSP at Duke.
16. Diary, July 9, 1974, in CCSP at Duke.
17. Contemporary definitions of MPD terms include: "(1) *unification,* an overall term for the personalities blending into one, (2) *fusion,* the point in time at which the patient satisfies certain stringent criteria for the absence of residual MPD for three continuous months, and (3) *integration,* a more comprehensive process of undoing all aspects of dissociative dividedness that begins long before

the first personalities come together and continues long after fusion until the last residua of dissociative defenses are more or less undone." Richard P. Kluft, M.D., "The Postunification Treatment of Multiple Personality Disorder: First Findings," *American Journal of Psychotherapy*, Vol. 42, No. 2 (April 1988), p. 213.

18. Diary, July 16, 1974, in CCSP at Duke.
19. Diary, July 21, 1974, in CCSP at Duke.
20. Ibid.
21. Diary, July 28, 1974, in CCSP at Duke.

Chapter Two

1. Bennett G. Braun, M.D., "The BASK (Behavior, Affect, Sensation, Knowledge) Model of Dissociation," *Dissociation*, Vol. 1, No. 1 (March 1988), pp. 4–23.
2. Ibid.
3. Evelyn Lancaster with James Poling, *The Final Face of Eve* (New York: McGraw-Hill, 1958).
4. Diary, August 23, 1974, in CCSP at Duke.
5. Compare to Chris Costner Sizemore and Elen Sain Pittillo, *I'm Eve* (New York: Doubleday, 1977), pp. 393–97.
6. Diary, August 26, 1974, in CCSP at Duke.
7. Diary, August 26, 1974, in CCSP at Duke; compare to Sizemore and Pittillo, *I'm Eve*, pp. 431–33.
8. Diary, September 2, 1974, in CCSP at Duke.
9. Diary, September 20, 1974, in CCSP at Duke.
10. Diary, October 9 and 10, 1974, in CCSP at Duke.
11. Diary, October 14, 1974, in CCSP at Duke.
12. For details, see Sizemore and Pittillo, *I'm Eve*, pp. 428–31.
13. Letter, Corbett H. Thigpen, M.D., to Mrs. Christine Sizemore, October 18, 1974, in CCSP at Duke.
14. Diary, October 28, 1974, in CCSP at Duke.
15. Diary, October 30, 1974, in CCSP at Duke.
16. Diary, November 1, 1974, in CCSP at Duke.
17. Diary, October 24, 1974, in CCSP at Duke.
18. Ibid.

Chapter Three

1. Jay Mathews, "Suddenly, Her Paintings Sell," *Washington Post*, October 3, 1975, p. A8, col. 2.
2. Diary, November 25, 1974, in CCSP at Duke.

3. Tom Harrison, "'Eve' Reflects on Past," *Augusta Chronicle* (Georgia), January 18, 1975, p. 1B, col. 2.
4. Charles Moore, "Edgefield Native Recalls Life with 'Three Faces of Eve,'" *Index-Journal* (Greenwood, South Carolina), January 10, 1975, p. 1B, col. 6.
5. Diary, January 9, 1975, in CCSP at Duke.
6. Kenneth L. Higbee, "Psychological Classics: Publications That Have Made Lasting and Significant Contributions," *American Psychologist* (February 1975), pp. 182–84.
7. Diary, February 20, 1975, in CCSP at Duke.
8. Diary, February 28, 1975, in CCSP at Duke.

Chapter Four

1. Donnel Nunes, "Many Faces of Eve Revealed," *Washington Post*, September 14, 1975, p. A6, col. 4.
2. This gap in professional literature persisted into the eighties. In fact, Dr. Richard P. Kluft, a leading MPD authority, concluded in 1988 that "the problems and treatment needs of unified MPD patients have received relatively little discussion in the literature." His overview of publications about postunification treatment cited only twenty-seven sources from among the hundreds available on MPD in general; and all of Kluft's citations were published between 1981 and 1987. Kluft, "The Postunification Treatment of Multiple Personality," pp. 214, 226–28.
3. Rollo May, *The Courage to Create* (New York: Norton, 1975), p. 120.
4. Diary, March 1, 1975, in CCSP at Duke.
5. Diary, March 5, 1975, in CCSP at Duke.
6. See "Chronology of Personalities," ca. Autumn 1975, in CCSP at Duke.
7. Diary, March 22, 1975, in CCSP at Duke.
8. Emphasis added. Kluft, "The Postunification Treatment of Multiple Personality," p. 221.
9. Diary, June 26, 1975, in CCSP at Duke; also compare to Sizemore and Pittillo, *I'm Eve*, pp. 449–52.
10. May, *The Courage to Create*, pp. 116–18.
11. Compare "Reporter's Notebook," *Fairfax Journal* (Virginia), October 16, 1975; see Donnel Nunes, "Many Faces of Eve Revealed," *Washington Post*, September 14, 1975, pp. A1, A6; Margaret Scherf, "Real 'Eve' Steps Forward," *Birmingham News*, September 15, 1975, p. 1; and "People and Places," *Evening News*, (Harrisburg, Pennsylvania), September 16, 1975, p. 17; also Sizemore and Pittillo, *I'm Eve*, pp. 453–61.

12. See "Correspondence 1952–March 1978," box 16-D, in CCSP at Duke.

13. Letter, Denver H. Graham, attorney, to Mrs. Christine Sizemore, September 19, 1975; Letter, Denver H. Graham, attorney, to Corbett H. Thigpen, M.D., September 19, 1975; Letter, Donald L. Bowman, attorney, to Hervey M. Cleckley, M.D., and Corbett H. Thigpen, M.D., September 6, 1974; all in CCSP at Duke.

14. Letter, Corbett H. Thigpen, M.D., to Donald L. Bowman, attorney, September 10, 1974, in CCSP at Duke.

15. Jay Mathews, "Suddenly, Her Paintings Sell," *Washington Post,* October 3, 1975, p. A8, col. 3.

16. Letters, Lisa Drew, Doubleday & Company, Inc., to Ms. Chris Sizemore, November 3, 4, and 7, 1975; Letter, Denver H. Graham, attorney, to Ms. Lisa Drew, Doubleday & Company, Inc., November 20, 1975; Letter, Janice March Friedman, assistant to Lisa Drew, to Denver H. Graham, attorney, November 24, 1975; Letter, Corbett H. Thigpen, M.D., to Denver H. Graham, attorney, December 1, 1975; all in CCSP at Duke.

Chapter Five

1. Donnel Nunes, "Many Faces of Eve Revealed," *Washington Post,* September 14, 1975, p. A6, col. 1.

2. Kluft, "The Postunification Treatment of Multiple Personality," p. 225.

3. Emphasis added. Ibid.

4. Erik Erikson, *Identity and the Life Cycle* (New York: Norton, 1979), p. 98.

5. For a selection of these, see the following in CCSP at Duke: Poem, "Lost Enchantment," February 7, 1976; Poem, "The Black Tambourine," February 25, 1976; Poem, "Heartbreak," March 9, 1976; Poem, "From Ashes," April 5, 1976; and Poem, "Eve's Eden," April 29, 1976. Note that these dates represent the day the poems were typed, which would be the morning after the night when they were written.

6. Compare to a special section, "The Facts on Transcendental Meditation," *Psychology Today* (April 1974), pp. 37–46; Harold H. Bloomfield et al., *TM: Discovering Inner Energy and Overcoming Stress* (New York: Delacorte, 1975); R. Keith Wallace and Herbert Benson, "Physiological Effects of Transcendental Meditation," *Science,* March 27, 1970, pp. 1751–54; and Claudio Naranjo and Robert Ornstein, *On the Psychology of Meditation* (New York: Viking, 1971).

7. Sizemore and Pittillo, *I'm Eve,* pp. 457–60; Letter, Elen Sain Pittillo

to Tony A. Tsitos, M.D., May 14, 1976, in CCSP at Duke; and compare to research in 1988 by Katharine Cutts and Stephen J. Ceci at Cornell University, which suggests that children age eight months to eighteen months have a form of "primitive memory" that exists for up to four months, or longer than previously thought. The researchers also hypothesize that this latent memory can influence memory, preferences, and tastes in adulthood. "Babies' First Memory in the Early Months," *Insight,* October 3, 1988, p. 52, col. 1.

8. Taped response to questionnaire, Richard P. Kluft, M.D., to Chris Costner Sizemore, July 1988.

9. Letter, Lisa Drew, Doubleday & Company, Inc., to Chris Sizemore and Elen Pittillo, July 21, 1976, in CCSP at Duke.

10. Compare to Mitchell J. Shields, "Looking for Mrs. Sizemore," *Atlanta Journal and Constitution Magazine,* August 14, 1977, pp. 6–7, 22–26.

11. Kitty Hanson, "The Real Faces of Eve," (New York) *Daily News,* July 25, 1977, p. 27, col. 4.

12. Excerpts in *Ladies' Home Journal* (May 1977), pp. 92–94, 100, 200–210; AP news feature, Andrew Rosenthal, "Multiple Personality 'Eve' Tells of Her Many 'Faces,'" released August 12, 1977; *Kirkus Reviews* (May 1977).

13. Dave Smith, "Twenty-two Faces of Eve—Now There Is One," *Los Angeles Times,* August 12, 1977, part 4, p. 1, col. 4–p. 13, col. 2.

14. Ibid.

15. Interview, President and Mrs. Jimmy Carter, *Larry King Show,* CNN, September 1, 1988.

16. Richard R. Lingeman, "Woman of Many Faces," in "Books of the Times," *New York Times,* August 20, 1977, p. 4, col. 1; and Martha Friday, "Real Story Behind 'Eve' Told," *Pittsburgh Press,* August 25, 1977.

17. Cathy Siepp, "All About the Aftermath of Eve," in *Los Angeles Times Book Review,* August 14, 1977, p. 1, 10; also a shorter version of Siepp's review was syndicated, appearing in such publications as the *Atlantic City Sunday Press,* August 21, 1977, *Vancouver Sun,* August 19, 1977, and *Portland Oregonian,* November 13, 1977, among others; and Barbara Kahn, "Real Multiple-personality 'Eve' Tells Story," *Seattle Times Magazine,* September 4, 1977.

18. Earl Waters, untitled review, *Chattanooga Times,* September 11, 1977; and Kitty Plunkett, "Facing the Real Eve," *Memphis Commercial Appeal,* October 16, 1977.

19. Excerpts of *I'm Eve* in *Viva* (November 1977), pp. 99–109, and *Viva* (December 1977), pp. 115–27.

Chapter Six

1. Letter, Livia Gollancz, Victor Gollancz Ltd., to Mrs. Chris Sizemore, January 25, 1978; and Letter, Mrs. Chris Costner Sizemore to Ms. Livia Gollancz, February 13, 1978; both in CCSP at Duke.

2. Letters, Livia Gollancz, Victor Gollancz Ltd., to Mrs. Chris Sizemore, February 6 and 10, 1978, in CCSP at Duke.
3. Letter, David W. Stevens, astrological counselor, to Chris C. Sizemore, February 15, 1978, in CCSP at Duke; and *Jerusalem Bible* (New York: Doubleday, 1966), John 9:1–3.
4. Letter, Tony A. Tsitos, M.D., to Mr. Denver H. Graham, attorney, April 24, 1975, in CCSP at Duke.
5. Compare to Letter, Chris C. Sizemore to Nellie Flexner, Victor Gollancz Ltd., March 24, 1978, in CCSP at Duke; and Letter, Nellie Flexner to Mrs. Chris Sizemore, March 10, 1978, in CCSP at Duke.
6. Letter, Lisa Healy, Doubleday & Company, Inc., to Ms. Chris Sizemore, April 12, 1978, in CCSP at Duke.
7. Compare to a third-party confirmation, written about a year after the unification and four years before Twentieth Century-Fox purchased an option on *I'm Eve*. It confirms the author's memory of the documents. Letter, Tony A. Tsitos, M.D., to Mr. Denver H. Graham, April 24, 1975, in CCSP at Duke.

   "Mrs. Sizemore is presently quite concerned in writing her second book, and she is interested in obtaining a release from the contract that she signed, supposedly in 1952, while she was under treatment with Dr. Thigpen.

   "For your information, Mrs. Sizemore claims that she does not recall signing any papers with Dr. Thigpen, but she is aware of the fact that she has signed some papers of some nature when she was contacted by the Twentieth Century-Fox Company in 1954 in regards to the movie made, based on the book entitled *The Three Faces of Eve*. She was told also that there were such papers and they were signed somewhere around 1952 by her agent in New York."

8. Thigpen and Cleckley, *The Three Faces of Eve*, pp. 223–24.
9. Ibid.
10. National Film Theatre Programme note, special event during "The New Australian Cinema" series, May 2, 1978, quoting an untitled review of "The Three Faces of Eve," *Manchester Guardian*, October 19, 1957.
11. Ibid.
12. Letter, William Wood, screenwriter, to Chris C. Sizemore, May 22, 1978, in CCSP at Duke.
13. Compare to Ed Tiley, "The Real Eve," Northern Virginia *People* (January/February 1978), pp. 21–25, which quoted the author as having said, "There is a dire need to stand up and say, 'So what if I did have this illness? I'm me, and I'm going to have a good life in spite of it.' And as long as people are interested, I'm going to share my experiences. Not the illness, but the need for more acceptance and understanding of the mentally ill. If they could just understand

that there is nothing to be ashamed of. . . . If people can accept it the same as a broken leg, then we're getting there."

14. Herald Grandstaff, "Life 'Begins' for 'Eve,' Now Well," *Greater Manassas News* (Virginia), September 21, 1978, p. A2, cols. 1–6.

15. Compare to Letter, Chris C. Sizemore to Shokichi Kawaguchi, translator, July 23, 1978, in CCSP at Duke.

16. Letter, Shokichi Kawaguchi, translator, to Mrs. Chris Sizemore, February 3, 1975, in CCSP at Duke.

17. Letter, Chris C. Sizemore to Shokichi Kawaguchi, translator, July 23, 1978, in CCSP at Duke; and Telegram, Shokichi Kawaguchi, translator, to Mrs. Chris C. Sizemore, October 27, 1978, in CCSP at Duke.

18. Compare to Ad, "Two Artist Show: Chris Sizemore, Pupil, and Ardeshir Arjang,. Teacher," *Zest: Houston Chronicle Magazine,* December 3, 1978, p. 51, cols. 7–8; Ad, "Chris Sizemore Exhibition," *Southwest Art* (December 1978); and a chronological listing of paintings, subsequently published in a brochure, "The Paintings of Eve/Chris Costner Sizemore," March 25, 1980, Fenwick Library, the Arts Gallery, George Mason University, in CCSP at Duke.

19. Letter, Mary C. Trone, Doubleday & Company, Inc., to Ms. Chris Sizemore. December 7, 1978, in CCSP at Duke.

20. Joyce Herndon, "Sizemore Had Twenty-two Personalities," *Communicator* (Houston, Texas), December 14, 1978, p. 8, col. 5; and for further consideration of how *fugue states* were clinically viewed in the late seventies, see American Psychiatric Association, *Diagnostic and Statistical Manual of Mental Disorders,* 3rd edition (Washington: American Psychiatric Association, 1980), pp. 255–57.

21. Tennessee Williams, *A Streetcar Named Desire,* in *Eight Plays* (New York: Nelson Doubleday, 1979), p. 196.

Chapter Seven

1. Emphasis added. Thomas Merton, *Contemplation in a World of Action* (New York: Doubleday, 1973), pp. 222–26, based on Reza Arasteh, M.D., *Final Integration in the Adult Personality* (Leiden: L. J. Brill, 1965).

2. Letter, Chris C. Sizemore to [name withheld], January 13, 1979, in CCSP at Duke.

3. Merton, *Contemplation in a World of Action,* pp. 222–26.

4. Beverly Mills, "After Living Twenty-two Lives, She Found One for Herself," *The News and Observer* (Raleigh, North Carolina), May 23, 1979, p. 10, col. 4.

5. Compare to E. M. Wood, "Behavior: Drugging Mental Patients,"

1979 Year Book: Annual Supplement to Collier's Encyclopedia (New York: Macmillan, 1978), pp. 153–54; and Wade Hudson, "The Mental Health Professional as Advocate," *Advocacy Now* (Van Nuys, California: San Fernando Valley Community Mental Health Centers, March 1980), pp. 12–15.

6. Program, "A Salute to Rosalynn Carter," Omni International Hotel, Atlanta, Georgia, June 23, 1981, p. 5.

7. Compare to Letter, John H. Cooper, Ph.D., George Mason University, July 30, 1979, in CCSP at Duke.

8. Compare to ad, "Original Oil Paintings by Chris Sizemore," *The Chronicle* (Duke University newspaper), September 11, 1979, p. 9, col. 2.

9. Compare to Letter, Gregory A. Kimble, Duke University, to Ms. Chris C. Sizemore, June 6, 1979, in CCSP at Duke.

10. Letter, Corbett H. Thigpen, M.D., to Mrs. Christine Sizemore, March 4, 1975, in CCSP at Duke.

11. Philip M. Coons, M.D., "Multiple Personality: Diagnostic Considerations," *Journal of Clinical Psychiatry,* Vol. 41, No. 10 (October 1980), pp. 330–36; and American Psychiatric Association, *Diagnostic and Statistical Manual of Mental Disorders,* 2nd edition (Washington: American Psychiatric Association, 1963).

12. Based on Myron Boor and Philip M. Coons, "A Comprehensive Bibliography of Literature Pertaining to Multiple Personality," *Psychological Reports* 53 (1983), pp. 295–310. This bibliography cites 350 publications. The vast majority, or 191 publications, were released before or during 1969, though most date from the turn of this century. However, during the years of 1970 through 1979, another 100 publications on MPD were issued, including the first major *biographical* or *autobiographical* accounts by MPD patients: Flora R. Schreiber, *Sybil* (Chicago: Regnery, 1973), R. J. Stoler, *Splitting: A Case of Female Masculinity* (New York: Quadrangle, 1973), Sizemore and Pittillo, *I'm Eve* (New York: Doubleday, 1977), Henry Hawksworth and Ted Schwarz, *The Five of Me* (Chicago: Regnery, 1977) and C. Peters and Ted Schwarz, *Tell Me Who I Am Before I Die* (New York: Rawson, 1978).

13. Thigpen and Cleckley, *The Three Faces of Eve,* p. 159.

14. Compare to Philip M. Coons, M.D., "Report on the American Psychiatric Association's Workshop on Multiple Personality," *Mnemonic* 19 (1978), pp. 39–43, and Philip M. Coons, M.D., "Report on the Second American Psychiatric Association's Workshop on Multiple Personality," *Mnemonic* 20 (1979), pp. 37–42.

15. Ralph Allison, M.D., with Ted Schwarz, *Minds in Many Pieces* (New York: Rawson, Wade, 1980), pp. 155–58.

16. Richard P. Kluft, M.D., "An Update on Multiple Personality Disorder," *Hospital and Community Psychiatry,* Vol. 38, No. 4 (April

1987), p. 363; American Psychiatric Association, *Diagnostic and Statistical Manual of Mental Disorders,* 3rd edition (Washington: American Psychiatric Association, 1980), pp. 257–59.

17. George B. Greaves, Ph.D., "Multiple Personality: 165 Years after Mary Reynolds," *The Journal of Nervous and Mental Disorders,* Vol. 168, No. 10, Serial No. 1175 (October 1980), p. 578.

18. "Numerous large contemporary series of such patients have been reported since 1980, leading *DSM-III-R* to discontinue designating MPD as a rare condition." Kluft, "The Postunification Treatment of Multiple Personality," 212; and American Psychiatric Association, *Diagnostic and Statistical Manual of Mental Disorders,* 3rd edition, revised (Washington: American Psychiatric Association, 1987).

19. Letter, [name withheld] to Mrs. Chris Sizemore, October 12, 1979, in CCSP at Duke.

20. Letter, Katharine E. Barrett, Virginia Tau president, to Chapter Honorary Membership Committee, Alpha Delta Kappa, October 15, 1979, in CCSP at Duke; and brochure, "Alpha Delta Kappa," no date, in CCSP at Duke.

21. Susan Baer, "The Paintings of the Many Eves," *Washington Star,* April 2, 1980, p. E1, cols. 2–4, p. E12, cols 1–4.

22. Emily L. Bull, "Chris Sizemore's Art Hung in Virginia University," *Edgefield County Press* (South Carolina), April 10, 1980, p. 1., cols. 1–6.

23. Liz McNulty, "Family Members Describe Home Life With 'Eve,'" *Reston Times* (Virginia), April 10, 1980, p. C1, cols. 1–6, p. C8, cols. 3–8.

24. William Keesler, "'Eve' Tells High Pointers About Many Personalities," *Daily News* (High Point, North Carolina), May 20, 1980; and Letter, Billie Ruth Sudduth, MHA of Craven County, North Carolina, to Hernando Palmer, president, MHA in North Carolina, July 17, 1980, in CCSP at Duke.

25. Compare to Letter, Mattie U. Russell, curator, to Mrs. Chris Sizemore, May 27, 1980; also Jim Buie, "'Three Faces' Was Only Part of Eve's Story," *Durham Morning Herald,* May 27, 1980, p. C1, cols. 1–5; and Robert L. Byrd, "Notable Acquisitions: The Sizemore Papers," *Duke University Library Newsletter,* No. 25 (October 1980), p. 9.

26. Emily L. Bull, "Duke Welcomes Mrs. Sizemore," *Edgefield County Press,* May 29, 1980, p. 1, cols. 2–24.

27. Editorial, "Bringing Honor to Town," *Edgefield County Press,* May 29, 1980, p. 4, cols. 1–3.

28. Liz McNulty, "Sizemore Donates Her Papers to Duke University," *Reston Times* (Virginia), July 3, 1980, p. C1, cols. 1–4, p. C2, cols 3–4.

Chapter Eight

1. Roger Rosenblatt, "The People's Analyst," *Time* magazine, September 29, 1980, p. 92, col. 1.
2. Philip M. Coons, M.D., "Multiple Personality: Diagnostic Considerations," *Journal of Clinical Psychiatry,* Vol. 41, No. 10 (October 1980), pp. 330–36.
3. George B. Greaves, Ph.D., "Multiple Personality: 165 Years after Mary Reynolds," *The Journal of Nervous and Mental Disease,* Vol. 168, No. 10 (October 1980), pp. 577–96.
4. Nomination book, Mental Health Association in North Carolina, Inc., to National Mental Health Association's 1980 Awards Panel, July 30, 1980, pp. 1–3.
5. National Mental Health Association, "Implementing Rather Than Repealing the MHSA," *Legislative Briefing Sheet* (Arlington, Virginia: NMHA, March 23, 1981).
6. National Mental Health Association, "Television Images of Mental Illness," *In Touch,* Vol. 4, No. 5 (Arlington, Virginia: NMHA, July/August 1981), p. 1–3.
7. Ibid., p. 3.
8. Ibid., p. 4.
9. Ibid.
10. National Mental Health Association, *Public Affairs Info & Action, Bulletin,* No. 118 (Arlington, Virginia: NMHA, March 13, 1981), p. 2.
11. Compare to Charlotte Hays, "The Seven Facets of Eve: From a Troubled Psyche, A Gallery of Artists Has Emerged," *The Washingtonian* (August 1982), p. 11.
12. National Mental Health Association, "Rosalynn Carter: A Georgia Gala," *Focus,* Vol. 2, No. 3 (Arlington, Virginia: NMHA, July/August 1981), pp. 1,7.
13. David H. Hubel and Torsten N. Wiesel, "Brain Mechanisms of Vision," *Scientific American* (September 1979), as reprinted in *The Mind's Eye* (New York: W. H. Freeman, 1986), p. 48.
14. Ibid., p. 52.
15. Iona Deering, an unpublished dissertation, written after an interview with the author, June 27, 1983.

Chapter Nine

1. Donald Goodman, "Crime and Crime Prevention: Murders," *1980 Year Book: Annual Supplement to Collier's Encyclopedia* (New York: Macmillan, 1979), p. 237; and Nicholas P. Spanos, John R. Weekes, and Lorne D. Bertrand, "Multiple Personality: A Social Psy-

chological Perspective," *Journal of Abnormal Psychology,* Vol. 94, No. 3 (1985), pp. 365–75.

2. Spanos, Weekes, and Bertrand, "Multiple Personality," p. 365; also compare to use of insanity defense in *State* v. *William Milligan,* Case no. 77-CR-11-2908 (Franklin County, Ohio, December 4, 1978).

3. Spanos, Weekes, and Bertrand, "Multiple Personality," p. 366.

4. Ibid.; and Ellen Hale, "When a Mind Goes to War with Its Own Body," part one of a four-part series, the Gannett News Service (December 1982).

5. Goodman, "Crime and Crime Prevention," p. 237.

6. Cheryl Haven, "Chris Sizemore Talks about Multiple Personality Cases," *Brunswick News,* October 7, 1982, p. 3A, cols. 3,4.

7. Compare to Haven, "Real-life 'Eve' of 'Three Faces of Eve' Fame Tells Her Story," *Brunswick News,* October 6, 1982, p. 3A, col. 6: "Mrs. Sizemore said . . . her recollection of the personalities is in picture form. 'All multiples remember in picture form. I wasn't there with my personalities as I am here now, because if I had been, there would have been no need for them.'"

8. Julian Jaynes, *The Origins of Consciousness in the Breakdown of the Bicameral Mind* (Boston: Houghton Mifflin, 1976), p. 23.

9. Charles Sheperd, "Reflections on Georgia's Insanity Defense Options," *Mental Health Notes,* Vol. 38, No. 3 (Atlanta, Georgia: Mental Health Association of Metropolitan Atlanta, September 1982), p. 4.

10. Ibid.

11. "Beers, Clifford Whittingham," *Collier's Encyclopedia,* Vol. 3 (New York: P.F. Collier, 1960), p. 182.

12. "1982 Mental Health Month Tour, 'I'm Eve': Record-breaking Success," *MHA Florida Focus,* Vol. 12, No. 3 (May–June, 1982), p. 1.

13. Ian Wilson, *All in the Mind* (New York: Doubleday, 1982) pp. 119–28.

14. Frank W. Putnam, M.D., "Traces of Eve's Faces," *Psychology Today* 16 (October 1982), p. 88; also compare to "Multiple Personality: Distinctive EEGs Suggest That It's More Than a Metaphor," *Brain/Mind Bulletin,* July 12, 1982, pp. 1–2, based upon research by Putnam and Collin Pitblado, first reported in *Science News* 121 (1982), p. 356.

15. Associated Press, "Woman Feels Mental Problem Like Illness," reprinted in *Morning Sun* (Pittsburg, Kansas), October 13, 1982, p. 4, col. 1.

16. George B. Greaves, Ph.D., *Newsletter, International Society for the Study of Multiple Personality,* Vol. 1, No. 1 (March 1983), p. 1.

17. Charlotte Hays, "The Seven Facets of Eve: From a Troubled Psyche, A Gallery of Artists Has Emerged," *The Washingtonian* (August 1982), p 11

18. Bethany Korwin-Pawlowska, "Eve of the Three Faces Has a Cause," *Oakland Tribune/Eastbay Today* (California), October 20, 1982, p. 1B, col. 3.

Chapter Ten

1. Ellen Hale, "Can Doctors Treat Multipersonalities?" part four of a four-part series, the Gannett News Service, released in December 1982.
2. Ibid.
3. Ibid.
4. Compare to The Troops for Truddi Chase, *When Rabbit Howls* (New York: Dutton, 1987), pp. 359–60. Although Chase's autobiography does not make the dates clear for this period, she apparently came to the author's lecture when she was experiencing tremendous conflict concerning integration. The phrase—"Two, four, six, eight, we don't wanna integrate!"—appears in her book as having been "lettered in a childish scrawl, with a lipstick on the side of the claw-legged tub" in Chase's bathroom. The implication is that one of her child alters, possibly the one named Lamb Chop, had originated the chant.
5. Hale, "Can Doctors Treat Multipersonalities?" (December 1982), reports Dr. Putnam's estimates at 80 percent; Chase, *When Rabbit Howls,* p. 159, reports Dr. Putnam's estimates at 98 percent.
6. Chase, *When Rabbit Howls,* p. 156.
7. Morton Prince, *The Dissociation of a Personality* (first published, New York: Longmans, Green, 1905; paperback reprint, New York: Oxford University Press, 1978).
8. Charles Downey, "Personalities Plus," *American Way* (April 1983), pp. 63–64.
9. Ibid.
10. Myron Boor, Ph.D., "The Multiple Personality Epidemic," *The Journal of Nervous and Mental Disease,* Vol. 170, No. 5 (Brown University, 1982), p. 302.
11. Corbett H. Thigpen, M.D., and Hervey M. Cleckley, M.D., "On the Incidence of Multiple Personality Disorder: A Brief Communication," *The Journal of Clinical and Experimental Hypnosis,* Vol. 32, No. 2 (1984), pp. 63–66.
12. Daniel Keyes, *The Minds of Billy Milligan* (New York: Random House, 1981).
13. Iona Deering, an unpublished dissertation, written after an interview with the author, June 27, 1983.
14. Emphasis added. Ibid.

Chapter Eleven

1. Poem, "Wholeness," March 9, 1983, in CCSP at Duke.
2. Moira Bailey, "Eve's Many Faces Are Now Ghosts of Days Gone By," *The Houston Chronicle,* December 6, 1984, sec. 4, p. 20, col. 3.; reprinted in an edited version by the Associated Press, "'The Three Faces of Eve' Woman Lectures," *USA Today,* November 27, 1984, p. 2A, cols. 5–6.
3. Compare to A. D. Feinstein and Stanley Krippner, "Personal Mythology and Dreams," *Svensk Tidskrift for Hypnos* 8 (1981), 97–99; and subsequently, Stanley Krippner, "Dreams and the Development of a Personal Mythology," *The Journal of Mind and Behavior,* Vol. 7, Nos. 2 and 3 (The Institute of Mind and Behavior, Inc., Spring and Summer, 1986), pp. 449–62 and 319–32.
4. Emphasis added. Letter, Stanley Krippner, Saybrook Institute, to Chris Costner Sizemore, February 28, 1984, in CCSP at Duke.
5. Richard M. Restak, M.D., "People With Multiple Minds," *Science Digest,* Vol. 92, No. 6 (New York: The Hearst Corporation, 1984), pp. 76–77.
6. Richard M. Restak, M.D., *The Brain* (New York: Bantam, 1984), p. 336.
7. Ibid.
8. See the *American Journal of Clinical Hypnosis,* Vol. 26, No. 2; *Psychiatric Annals,* Vol. 14, No. 1; *Psychiatric Clinics of North America,* Vol. 7, No. 1; and *International Journal of Clinical and Experimental Hypnosis,* Vol. 32, No. 2.
9. Compare to Philip M. Coons, M.D., "Child Abuse and Multiple Personality Disorder: Review of the Literature and Suggestions for Treatment," *Child Abuse & Neglect* 10 (Pergamon Journals Ltd., 1986): pp. 455–62. "Like child abuse, particularly incest, there is a professional reluctance to diagnose multiple personality disorder. In all likelihood, this reluctance stems from a number of factors including the generally subtle presentation of the symptoms, the fearful reluctance of the patient to divulge important clinical information, professional ignorance concerning dissociative disorders, and the reluctance of the clinician to believe that incest actually occurs and is not the product of fantasy." Also compare to George K. Ganaway, M.D., "Multiple Personality Disorder: Myths and Facts," *Insight,* 1 (Smyrna, Georgia: Ridgeview Hospital, 1986), p. 8. He confirmed that "practically all of the definitive journal articles and textbooks on [MPD] have been published since 1980" and that, even in 1986, though most psychiatrists are "fascinated" by MPD, "few want to commit themselves on record in defense of its validity."
10. Richard P. Kluft, M.D., "Multiple Personality in Childhood,"

Psychiatric Clinics of North America 7 (1984): 121–34; Thomas J. Hurley III, "From Abuse to Alter Personalities," *Investigations,* Vol. 1, Nos. 3–4 (Sausalito, California: Institute of Noetic Sciences, 1985), p. 12; and "AMA Issues Guidelines for Diagnosis and Treatment of Child Abuse and Neglect," *Hospital and Community Psychiatry,* Vol. 37, No. 1 (January 1986), p. 89.

11. Wilson, *All in the Mind,* pp. 2, 3, and 25; Ian Stevenson, *Twenty Cases of Reincarnation* (New York: American Society for Psychical Research, 1966; 2nd edition, Charlottesville: University Press of Virginia, 1974); Ian Stevenson, "The Explanatory Value of the Idea of Reincarnation," *Journal of Nervous and Mental Disease,* Vol. 164, No. 5 (May 1977), pp. 305–26; Ian Stevenson, "Research into Evidence of Man's Survival After Death," *Journal of Nervous and Mental Disease,* Vol. 165, No. 3 (September 1977), pp. 152–70; and Ian Stevenson, "Some Questions Relating to Cases of the Reincarnation Type," *Journal of the American Society for Psychical Research* 68 (1974), p. 409.

12. Wilson, *All in the Mind,* pp. 2,3.

13. Michele Clements, M.D., "What a Fetus Hears, an Adult Remembers," *General Practitioner,* April 13, 1979, p. 38; Carl Sagan, *The Dragons of Eden* (London: Hodder & Stroughton, 1978), p. 148.

14. Wilson, *All in the Mind,* pp. 25–26.

15. At the time, Dr. Braun was the ISSMP&D's president, Dr. Kluft was the society's president-elect, and the author was one of the society's representatives-at-large; also see Brendan O'Regan, "Mirrors of New Models of the Mind," *Investigations,* Vol. 1, Nos. 3–4 (Sausalito, California: The Institute of Noetic Sciences, 1985), p. 1.

16. William Dunn, "'Eve' Wins Over Many Selves," *Detroit News,* December 11, 1984, pp. 1A, 9A, and 12C.

17. Quoted in Thomas J. Hurley III, "Possession, Dynamic Psychiatry and Science: The Historical Fortunes of MPD," *Investigations,* Vol. 1, Nos. 3–4 (Sausalito, California: Institute of Noetic Sciences, 1985), p. 9.

18. Ibid.

Chapter Twelve

1. The author's endorsement stated, "*Multiple Man* is a remarkable study of the phenomenon of multiple personality disorder, and I am pleased that Adam Crabtree chose to include my life experience as a multiple personality patient in this fascinating work. His concepts of possession are not only intriguing and thought-provoking but also highly illuminating revelations of the innermost recesses of the mind." Adam Crabtree, *Multiple Man: Explorations in Possession*

and Multiple Personality (Toronto: Collins, 1985), p. ii; also compare to Letter, Sally Rogers, Collins Publishers, to Chris Costner Sizemore, April 26, 1985, in CCSP at Duke.

2. Emphasis added. Crabtree, *Multiple Man,* p. 261.

3. Compare to Adam Crabtree, "Dissociation as a Way of Life," an unpublished talk at a conference sponsored by the American Society for Psychical Research, New York City, October 10, 1987, msp. 17: "Those who suffer from multiple personality . . . do not think of themselves as possessed. The alter personalities are there alongside each other, but one personality never possesses or takes over another."

4. Crabtree, *Multiple Man,* p. 261.

5. George B. Greaves, Ph.D., Untitled Review of *Multiple Man* by Adam Crabtree, *Newsletter, International Society for the Study of Multiple Personality and Dissociation* (Fall 1986), pp. 3–4.

6. Crabtree, *Multiple Man,* pp. 230–31.

7. Ibid.

8. Stanley Krippner, Ph.D., "Cross-cultural Approaches to Multiple Personality Disorder: Practices in Brazilian Spiritism," *Ethos,* Vol. 15, No. 3 (September 1987), p. 293.

9. Compare to Transcript, Canadian Broadcasting Corporation, "The Splitting of the Mind," a three-part series on the radio show "Ideas," hosted by Adam Crabtree, April 22–May 6, 1985, pp. 30–33, which quotes John Watkins, a psychologist at the University of Montana, as saying, "I don't want to say we're all multiple personalities. . . . But we are multiple in the sense that we have different segments or components of our personality that become active at different times. . . . We believe that dissociation . . . exists on a continuum, and that at one end of the continuum are simply the normal experiences of mood changes, and at the other extreme end of it is the true multiple personality, one that emerges without hypnosis, emerges overtly and shows entirely different personality structures. . . . [Individuals are] a family of selves. . . . So we're actually doing group and family therapy with a single person. . . ."; also compare to Eve M. Bernstein, Ph.D., and Frank W. Putnam, M.D., "Development, Reliability and Validity of a Dissociation Scale," *The Journal of Nervous and Mental Disease,* Vol. 174, No. 12 (1986), pp. 727–35.

10. Compare to Millie Ball, "The Woman Behind the Multiple Faces of 'Eve,'" *Times-Picayune,* November 3, 1985, p. B4, cols. 1–5.

11. Tom Minehart, "From 'Three Faces' to Energy of Three People," *Durham Morning Herald* (North Carolina), October 5, 1986.

12. Nicholas P. Spanos, John R. Weekes, and Lorne D. Bertrand, "Multiple Personality: A Social Psychological Perspective," *Journal of Abnormal Psychology,* Vol. 94, No. 3 (American Psychological Association, Inc., 1985), p. 365.

13. J. P. Sutcliffe and J. Jones, "Personal Identity, Multiple Personality and Hypnosis," *International Journal of Clinical and Experimental Hypnosis* 10 (1962), pp. 231–69.

14. Compare to Moshe S. Torem, M.D., "My Philosophy of Treatment for MPD," in *Handbook, Second Regional Conference on Multiple Personality and Dissociative States,* April 24 and 25, 1987 (Akron General Medical Center, Department of Psychiatry and Behavioral Sciences).

15. Ludel Sauvageot, "Chris Sizemore—A Real Person," *Helping Tomorrow Happen,* Vol, 2, No. 2 (Summer 1987), pp. 4–5.

Index